Parenting with a Story

PARENTING WITH A STORY

REAL-LIFE LESSONS IN CHARACTER FOR PARENTS AND CHILDREN TO SHARE

Paul Smith

AMACOM
AMERICAN MANAGEMENT ASSOCIATION
New York • Atlanta • Brussels • Chicago • Mexico City
San Francisco • Shanghai • Tokyo • Toronto • Washington, D.C.

This publication is designed to provide accurate and authoritative information in regard to the subject matter covered. It is sold with the understanding that the publisher is not engaged in rendering legal, accounting, or other professional service. If legal advice or other expert assistance is required, the services of a competent professional person should be sought.

Any time characters are introduced by only a first name in this book it is an indication that their names (and perhaps other personal details) have been changed to protect their anonymity.

LIBRARY OF CONGRESS CATALOGING-IN-PUBLICATION DATA
Smith, Paul, 1967 July 3–
Parenting with a story : real-life lessons in character for parents and children to share /
Paul Smith.
pages cm
Includes index.
ISBN-13: 978-0-8144-3357-7 (pbk.)
ISBN-10: 0-8144-3357-X (pbk.)
1. Parenting. 2. Parent and child. 3. Storytelling. I. Title.
HQ755.8.S63287 2014
306.874--dc23
2014021477

About AMA

American Management Association (www.amanet.org) is a world leader in talent development, advancing the skills of individuals to drive business success. Our mission is to support the goals of individuals and organizations through a complete range of products and services, including classroom and virtual seminars, webcasts, webinars, podcasts, conferences, corporate and government solutions, business books, and research. AMA's approach to improving performance combines experiential learning—learning through doing—with opportunities for ongoing professional growth at every step of one's career journey.

Printing number
10 9 8 7 6 5 4 3 2 1

To my sons, Matthew and Benjamin,
that you may benefit from more wisdom than my one lifetime can provide.

Contents

Acknowledgments

First and foremost, I'd like to thank the people whose names and stories grace the pages of this book. I'm grateful to all of you for sharing such intimate moments of your life so that others could benefit from your experience.

For most, your names are already included elsewhere in the book, so I won't repeat them here. But I am just as humbled by those who contributed their time and wisdom in lengthy interviews, but whose names do not show up as characters in the stories. You include Moe Abdou, Steve August, Preston Becker, Tikica Benjamin, David Boje, Rani Bookvich, Rita Bosel, Clay Brizendine, Roby Brock, Theresa Cornett, Ji-Hoon Dierckx, Karen Dietz, Felecia Favroth, Kim Fullerton, Scott Gaudi, Pilar Gonzalez, Jessica Hall, Kelley Bridges Herbez, Dann Hotelling, David Hutchens, Jean Ibrahim, Doyle Jackson, Margaret Layding, Chad Leland, Dejah Meldem, Ruth Milligan, Curtis Munk, Christina Parisi, Sue Ransohoff, Butch Renfroe, Rupa Sharma, Kristin Sharp, Aimee Shouse, Annette Simmons, Bob Smith, John Stagliano, Maki Tahara, Scott Tilford, Leslie Tse, Berenike Ullmann, Paul Wesselmann, Andrew Wong, and Tiffany Yang.

Thanks also to my editors at AMACOM Books, Stephen S. Power and Erika Spelman, and to Dan Dorr for being an early sounding board for these stories. And a special thanks to Ed Tanguay for brainstorming questions for the discussion guide with me, and to my wife, Lisa, for patiently listening to me retell each story over and over again until I found my voice in them.

Parenting with a Story

Introduction

> The destiny of the world is determined less by the battles that are lost and won than by the stories it loves and believes in.
>
> —HOWARD GODDARD

Perhaps the most memorable lesson I ever learned about becoming an adult occurred at the most unexpected place and time: in a crowded restaurant on Secretary's Day, April 1986. Still a teenager and a freshman in college, I had a part-time job at a local furniture manufacturing company. My father was an executive there, and he helped me get a job as a file clerk in the personnel office. I discovered that each year on that day, all the bosses took their administrators and clerical staff out to lunch. That meant a free lunch for me.

To make it easy, the company reserved every seat in a local restaurant. About fifty managers and more than a hundred "secretaries" showed up that day. In preparation for so many guests, the restaurant prepared only two meal options: a club sandwich and quiche lorraine. It's important to recognize that this event happened shortly after the publication of the bestselling book *Real Men Don't Eat Quiche* by Bruce Feirstein, a tongue-in-cheek look at the feminization of the American male.

So as the waitress was making her rounds taking orders, it was no surprise that all the men ordered the club sandwich and most of the women ordered the quiche. Until they got to my dad, that is, who was sitting within earshot of me. He looked up from the menu and said, "Hmm . . . I've never had quiche before. I tell you what, why don't you bring me half a quiche and half a club sandwich. That way, if I don't like the quiche, I'll still have the sandwich."

Within seconds, the abuse began. The men at the table called my father's masculinity into question in more creative ways than I had imagined possible at that point in my life. Awkward and embarrassing don't begin to describe how it feels for a boy still in his teenage years to watch his father be ridiculed in such a manner. Needless to say, when it was my turn to order, I quickly picked the club sandwich.

After ten or fifteen minutes of ribbing, my father seemed to have had enough and called the waitress back over. "Thank God!" I thought. "Just pacify these jerks and let's get on with lunch." The waitress arrived and Dad said, as expected, "I'm sorry. I need to change my order. I ordered half a quiche and half a club sandwich." Howls of success and a round of high fives erupted at the table as the other men celebrated their victory. Their aim had been to break my father's will with their ridicule, and apparently they had just done it.

What came next, however, shocked me and everyone else. He continued, "Take back the half a club sandwich and bring me the whole damn quiche!" A stunned silence fell over the table of now slack-jawed men.

To this day, I still don't know if my father likes quiche. But on that particular day he ate every bite with a smile on his face.

My respect and admiration for my father rose to a whole new level that day. He showed everyone at that table that he was man enough to eat anything he liked and didn't care what they thought about it. He showed them that he refused to be defined by social norms. And he showed me, his son, something of what it means to be a real man.

Twenty-eight years later, I have two sons of my own. I've shared this story with both of them on several occasions when I saw them confronting peer pressure. My goal, of course, is to give them the courage to stand up to that pressure, but also to give them a successful way to respond.

If a classmate teases my son Matthew that his pants aren't sagging off his waist enough, as is unfortunately fashionable these days, now I simply prompt him, "Eat the quiche, son." Recalling the story, he'd then follow the example set by my father. Instead of doing less of what he's being teased for, he'd do it more! He'd pull his pants up even higher and say, "There, is that better?"

You can imagine the confused look on his tormentor's face and the retort, "No, you dummy, I said they're too high!" Another tug and his pants are now up to mid-torso, followed quickly by "How about now?" You can see how his adversary would rapidly become exasperated and give up.

But notice three other things about this story. First, I hope you can see how simply advising children to "stand up to peer pressure" or to "be yourself" is less likely to help them navigate this situation. Platitudes that seem profound in a pithy piece of prose are surprisingly unhelpful to children in a real-life situation. They're too vague and abstract. "What exactly does it mean to 'be myself' or to 'stand up to peer pressure'? Should I walk away, start a fight, or just ignore them?" At the other end of the spectrum, telling children exactly what to do in every situation is overly prescriptive and doesn't leave them room to think for themselves. But a story like the one above gives them a concrete idea for how to respond without just telling them what to do. As keenly observed by Hannah Arendt, "Storytelling reveals meaning without committing the error of defining it."[1]

Second, the story does something else platitudes and advice won't do. It shows the hero in the story succeeding, a success that could be theirs if they follow the hero's lead. My experience with children (and especially teenagers) is that they have a natural distrust of advice doled out by old people (i.e., you!). So why should they believe that "standing up to peer pressure" would have an outcome they'll be happy with? But after hearing that story, they can judge for themselves and won't have to take your word for it.

Last, notice that the story represents an unexpected moment of clarity in someone's life, in this case, mine. I was just having lunch. I wasn't expecting to learn anything, much less anything important in my journey to manhood. Almost thirty years later, after spending most of my career as a consumer researcher and the last five years as an author, conducting hundreds of interviews and documenting more than 1,500 personal stories, I've concluded this: To most people, these unexpected moments of clarity represent their most meaningful, insightful, and memorable experiences that have the longest-term impact on their lives. When such a moment is shared with a loved one, it can become one of that person's most impactful moments as well.

PURPOSE OF THIS BOOK

Like me, most parents desperately want to impart the wisdom of our age to the children in our lives, thus sparing them the painful and time-consuming task of making all of life's possible mistakes. And as we've learned from experience, a great personal story (perhaps about one of those unexpected moments of clarity) is often the best way to do that. The problem, though, is that none of us has had the breadth of life experience to have enough great stories all by ourselves. So we inevitably resort to handing out ineffective platitudes or directives, as discussed above. That conundrum is what led me to create this book.

Wouldn't it be great if we had at our disposal the collective life experience of not just ourselves but of scores of other people around the world to draw upon when looking for exactly the right story to teach the lesson we need to teach at the moment? I thought so. That's the book I wanted to have when I became a parent. And this is my attempt to create it.

The purpose of this book, then, is to give parents, grandparents, aunts, uncles, teachers, counselors, clergy, and others important in the lives of young people a collection of 101 compelling stories from people all over the world and from all walks of life to help them teach life's most important lessons to the next generation of humanity. And it doesn't matter whether the child is five or fifteen or even fifty. We're never too old to learn from a good story.

WHERE THESE STORIES CAME FROM

To find those stories, I embarked on a yearlong process to interview one hundred people from all over the world and from all walks of life. The stories I've captured come from Australia, Belgium, England, France, Germany, India, Israel, Italy, Japan, Mexico, the Philippines, Poland, Russia, Scotland, Singapore, Switzerland, Tanzania, Venezuela, and eighteen U.S. states plus the District of Columbia. I interviewed old people and young people, straight people, gay people, the rich and the poor, the hearing and the deaf, Christians, Jews, Hindus, agnostics, and people from an astonishing variety of professions (including a navy fighter pilot, teachers, authors, scientists, comedians, bankers, nurses, CEOs, and statisticians), as well as people from a multitude of ethnic backgrounds too numerous to list.

Importantly, in my interviews I didn't ask anyone for their advice. My experience is that when you ask people for advice, you get the platitudes and prosaicisms I warned about above. Instead, I asked questions designed to elicit memories of concrete events in their lives where they learned their most valuable lessons—their unexpected moments of clarity. I asked questions like: Tell me about a time in your life when you learned an important but completely unexpected lesson. What personal stories do you recall hearing as a child that taught you so valuable a lesson you still remember them to this day? What's the biggest mistake you've ever made and why?

Most interviews yielded between five and ten unique stories. From that total of perhaps eight hundred, I selected the most compelling 101 to populate the pages of this book. I then categorized the stories based on the most obvious character traits each addressed. That resulted in the set of twenty-three traits that form the main chapters of this book. A review of history's noteworthy attempts to define the most important character traits gave me confidence I was on the right track. Noble thinkers like Aristotle, Charlemagne, Thomas Aquinas, and Ben Franklin advocated many of the same traits. And similar traits can be found in the teachings of many of the world's major religions and philosophies.

Even in modern times the importance of such traits is being rediscovered. In his groundbreaking book *How Children Succeed: Grit, Curiosity, and Hidden Power of Character*, author Paul Tough describes what a growing number of economists, educators, psychologists, and neuroscientists are now coming to believe. Just shoving information into our kids' brains isn't what matters most, he argues. It's "whether we are able to help her develop a very different set of qualities, a list that includes persistence, self-control, curiosity, conscientiousness, grit, and self-confidence. Economists refer to these as non-cognitive skills, psychologists call them personality traits, and the rest of us sometimes think of them as character."[2]

Most important, I trust that you, the reader, will conclude as you glance through the table of contents that if you send your children off into the world with a firm foundation in these character traits, they will be well prepared to succeed in life and in their careers, to be happy with themselves and those around them, to be productive and caring members of society, and to be the kind of people you will be proud to call yours and that others will want to emulate. In short, you will have made the world a better place through your children, and your job as a parent will have been honorably and exceedingly well done.

HOW TO USE THIS BOOK

First, notice I used the word "use" and not "read." That's because if all you do is read this book, much of its value will be missed. You need to put it to use by sharing the stories, having a conversation about them, and perhaps discussing a few similar stories of your own.

Second, this book is written to be read by you, the adult. It's incumbent on you to choose which stories to share with your young person and how to share them. You may or may not choose different stories to share with a five-year-old than you would with a fifteen-year-old. But you will almost certainly tell those stories differently. You'll use smaller words and shorter sentences with the youngest. For older kids or adults, you can share the stories largely as I've written them, or perhaps you can just hand them the book and ask them to read a particular story themselves. Keep in mind that just because a story is about a seven-year-old boy or a forty-five-year-old man does not mean it's not appropriate for your twelve-year-old girl. Most of the lessons in this book are widely applicable to all ages and most cultures. You'll find more advice on how to tell these stories in the last chapter, "Getting Started."

As for how to work through this book, there are several options. First, you can choose to move straight through from beginning to end, like you would most other books. Or you can skip around based on whatever topic suits your fancy. Either way, you can file those stories away in your head until you need them. Or you can share them with your young person as you come across them or at a regular time each day like you would a bedtime story.

But you can also use it opportunistically. When your child is having a problem with self-discipline or bullying or selfishness, turn to the appropriate chapter and read those stories. There's a detailed list of stories in the appendix to help you find just what you're looking for.

More important than how you read through it is how you go about sharing these stories. Consider each story not as the final word on the subject, but only as the beginning. After each telling, have a conversation with your young person. Much of the wisdom you impart will come from the discussion, not just from the story. Talk about the events in the story and how well or poorly you think the people in the story behaved. Would you have done the same thing if you'd been in their situation? Or something entirely different? Recall that these stories are experiences in the lives of ordinary people as they confronted life's most important crossroads. You and your child can draw wisdom from them by following the path of the people in the story. Or you may recommend the opposite. That's up to you. Most important, have your young person brainstorm ways he or she could apply the wisdom in the story (or from your discussion) to his or her life. You can download a free set of suggested discussion questions at www.leadwithastory.com/resources. Use them. You'll get more out of this book if you do.

Let's get started.

PART 1

WHO YOU ARE

ONE

Ambition

The greater danger for most of us is not that our aim is too high and we miss it, but that it is too low and we reach it.

—MICHELANGELO

Ever since the 1960s, countless young boys and girls have spent their days dreaming of becoming an astronaut, orbiting Earth in the apparent weightlessness of space, or exploring strange new worlds as they saw their heroes do in episodes of *Star Trek* or movies like *Star Wars*.

Bob Woolley was one of them.

Bob describes himself as a child of the space age. He was born in 1953 in Little Falls, New York. One of his earliest memories, at the age of four, was learning about the first man-made satellite, Russia's *Sputnik*, as it orbited Earth. He was fascinated at the very idea that human beings could make something that could circle the entire planet in just ninety minutes.

He recalls watching on February 20, 1962 (his ninth birthday), the television coverage of John Glenn orbiting Earth in the *Mercury-Atlas 6*, the first American to do so. An autographed picture he received from Mr. Glenn on the thirtieth anniversary of that orbit is one of Bob's most treasured belongings to this day.

So the seeds of desire to become an astronaut were sown early. Most children's dreams of becoming an astronaut are long abandoned by the time they're in high school or college, but not Bob's. When it was time to make his first career decisions, he studied what career paths those early astronauts, like John Glenn, had followed. And there was a clear pattern. Almost all of them had been military pilots of high-performance fighter jets. So that's what he set out to do.

He studied astronomy, physics, and geology at the University of Maryland. And in 1981 he joined the U.S. Navy and was assigned as a naval aviator to fly the supersonic F-14 Tomcat popularized in the movie *Top Gun*. To listen to Bob describe the thrill of flying such a powerful machine is an adventure in itself: going from zero to 150 mph in 2.5 seconds as you're slingshot off the deck of an aircraft carrier; flying at top speeds around Mach 2 (over 1,500 mph); breaking the sound barrier the first time; doing 360-degree aileron rolls while flying straight up 25,000 feet off the ground; landing on a carrier deck that's only a thousand feet long and looked the size of a postage stamp only a few seconds earlier; then dropping the landing hook and coming to a dead stop two seconds after touchdown.

Bob's plan was definitely off to a great start. But as you can imagine, the competition to become an astronaut is intense. There have been fewer than 350 Americans admitted to NASA's astronaut program in the fifty years of manned space flight.[1] One of NASA's many selection criteria for astronauts was flight time as a military or commercial pilot. At the time, to be eligible for the program candidates needed to have a minimum of 1,500 flight hours. Even though Bob spent eleven years in the navy, assignment changes and medical issues kept him grounded for much of that time. As a result, by the time he left, he was still short of that number. Bob left the navy knowing he would never be an astronaut.

But his love of space remained, and it took him on two more life adventures he never imagined when he was nine years old. First, with his astronomy training and navy experience, Bob had the perfect background to work at Space Camp at the U.S. Space and Rocket Center[2] in Huntsville, Alabama. There, he managed the Aviation Challenge Program, where young people got to experience navy pilot training: flight simulation, land and water survival training, and ground school academics. He was inspiring future astronauts and loving it.

Next, he started his own tour company called Astronomical Adventures. He created one- to seven-day vacation programs under the beautifully dark skies thirty-five miles southeast of Flagstaff, Arizona. Picture yourself in the middle of a ninety-thousand–acre cattle ranch, miles from the nearest streetlight. By day, he took his guests on tours of the Grand Canyon, Meteor Crater, and the red rock formations in Sedona. Along the tour he explained the scientific and geological formation of each amazing structure. And at night he captivated and educated his guests with a personal tour of the night sky through enormous telescopes Bob built just for this purpose. Imagine a telescope three feet wide and eighteen feet long with a ladder alongside so you can reach the eyepiece. Again each awe-inspiring view came with a full scientific explanation.

Today, entering what most of us would describe as our retirement years, Bob is a high school teacher in math and science in Phoenix, where he lives. There, he shares his knowledge and passions with students, inspiring a whole new generation.

If you're waiting for a nice Hollywood ending where decades later Bob finally gets to become an astronaut, stop waiting. There isn't one. Life's rarely like that. No, Bob never did get to become an astronaut. But the point is, look at the amazing life he's been living largely in pursuit of that dream. He flew supersonic jets in the navy, taught aviation at U.S. Space Camp, led his own personal exploration of the stars through Astronomical Adventures, and inspired hundreds of students with his passion and knowledge of astronomy, math, and science. And he's loved every minute of it. When asked to reflect on what he started out to do and who he's become, Bob smiles and observes, "What's not to love? I'm an adult who was raised on my childhood dreams."

Imagine instead if Bob had set his sights on less lofty goals. He may never have gotten to do the amazing things he's done. Life has a way of getting in the way of whatever goals you set for yourself. Set them high enough, and you'll not be disappointed wherever you land.

• • •

Now let's look at an example of what happens when you don't set lofty enough goals. It's a simple one. And unfortunately it's one that's more common than you might imagine.

At some point in Kelly Olson's senior year at Conway High School in Arkansas, it came time to do what many high school seniors do: apply to college. She took all the college entrance exams that might be necessary: the PSAT, SAT, and ACT. And she did very well. So well, in fact, that she was named a National Merit Finalist. Her scores put her in the top one-half of 1 percent of all college-bound high school seniors in the country. She probably could have gotten into any school she applied to, likely on scholarship. She just didn't fully realize it at the time. And since her family wasn't overly wealthy, she didn't want to burden her parents with Ivy League debt. So when it got right down to the application process, she only applied to one: Hendrix College, the same hometown college where her father worked as a professor.

After all, Hendrix was a private liberal arts college that attracted top high school graduates from several neighboring states. And since her father worked there, she could attend tuition-free. It was an excellent choice by any standard. And it had always been assumed she'd go there. So why apply anywhere else? Even after successfully completing graduate school at William & Mary in Virginia and many years in the working world, she's confident the education she got at Hendrix was top notch and allowed her to be competitive with any of her peers. But when asked thirty years later what her biggest regrets in life are, the first one she mentions is not applying to other schools.

Notice she didn't say not *attending* another school. She said not applying. The reason was this:

"Don't get me wrong," she'll tell you. "I loved my Hendrix experience. But I've always wondered what my life would have been like if I had applied to Ivy League schools, for example. Why didn't I at least apply? I might have been offered scholarships, and then I could have made a more informed choice."

Kelly might have still chosen Hendrix at the end of the day. But if she had set higher or at least broader goals for her college application process, she wouldn't suffer that lingering doubt thirty years later.

• • •

Recognize, of course, that the kind of goals deemed worthy could vary over time and across cultures. In Asia, for example, setting lofty goals and falling short of them might not be what most parents wish for their children. In fact, there's an ancient Chinese saying that it's "better to be the head of a dog than the tail of a lion." Let's look at how that value might play out in someone's life.

Junichi Endo grew up in Saitama City, Japan, about twenty miles north of Tokyo. Like every other student, when he entered O'Hara Junior High School he was encouraged to join one of the extracurricular clubs on campus. Junichi loved baseball in elementary school, so that's what he signed up for. It's important to understand that in Japan, baseball was the most popular sport among boys his age. So it attracted the best athletes in the school. The good news was that thirty boys were allowed to join the team, including Junichi. But since only nine can play at any given time, earning a starting position would be difficult. The other thing he discovered was that the first-year players had to collect the senior players' balls and equipment after practice—something of an initiation ritual.

By the middle of his first season, Junichi had racked up lots of time running drills and picking up after the other players. But he hadn't seen any actual playing time. That honor went to boys who were bigger and could hit and throw the ball farther. That left Junichi in a quandary. He loved baseball, but he didn't relish the idea of two more years of sitting on the bench. He was also painfully conscious that in Japan it was considered shameful to quit anything in the middle once you'd decided to do it. He talked to his coach and one of his teachers about his dilemma, and both encouraged him to stay on the team. Despite that guidance, Junichi decided to quit baseball and join the tennis team.

Because tennis was not as popular as baseball, the tennis team only had about ten players. And relative to the baseball team, as Junichi described it, "its performance was quite weak." But since tennis required more technique and skill than it did power, it suited him better, and his skill grew quickly. His second year he was even elected captain of the team. In that position, he was able to influence the practice routine and tournament schedule. He made adjustments to the training schedule to make the team stronger and added several practice tournaments.

By his third year, his team advanced all the way to the final round in the city tournament and won second place. That meant that for the first time in the school's history, the tennis team had earned a berth in the district-wide tournament. As for the baseball team that year, in their city tournament "they lost in the first round."

For Junichi, his time on the tennis team was the greatest experience of leadership he'd had at that point in his life. And it was one he would have almost certainly not had if he'd stayed on the baseball team. That leadership lesson was to become one of many that stayed with Junichi in the decades since and helped lead to many successes. In 2005 he became the youngest senior vice president in the history of Nissan Motors. And now he is the president and CEO of NMKV, a joint venture between Nissan and Mitsubishi, two of the largest and most prestigious Japanese firms today.

It turned out that spending time as the head of a dog in junior high school tennis helped Junichi today become the CEO of a lion.

• • •

A creative application of that philosophy for an even younger child involves my then seven-year-old son, Benjamin. When Ben was in the Cub Scouts, one of his favorite activities was the Pinewood Derby. Prior to the derby, each scout, with the help of a parent, builds a race car out of a block of wood about seven inches long. The car must meet several design specifications, including a maximum weight and the width of the wheels. On derby day, race officials place each car at the top of an inclined track about forty-five feet long. When let go, the cars race down the track pulled only by gravity. The first car to the bottom wins each heat. And electronic timers record every car's time, so an overall winner can be identified.

In Ben's pack, around sixty scouts compete each year, and they're competing for two main trophies: Fastest Car and Best in Show. The fastest car trophy goes to the car with the best time of the day and is the most coveted of the prizes. A smaller trophy is awarded for the fastest car in each scouting age bracket. Best in Show is the official name for what the boys generally refer to as the "coolest car." If you've never seen a Pinewood Derby race, it is a thing to behold. The boys (as well as many dads) spend weeks crafting unbelievably elaborate cars, including the most creative uses of modeling paint, chrome, and craft supplies you can imagine. It looks like a miniature Detroit auto show. Prior to the race, all the cars are displayed on a table and each scout gets to vote for the coolest car. At the end of the race, the winner is announced, just after the fastest car. And since building an elaborate "cool" car often comes at the expense of the best aerodynamics, usually the scout has to decide up front if he's designing a car for speed or for looks.

So with sixty scouts and only two overall winning trophies, competition is steep. And not just between the scouts. Many of the dads take the competition as seriously as they do their day jobs. Some are engineers or designers and spend weeks perfecting their cars. (Uh, I mean their child's cars, of course.) A quick web search will reveal countless professional articles defining the physics and optimal design of a Pinewood Derby car.

Well, Ben's dad is neither an engineer nor an artist. As a result, Ben's chances of winning either trophy have always been below average. So after his first year of not taking home either of the two major trophies, he decided on a different strategy.

Due to the weight and speed of these cars, any slight imperfection in the track or the wheels can result in a car crashing at the bottom or flying off the track. Any car suffering that fate loses all chances of winning the race and generally earns some good-natured teasing from the other boys. So to add some levity, one year Ben's pack leader added a third trophy to the mix: Best Crash. It wasn't a trophy anyone hoped to earn, but it did take away a bit of the sting out of defeat.

So for Ben's second year in the derby, instead of going for fastest car or coolest car, he decided to aim for a trophy nobody else wanted: Best Crash! His plan was to design a car guaranteed to crash in the most spectacular manner possible. Genius. After many designs, here's what we came up with. We built an average-looking race car. Then we cut it all the way through into three roughly equal sections: a front, middle, and back end of the car. We attached the segments with weak magnets, just strong enough to hold the car together if it wasn't bothered much. Then we put an antenna sticking straight up out of the middle section just tall enough that it wouldn't fit under the metal frame that held the checkered flag over the finish line. Every time his car crossed the finish line, the antenna slammed into the frame with a loud clang. That sent all three segments of the car flying in different directions, some even into the cheering crowd.

The first time his car raced, the crash took everyone by surprise. "How could a car just fly apart like that?" By the last heat, however, everyone was cheering "Crash, crash, crash, crash!"

It's no surprise who won the Best Crash trophy that year. Today it sits proudly on Ben's shelves in his bedroom, next to a race car designed to never win a single race.

• • •

As important as it is to set worthy goals, it's also important to know how to recognize unhealthy ones and let them go. Few people know that better than a woman we'll call Carrie.

Carrie entered the working world after graduating from Vanderbilt University. Her mother was a teacher and her father was in the construction business. Though these were both certainly respectable jobs, Carrie had long admired the status and prestige of the professional and corporate careers she saw on television and in the movies. "I thought it was cool to see women in suits and with briefcases," she explains. So she was pleased to land her first job at a big company in exactly the kind of position she'd imagined.

There was something about the corporate uniform that made her feel important and successful. She remembers the blue pinstriped suit with a bow tie, a skirt, and panty hose. And like all the women, she wore tennis shoes for the long walk from the parking lot, but had a nice pair of pumps in her hard, square briefcase to change into as soon as she arrived. She was an African American woman in her twenties playing in her starring role as the up-and-coming corporate executive. She had assumed exactly the image she'd dreamed of.

Then one day, a few years into her career and after a series of late nights at the office, Carrie realized the person she had become wasn't the person she really wanted to be. The trappings of success she had so desperately wanted were now keeping her from enjoying life.

She recalls the moment vividly. "It was eleven o'clock at night. I was sitting there at my gray metal desk that I shared with two other people, and I was working on probably the tenth version of my forecast. I knew I liked the prestige that came from working there. But I certainly wasn't feeling enriched. So I called my sister on the phone and told her, 'Tomorrow I'm going to walk into my boss's office and quit.'" Since Carrie had no other jobs or even prospects, what did her sister think? "She thought I had lost my mind."

Despite her sister's pleas, the next day Carrie did go into her boss's office and told him she wanted to resign. And in that instant, something amazing happened. "It was like this incredible moment of clarity. Quitting my job unleashed the tethering I had to this corporate persona. I was so caught up in the superficial status of wearing my corporate suit that I was afraid to do anything to risk losing it. It was liberating. I decided at that moment that never again would I be attached to something purely because of the status it offers."

Ironically, Carrie still works at the same company she did thirty-two years ago. Her boss convinced her to stay through his genuine concern and the promise of a new role and promotion. "So I ended up not quitting my job. But I did quit something more important that day. I quit the superficial part of me." And more than quitting something, she was also welcoming back a part of her that she'd lost sight of and the values she was raised with.

Today, Carrie still dresses very well. But it's her style, not something defined by a corporate image. More important, she no longer feels beholden to the unworthy goals of status and prestige. If she ever faces a dilemma in her job that requires her to compromise her values or sacrifice too much of her home life, "I know now I can walk away before I ever let something like that happen."

TWO

Open-Mindedness

> Those who cannot change their minds cannot change anything.
>
> —GEORGE BERNARD SHAW

There's only one person in the world whose opinion is always right. And it's me.

Well, to me, it's me. To you, it's you. And to teenagers, well, we know they're always right. To each of us, we are the only person in the world who agrees with us 100 percent of the time. That doesn't mean our opinions can't change. They do. But it usually takes a lot of evidence (sometimes more than it should). And the very second that compelling information registers in our brain, we change our opinion to fit our new understanding. And then, presto, our opinion is once again 100 percent correct, thus restoring balance and harmony to our self-centered universe.

Such is human nature. Learning to be open-minded to new information takes practice and humility. Just telling someone to be open-minded rarely works. Sharing the following story should be much more effective.

Jim Bangel is a statistician, a retired product development engineer, and an intellectually curious fellow. Many years ago, the company he worked for had just built a state-of-the-art office complex and laboratory, and Jim was attending one of his first meetings there. It was a beautiful building, with lots of windows, natural light, and a huge atrium. But Jim is a thinker. So while he could appreciate its attractiveness, he also couldn't help but assess its functionality as he went through his day. Jim is also a voracious reader. So it's not unusual to see him engrossed in a new book or trade journal article. Such was the case on this particular day. Jim had just started reading a fascinating twenty-page report when he realized he needed to go to the bathroom. So he did what men have been doing since the invention of the toilet. He took the report with him.

Jim walked down the hallway still reading the memo, looking up just often enough to not run into anyone. Reaching the restroom, he entered, quickly picked a stall, and sat down. But the memo was highly engaging, so he stayed to finish it.

While reading he couldn't help but continue his back-of-the-mind assessment of this new building. Since he had sat down, he'd been hearing the muffled sounds of women's voices through the walls from the ladies' bathroom next door. "Wow, they really built the walls cheap in this new building," Jim thought. One more tick on the "con" side of his assessment; then he went back to reading his memo.

A minute later, he noticed a small rectangular garbage receptacle attached to the wall of his stall. "Really? The new construction standards have some strange requirements for bathrooms," he thought (another tick on his mental ledger). Then he started speculating what possible use he could have for such a thing. "I thought maybe if I had a bloody nose, or cut myself shaving in the sink." It seemed like a real waste of money. And he continued with his memo.

Then, under the door to his stall, and accompanied by even closer sounding female voices, he saw two unmistakable pairs of ladies' shoes walk right past him! "Good Lord, there are women in this men's room!" They were chatting away, apparently completely unaware they were in the wrong restroom. "What's the proper etiquette for this?" Jim wondered. Should he say something to warn them? Or sit quietly and wait for them to leave? A few seconds later, he heard even more women's voices, and more ladies' shoes crossed right in front of him. Now his brain was really spinning. "What's going on here? How could all these women not know where they are? Didn't they see the sign, or the urinals against the wall when they walked in? Maybe there's a big women's conference in the building, and someone temporarily converted the sign on this men's room to 'ladies' after I walked in."

Then it occurred to him. He didn't recall seeing any urinals when he walked in. And that's when it hit him, first as a sick feeling in his stomach like he'd just been sucker punched. And then it hit his brain. "Oh my God, I'm in the women's bathroom!" In one mind-blowing instant, Jim's paradigm about where he had been for the past ten minutes was shattered. He instinctively jerked his knees up to his chest to hide his masculine pants and shoes from view. He huddled in this balled-up balancing act until the last woman left. When he was certain he was alone, he made a mad dash for the door, praying nobody would walk in or catch a glimpse of him on the way out.

On the way back to the meeting, Jim analyzed the entire event in his head. Why did it take him so long to admit he was wrong about where he was, despite several damning pieces of evidence? Because he was sure he was right. And to protect that belief, he concocted several elaborate fabrications to make sense of the conflicting information between what he thought was true and what he saw around him. We do the same thing every day. We're just so certain we're right, we can see things no other way.

If you find your child vehemently defending his or her position, despite all evidence to the contrary, tell this story. Then ask, "Is it possible that maybe, just maybe, you're in the wrong bathroom?"

• • •

Sometimes being open-minded doesn't mean having to admit being wrong. It just means admitting that someone else might be right. Those aren't the same thing. And to do that, you have to start by seeing things from that other person's perspective, which doesn't come easily or naturally to most people. Looking at things from a different angle was exactly the lesson Luigi Ciuti learned in quite an unexpected place: a college course on statistics. It was his first year in college, at the University La Sapienza in Rome, Italy. Growing up in Rome, he was used to a traditional grading system in school. Grades on several tests during the quarter plus homework and term papers all combined to yield your final grade in the course. But in his university statistics class, the entire course grade was based on the final exam. So his stress level was unusually high on exam day.

And if that wasn't enough, the other strange thing was that each student sat for the test individually, one after another. That meant Luigi was alone in the room with the professor looking over his shoulder, commenting on his work as he tackled each problem. Fortunately, throughout most of the test, all Luigi heard and saw were occasional grunts of approval and head nods. But that all changed when he got to a problem where he had to solve a matrix equation that involved division.

In mathematics, a matrix is a set of numbers arranged in a square grid with the same number of rows as columns. (Think of a tic-tac-toe or sudoku game with all the boxes filled in.) It turns out a matrix can be used in most of the same ways as any other number in mathematics. You can use them in equations with regular numbers, variables, or even other matrices, where they can be added, subtracted, or multiplied. But the one thing you cannot do with a matrix is divide by it. So mathematicians have invented a trick. Just like dividing by three is the same thing as multiplying by one-third, you can divide by a matrix by taking the "inverse" of the matrix first and then multiplying by it. So that's exactly what Luigi was attempting to do when the nods of approval from his professor suddenly stopped.

Inverting a matrix isn't as simple as just flipping it upside down. There is a complex and tedious set of steps you have to go through to calculate it. As Luigi started that process, he noticed his professor scowling at him. "I could tell he was becoming agitated," Luigi explained. "'Wait, back up. You're doing it wrong,' he said several times."

Now Luigi was really starting to sweat as he struggled to figure out what he was doing wrong. It was well known that this professor would throw students out of an exam if they couldn't progress according to his expectations. But as much as he tried, Luigi was still convinced he was doing it right. But he also knew his professor wouldn't be so adamant if he wasn't sure too. Luigi looked back and forth from the exam to his scowling professor. "Is it possible that we're both right," he thought, "and he's just looking at this from a different angle?"

That turned out to be the right question to ask.

That's when Luigi remembered another oddity of matrix math. In finding the inverse of a matrix, there's more than one way to do it. You can start off horizontally, going by rows first, or you can start vertically, going down the columns first. Luigi was used to doing the problem vertically. His professor, it turns out, liked doing them horizontally. He was literally looking at the problem from a different angle, ninety degrees different to be exact. If the professor had waited until Luigi was done with the problem, he would have seen the correct answer. But the intermediate steps looked all wrong to him.

So Luigi stopped working and explained his revelation to the professor. "I'm doing this vertically. I think you're expecting me to do it horizontally. Right?"

The professor's face froze. After a brief, and perhaps embarrassed, reflection, the professor said, "You're right. Go ahead." Luigi completed the problem, and the entire exam, with a new sense of confidence. And he ended up earning the highest marks in the class.

In the years since Luigi finished his degree and went into the working world, he hasn't found many occasions where he's needed to solve a matrix equation. But he's encountered countless uses for asking the question "Is it possible we're both right? Are they just looking at this from a different angle?" Life's not like the simple math we learned in grade school, where one plus one always equals two. It's more like inverting a matrix: challenging, complicated, and with more than one way to get the right answer. When embroiled in a disagreement with someone, ask the same questions Luigi did. You'll save yourself a lot of stress.

• • •

Since we're all so enamored of our own opinion, it's sometimes hard to imagine why anyone would do something we see no sense in. So it's easy to dismiss a decision we don't understand as being foolish, which means we think the person who made that decision is foolish. And it's certainly possible she is. But that assumption turns out to be wrong more often than it's correct. Thaler Pekar helped a good friend learn that lesson with just a little walk around a lake.

One of the places Thaler likes to spend her time away from the bustle of her office and home in Hoboken, New Jersey, is a lake house in Otsego County in the central part of New York State. It's known by many as the "leatherstocking district" in reference to one of its most famous former residents, James Fenimore Cooper, author of *The Leatherstocking Tales*. The sparsely populated and rural landscape where Thaler retreats sits in the middle of a wildlife preserve befitting the rustic images the name implies.

A few years ago, Thaler's best friend came to visit her there. As the two were walking around the lake, her friend noticed a small Japanese maple tree in the front yard of one of the local residents. But unlike any of the other countless trees in this bucolic neighborhood, this one had a small fence surrounding it on all sides. The woman remarked incredulously, "Who would put a tree in their front yard that needed a fence around it? That's so stupid! Why would anyone bother to do that?" Admittedly, it probably did look a bit out of place.

Even though it was certainly a rhetorical question, Thaler answered it flatly. "Well, if your daughter dies in her thirties, and your neighbors give you a tree to commemorate her life, that's what you do."

Her friend stood in a stunned silence, shocked at the answer and embarrassed at her own insensitivity.

Thaler went on to explain that the young woman had died of ovarian cancer. "And her parents who live in that house are Japanese," she said, which explained the choice of the Japanese maple tree. Lastly, she explained that with the high population of deer around the lake, "the fence was the only way to keep the deer from eating the tree while it was still young."

Thaler normally wouldn't have been so blunt. But she was talking to her best girlfriend and knew her words would be taken sincerely and not offensively.

Many of us, especially when we're young, are quick to conclude how silly some things in life are. But most of the time, it turns out there's a good reason for them. We just don't know what it is yet. We owe ourselves and our neighbors the benefit of the doubt and a dose of humility.

• • •

The above stories indicate how overconfident we can be, and how possible, even likely, it is that we miss other people's legitimate reasons for their opinions or decisions. Once young people realize that, it becomes much easier to find those legitimate reasons. Stories like this have made me start practicing it myself after a lifetime of arrogantly and quickly jumping to conclusions. Here's a recent example to illustrate the point.

I recently attended my son Matthew's junior high wrestling meet. Each match takes place on a mat with a circle twenty-eight feet in diameter as the wrestling area. The coaches are allowed to sit in chairs just outside the circle. But they're not allowed to venture far from their chairs or come inside the circle.

At one critical point, Matthew's opponent had him on his back, close to being pinned. Matthew's coach slid out of his chair and onto his knees to shout instructions and encouragement to help him break out of the hold. Although the coach was still outside the circle, and only a few inches from the seat of his chair, the referee waved him back. The rules are, after all, the rules.

After the match was over, I had about an hour until Matthew wrestled again. I tried to be productive, so I pulled out my laptop to get some work done (writing this book, actually). But the cheering for the other matches occasionally distracted me. At one point I looked up to see the coach of one of the other teams running all the way around the circle to coach her wrestler, madly waving her arms around. I knew what was supposed to come next, so I looked at the referee. But he did nothing. "How could he miss that?" I thought. A moment later, she ran around to the other side to get closer to her wrestler, and this time even stepped inside the circle waving more signals. "Well, that's not fair," I thought. In fact, I started feeling a bit of disdain for the referee who so strictly maintained the rules when it hindered my son, but was lenient when it was someone else's.

Then I thought of Thaler Pekar's lesson, and I asked myself, "Let's assume there is a legitimate explanation for this. What could it be?" Nothing came to mind, so I kept watching, looking for a clue. Importantly, I was looking for—and honestly hoping to find—a good reason this obvious infraction was being overlooked. And then I saw it. The woman running around the ring wasn't the boy's coach. She was his sign language interpreter. The boy was deaf. His coach was sitting in his chair outside the ring, exactly where he was supposed to be. This justifiable exception to the rule was made to level the playing field. Suddenly my son and his coach didn't seem unfairly judged. In fact, I gained a whole new level of respect for that official and the organizers of the meet for making these arrangements.

When we start with the open-minded assumption that the rest of the world isn't full of idiots, it's amazing what good sense we'll find in other people's decisions.

THREE

Creativity

> Every child is an artist. The problem is staying an artist when you grow up.
>
> —PABLO PICASSO

Creativity is considered by many to be a rare, elusive gift only musicians or bohemian New York artists possess. And to be sure, some people are born with more than an average amount of it. But everyone has the capacity to be creative. Many of us simply don't call on it very often. When you intentionally call on that capacity inside, really call for it, you'll realize it can be summoned. That's a lesson Michael Margolis learned at an early age.

Michael grew up in Lausanne, a city in western Switzerland perched on the north shore of Lake Geneva. He describes his father as "a mad scientist and inventor." His mother, Leslie, was a teacher, artist, and toy designer. "So I never knew if my day was going to be an art project or a science experiment," he muses. Importantly, Michael recalls climbing in the family station wagon on many weekends and driving around to rummage sales. "What everyone else was getting rid of, we would buy." They referred to other people's trash as "super-junk, because we would build things with it." As a result, their basement was always well stocked with super-junk.

When Michael was six years old, he remembers his older brother David working on an art project at home with some clever material their mom had given him. And, as can happen between siblings, Michael got jealous. "Why does David always get the cool stuff? That's not fair!" Most such squabbles were tame enough. But for whatever reason, this time Michael was hysterical over it. "I threw a complete tantrum. I was kicking and screaming and huffing and puffing."

Mom quickly intervened. "Michael, Michael, take a breath, son. Just wait here. I'll be right back." She soon emerged from the basement with something in her hands. Michael was still upset and sniffling, so Mom had to work to get his attention.

"Michael, look here, son. Look at this. I have something for you." And she handed him an old wooden box.

Michael didn't know it at the time, but what she handed him was an old sewing box, part of her collection of super-junk. And it was no longer in any shape to serve as a sewing box. One of the covers was missing. It was badly chipped on another side. And the hinges were rusty. But she got him to at least look at it. He quickly noticed that this box didn't open from the top like most boxes. It opened from the sides, with nested layers of trays that splayed out like a fishing tackle box the further you pulled them. And then she asked Michael the critical question. She said, "Michael, what do you see?"

Still sniffling and cranky, all Michael could come back with was, "I don't know what you're talking about, Mom. It's just a box!"

Undaunted, Mom repeated slowly, "Michael, what do you see?"

So Michael calmed himself and finally took a good look at the box for a moment. And then another moment. And then finally, with a bolt of excitement and discovery, he shouted, "Oh, it's a pirate ship!"

"Well done, Michael," Mom said with a smile. "Now let's go build it."

And with that the two struck off to the basement for more supplies. They found some old empty shotgun shells that became cannons for the deck. An old wooden centipede toy held together with springs sacrificed its legs, each of which became a crew member on board the ship. Then Leslie dug into a cupboard full of old wedding gifts and mementos and pulled out a set of doily napkins that had never seen use. When she presented them to Michael, he beamed, "Hey, you found sails!"

By the time they were done, it was a beautiful piece of art and a finely functioning pirate ship Michael is still proud of today.

Michael took away two lessons from that day. First, the joy of reinvention and reinterpretation: "How you can take things that are old and discarded and remake them in a new way." And second, he learned to see possibilities where none readily appear, like seeing a pirate ship in an old sewing box.

For our purposes here, however, what's important is the brilliant way Michael's mother taught him to summon that creativity. She did it by asking him the simple question, "Michael, what do you see?" And she didn't let up until he'd given her an answer. It wasn't simply a question. It was an invitation to use his imagination.

If you want to summon creativity—in your young person or in yourself—try following Leslie Margolis's lead. Look at your subject, and ask the question, "What do you see?"

• • •

Fortunately, you don't have to be an artist, inventor, or professional toy designer to help a young person develop creativity. It turns out all you really have to do is remove less creative ways for her to spend her time. That's a lesson Emma Sartini didn't even know she was learning as a child. But she's glad she did.

Emma was the oldest of three children of a stay-at-home dad and a mom who worked as a retail executive. As Emma explains, one of the rules they established early on for all three of their children was this: "We weren't allowed to have toys with batteries or that needed electricity." Many kids would consider that cruel and unusual punishment. But to Emma, that's just the way things were. She recalls the only exception to the rule was for toys like Lite Brite or K'Nex where they were actually building a creation of their own design. "Mom thought we shouldn't have toys where we had to be told what it was and how we had to play with it."

So how did they entertain themselves? "We had to be more creative. I played with Lincoln Logs and paper dolls I made. We would go for walks and collect rocks. Then we painted the rocks into different animals and created whole scenes with them. I even remember my brother making wallets out of duct tape."

Spending an entire childhood that way led to some powerful character traits for Emma and her siblings. Today, Emma is always trying to make something from nothing. She says, "I don't mind buying something that isn't perfect. And it doesn't have to be a designer name brand either. I can get something from a thrift shop and fix it up. Or if I see a painting I like, I buy a blank canvas and make it myself. If I cut the sleeves off of a shirt, I keep the scraps and make something out of them—maybe turn it into a bracelet or headband."

And if you think you see something other than creativity being developed here, you're right. Her parent's rule helped her develop a sense of frugality and resourcefulness. "I still don't like things with batteries," she says. "I think it's wasteful. I even wash and reuse plastic Baggies."

But the rule may have had an even longer-term impact. All three children grew up to pursue a career in some kind of creative design. Emma studied industrial design and grew up to be a product designer, using her creativity on a daily basis. Her brother went to school for digital design. And her sister, who learned how to knit and crochet in elementary school, ended up making her own purses and hats in junior high, then went on to college to study fashion design.

Emma's parents raised a whole family of highly creative people. And it all started with a simple rule.

• • •

Think you're doing enough to foster a creative environment for your kids? You might be squelching it and not even know it, as this next story illustrates.

One evening, nine-year-old James was sitting with his aunt in the kitchen having tea. Frustrated with his apparent laziness, his aunt barked out at him, "James, I never saw such an idle boy! Take a book or employ yourself usefully. For the last hour you have not spoken one word, but taken off the lid of that kettle and put it on again."[1] It seems he was fascinated with the steam coming from the kettle. He held a silver spoon over the jet of steam and watched as drops of water formed on the spoon and ran down the handle. Over and over again he studied this simple phenomenon. "Are you not ashamed of spending your time this way?" she scolded.

Fortunately, the boy was undaunted by her admonishment. His childhood fascination with steam stuck with him. Two decades later, in 1765, a now twenty-nine-year-old James Watt invented a new and improved steam engine that helped usher in the Industrial Revolution.

As observed by William Bennett, "The opposite of work is not leisure or play or having fun, but idleness—not investing ourselves in anything."[2] Be careful not to discourage play. Discourage idleness. And for the record, watching TV is usually not play.

FOUR

Curiosity and Learning

> I have no special talents. I have only been passionately curious.
>
> —ALBERT EINSTEIN

Consistent with Einstein's observation above, being passionately curious paves a strong path to learning. It's akin to necessity being the mother of invention. If you have an insatiable desire to know something, you'll eventually find a way to learn it. So if you wish to learn anything, start by learning to be curious.

How does one learn to be curious? One of the surest paths to a strong sense of curiosity is to experience the thrill and joy of discovery. Like a drug whose effect the addict craves, discovering something you've tried in earnest to find (as opposed to being given the answer with no effort) creates a joy and elation like nothing else. Anyone who's known that thrill is apt to want to experience it again and again. Giving yourself, or someone else, that joy of discovery is a gift that continues to reward its recipient for years to come.

The best example of this I've come across was from a Boy Scout camping trip to Ferne Clyffe State Park in southern Illinois.

Rick was a sixteen-year-old high school student in Carbondale, Illinois, at the time and a senior patrol leader in the scouts. That meant on a campout he was in charge of a small cadre of scouts four or five years younger than him. It had just started to rain as they left home for the hour-long drive to Ferne Clyffe. By the time they arrived, everything was thoroughly soaked. They set up their tents in the rain, and then turned their attention to dinner. The stew was already made but needed to be heated on a fire. But how can you make a fire when all the firewood is wet? You can't, of course. So that's when Rick posed this question to his troop of eleven- and twelve-year-olds. "Where is the dry wood?" And with that, off they went in search of this elusive dry wood in a soaking wet forest.

For fifteen or twenty minutes they tried, but no amount of climbing or digging produced anything other than a slightly less wet piece of unburnable wood. So Rick asked, "Well then, where is it *not*?" This started a vigorous debate among the young scouts as they struggled with this worthy puzzle that stood between them and dinner. After another dozen minutes without an answer, Rick picked up a thick branch from the ground and asked an even more leading question: "Where on this log is the wood *not* dry?"

"On the outside, of course," came a chorus of answers almost in unison. Then, almost as quickly, came the realization that the "dry wood is on the inside!" Rick took an extra measure of pride in the shrieking prepubescent voices of half a dozen boys and their elation of finding the dry wood that had been right at their feet the whole time. They quickly determined safe and effective ways to shave and chisel off the wet bark on the outside to reveal dry wood for their fire.

In less than an hour, while enjoying warm stew and a roaring fire, each boy took turns taking credit for the amazing discovery of dry wood in a wet forest. Each one was more certain than the last that he was the first to yell out the correct answer.

Rick vividly remembers hoping none of them would realize how blatant his efforts were to lead them to the answer. They worked hard for this victory and he wanted them to enjoy it. He also remembers being conscious of the fact that at the previous year's camping event, he probably wouldn't have had the patience to let them find the dry wood themselves, or the maturity to stand by silently as they took credit so quickly for it. In helping his troop grow into young men, he was actually taking his own step into manhood.

If you want to instill in someone a strong sense of curiosity, find a way to give him the gift of discovery, like Rick did for these Boy Scouts. You may find it helps both of you grow.

• • •

So having the curiosity to learn is part of the battle. Knowing *how* to learn—and how not to learn—is another. This next story contains one of the simplest yet most powerful lessons I've ever learned about how to learn.

When Louise-Audrey Zenezini was six years old, her family moved from Italy to the United States. Her father, Stefano, had been transferred to a new assignment in his company. Shortly after they arrived, both father and daughter knew it was time for her to learn to ride a bike. And the wide-open front yard of Louise-Audrey's new school was the perfect place to do it. It was a lush, green lawn that stretched out flat for dozens of yards in all directions, with nothing to get in her way. Nothing, that is, except for one thing: the flagpole.

Stefano took off the training wheels, saddled his girl onto her little pink bike, and gave her the expected instructions: "Keep pedaling, lean into a turn, and whatever you do, don't run into that pole." Then he gave her a gentle push, and she was off, keeping an eye, of course, on the flagpole. She made it a few turns of the pedals before her first stop. Dad was there for her and got her started again. This time there were a few more rotations and shouts of encouragement from Dad before another tenuous stop. And as anyone who's taught children to ride a bike knows, the direction you push them has little to do with the direction they end up going. Each wobble reorients the bike as they lean into their fall to right themselves.

Finally, with a big push, Louise-Audrey was doing it, pedaling all on her own, hands on the handlebars, and eyes on the flagpole. Stefano was beaming as only a proud father can as he saw his little girl riding a bike all on her own. But with just a few more wobbles, Louise-Audrey was now getting closer and closer to the flagpole. Stefano managed to get out one last shout, "Don't hit the flagpole!" right before his little girl took her last wobble-righting turn and ran straight into . . . the flagpole. She had 359 degrees of freedom to ride her bike wherever she wanted, and somehow she ended up on a path that led her to the only three-inch-wide obstruction on the entire field.

What are the odds of that happening? Actually, quite high, according to Steven Vannoy and Craig Ross, authors of *Stomp the Elephant in the Office.*[1] As part of their work as workplace and leadership consultants, two of their observations about human behavior are (1) the mind cannot avoid a "don't," and (2) we go toward our focus.

Most of us know if you tell a child to not put a shiny quarter in his or her mouth, that's the first place it will go. But adolescents and adults aren't immune to this phenomenon either. The authors demonstrate this brilliantly by telling the reader, "Don't take time to look now, but when you examine the front cover of this book, you will notice that the elephant is in a peculiar shape. . . . When you look at it later, you will see what we are talking about." Two paragraphs later they ask about it, and most readers have to admit that they immediately looked at the elephant on the cover. So none of us are exempt from this.

And that's exactly what happened to little Louise-Audrey. Her father told her, "Don't hit the flagpole." So that's what she was focusing on the whole time—the flagpole. And since we go toward our focus, that's exactly where she ended up.

So, whether as the parent teaching, or the child learning, focus on what to *do* instead of what *not* to do. For Louise-Audrey, that might have been, "Ride your bike anywhere on this side of the yard." Or for the child with the shiny quarter, it would be "put this in your pocket." For older children it's the difference in focusing on winning instead of not losing, or passing the exam instead of not failing, or developing healthy relationships instead of avoiding bad influences. That positive focus will take you a long way toward more effective learning. Plus you won't run into any flagpoles.

• • •

Since we're talking about learning, let's devote some attention to the many choices young people have to make in life about their education, from whether to pursue it at all, to what to study, to what extracurriculars to sign up for. And let's start with a teenager named Austin Channell.

By the time Austin was thirteen years old, he'd completed the Boy Scout requirements to be a life scout, just one rank below the highest rank of eagle scout. He loved the outdoor activities and all the experiences that came with being a scout. And as an active senior patrol leader with five years remaining to complete the eagle scout requirements, he was almost certain to achieve that rank, earned by only 5 percent of scouts.

But then in the eighth grade, Austin achieved something else impressive. He landed a role in a community performance of the Tony Award–winning musical *The Music Man*. It was the largest part he'd had up to that point. And unlike school shows he'd previously performed in, this show was a charity event to be performed at the Palace Theater in Columbus, Ohio, in front of 2,700 people. But while Austin was excited about this opportunity, his scoutmaster and the other boys in his troop were not. Rehearsals for such a performance were frequent and demanding. As Austin explained, "It was going to hurt my attendance a little at scouting events. I think they just didn't like the distraction. In fact, my scoutmaster told me, 'You need to get your priorities straight and pick one or the other.'" And while the choice was Austin's, it was clear which decision he was feeling pressure to make. Eagle scout was a highly valued honor he could put on his resume and that might even help him get college scholarships. Being in a play was viewed as nice but not nearly as important. "Having to pick was devastating to me," he recalled. "Eventually I chose to leave scouting to do theater, something I loved even more."

Austin went on to perform his role in the musical, which raised close to $200,000 for nationwide children's hospice care. But afterwards, he was uncomfortable around the boys from his old troop at school. He felt ostracized. His decision was clearly unpopular and contrary to the conventional wisdom he'd been offered. But he knew it was the right one for him. And it gave him some practice making unpopular decisions, which it turns out he needed just a few years later.

By the time he was a high school senior in 2013, Austin had an impressive academic record. He completed twelve advanced placement courses before he graduated. But because he still loved the arts, he also continued with theater and auditioned for a competitive seat in the choir. Once classes were under way, he began to do the math on his grade point average. He was earning an A in each of his AP classes, which meant he could have a 5.0 GPA for the year, putting him first in his class and making him the presumptive valedictorian. But then he realized that choir class, even the most competitive group he was part of, was a regular four-point class. Even if he got an A in the course, it would bring his GPA down to a 4.8 and likely put him out of the running for valedictorian. The senseless irony was that his GPA would be higher if he just took a study hall instead of choir! And nobody had to explain to Austin what an honor it is to be valedictorian and the benefits that can have on future college and job prospects.

So once again, Austin faced a difficult choice: drop choir and work to be the valedictorian, or stay in choir and likely lose that opportunity. Once again, Austin made the difficult decision and stayed in choir. But the whole ordeal made him question the values inherent in the conventional wisdom. "It made me think we should reevaluate society's definition of success," he said.

After all, in both situations, Austin was engaging in pursuits that were just as worthy but did not have the recognizable accolades of success that comes with being an eagle scout or valedictorian. So he had to ask himself, am I doing what society tells me is the best thing to do, or what I know in my own heart and soul is the right thing for me?

If you were Austin, what choices would you have made?

• • •

Now let's shift our attention to learning after high school, specifically, the choice to attend college or not. Only a couple of generations ago, less than half of all high school graduates in the United States went on to college. Today, 84 percent of twenty-seven-year-old Americans have attended at least some college courses.[2] But with skyrocketing tuition costs, many families are still struggling with this expensive decision. And if you think it's tough here, imagine what it's like in the developing world. In many places it's still a rare opportunity, so the decision is harder. Just like in the United States, in those places people have to consider carefully the long-term costs and benefits of such a choice. And no matter what you choose, you can never really be sure how things would have turned out had you made a different decision. But every once in a while, a lucky few are given as close a glimpse as the laws of nature allow. Two of those people are Marvin Abrinica and his father, John.

John grew up in the Philippines on the island of Negros, the twelfth of thirteen children. Like most people on the island, John's family were farmers working the sugar cane plantations. In his late teens, John decided he wanted more than a farmer's life. So he ran away to Manila, where he attended a small engineering college. He was the first in his family to get a college degree, and one of only two to ever leave home. In Manila, he met a schoolteacher named Noemi, and the two married and immigrated to the United States. The couple settled in Wisconsin, where John got a job as a draftsman and Noemi worked as a maid at a Red Roof Inn. Both jobs were beneath their education and training, but it was a start. John eventually went on to become a successful engineer at General Electric. Noemi ran several of her own businesses before becoming a real estate agent and investor.

When Marvin was born, he was raised with "a healthy dose of Filipino culture," as he described it. Mom and Dad maintained their traditional food, language, and values, which Marvin was immersed in at home. But he still knew little else of where he came from. Like his father, Marvin eventually attended college, went on to graduate school, and landed a great job at a Fortune 500 company where he's enjoyed a rewarding and challenging career ever since.

But about six years ago, at the age of sixty-nine, John was diagnosed with dementia. His short-term memory began slipping away. As Marvin explained it, "it's like a candle that slowly burns away. After the short-term memories are gone, it continues to burn until the rest of your memories disappear too." As it became clear that John wouldn't always have clear memories of life in the Philippines, Marvin started feeling a sense of urgency to make a journey there. He called it a "roots journey." So he made arrangements to take both his parents on a trip.

Their first stop was in Manila to visit his mother's family. Then John and Marvin moved on to Negros. It took several hours of navigating long back roads on the island until they finally arrived at the village where John grew up. Looking around, Marvin describes the homes as "shanties with tin roofs and dirt floors, with no running water or electricity." And it was there that Marvin got his first glimpse of the family he'd never met—one of his surviving uncles and his son, Marvin's cousin.

"My uncle was seventy-nine years old. He'd lived and farmed there his whole life. And my cousin, to greet us properly, climbed thirty feet up the nearest coconut tree with a machete and cut down some coconuts for us to eat. I quickly realized how simply these people lived. And they were happy. So I was happy for them." But it wasn't the life Marvin would have chosen for himself. And that's when he had his unexpected moment of clarity. As he explains, "It was just the four of us—two brothers and two cousins—on this dirt road lined with sugar cane and coconut trees. And it was so strange. It was like looking in the mirror. I was looking at two people, my blood, and it occurred to me for the first time the gravity of my father's decision fifty years ago. It must have taken a lot of courage for him to do what he did. And if he hadn't, I very much could have been this other man in front of me.

"That moment really clarified for me the importance of making courageous decisions in the defining moments of your life. My dad saw generations of his family grow up in poverty. And he decided that wasn't the life he wanted for himself, or eventually his children. His decision to leave and get an education changed life forever for him and generations to come."

The value of getting an education is something many parents try, often unsuccessfully, to impress upon their children. It's certainly not the only route to success and happiness in life. But it clearly creates more opportunities and paths to get there, as evidenced by Marvin's story. But his story illustrates another point rarely mentioned in those conversations: the impact that choice will have on their children and their children's children.

So if they find themselves someday with one of those rare opportunities to see what life might have been like for them and their children, will they be happy with the choice they made?

• • •

With all the pressure on kids today to go to college, and the high cost of doing so, there's mounting anxiety for them to choose the "right" field of study. In the United States, for example, delaying that choice or changing direction even one year in can cost tens of thousands of dollars in added tuition. But even where cost isn't a major concern, pressure to make the right choice can be paralyzing. Someone who hears about that anxiety firsthand is Anne Favrelle.

Anne is an artist living in Annemasse, France, just across the French border with Switzerland, seven miles east of Geneva. She works primarily with acrylic, chalk, pencil, markers, and even some ceramics. And when she's not working on her own creations, she runs an art gallery[3] for fledgling artists hoping to update the public's perception of what contemporary art looks like.

And if that weren't enough, she also finds time to tutor local high school students in math and English. Spending those few hours a week with several teenagers, she gets to hear about their hopes and dreams and of course their fears. One of those fears, she confirms, is making the right choice for higher education. She explains, "In France, the first choice you have to make about higher education is around the age of fifteen or sixteen. So from the age of twelve, they're told 'you need to start thinking about what direction you want to take, and make good grades so you have options.' That puts a lot of pressure on these very young people. They feel like they have to choose what they will do for the next forty years!" It's a concern shared by young people in many places around the globe.

To allay their anxiety, Anne explains that they're not really making a forty-year decision. She reminds them of the now ubiquitous statistics that the average person changes careers seven times during his or her working lifetime.[4] And even if that's an exaggeration, clearly the correct number is greater than one. "You're making at most a ten-year decision," she ventures.

That seems to comfort some of them. But what they find more comforting is hearing her personal story. Her first sentence usually gets their attention. "In my early twenties, I completed a master's degree in genetics from Pierre-and-Marie-Curie University in Paris." Not exactly the background they expected to hear from their English tutor and French artist.

She goes on to explain that her plan was to become a research scientist and university professor. So her next step would be to complete a Ph.D. But after finishing her master's degree, she had an opportunity to do a research internship in exactly the kind of academic environment she would eventually work in after getting her doctorate. By the end of the internship, she explains, "I didn't like the work at all." Doing more of the same for a living was out of the question. "So I decided to study marketing."

Anne relocated three hundred miles south, to the Institute of Management for the Health Industry in Lyon. A little more than a year later, she completed her degree in marketing and took her first job as a marketing research manager for a big pharmaceutical company. This change is probably the most telling to her young audience. In just over a year, Anne went from having completed a master's degree in genetics and working at an active internship in the field, to a completely different industry and career, completing an advanced degree in that new field, and landing a job at a prestigious firm in the industry. But she obviously wasn't done yet.

After two years, she moved to a global consumer products company, still in the market research field, where she stayed for eleven years. After a few months with a market research agency, she decided to follow her greatest passion and become an artist, which is how her students know her today.

So in the span of eighteen years, Anne has gone from geneticist, to marketing researcher, to artist and gallery owner and tutor. And she's been successful with each new venture.

At that point she can get back to tutoring her student, who's now settled down enough to focus on her math instead of stressing about her future.

FIVE

Courage

. . . being brave does not mean being unafraid. It . . . means being afraid and doing it anyway.[1]

—RACHEL NAOMI REMEN

One of the most common fears young people face early in their lives is trying something new. The uncertainty and apprehension of failure can be crippling. And if it's not overcome as a child, it can haunt someone throughout life. One person who's earned some valuable wisdom struggling to find courage is Kerri Whitfield.

Two years after her family's move, Kerri was still feeling a bit like the new kid in town. She'd made a few friends but still didn't know that many other twelve-year-olds. Watching one of her girlfriends play on a softball team that summer, Kerri sat in the bleachers and secretly wished she was on the field with her. "It looks like fun to play," she thought. And she'd make so many new friends that way, too. Eventually her friend asked Kerri if she wanted to join the team. This was her big opportunity! What did Kerri do?

"I told her, 'No.'"

Three-plus decades later, Kerri explains that decision this way. "I was so scared. I'd never played softball before. I'd never played any organized sport before! So I didn't know anything about the game. I didn't know the rules, or how to play. All I could think about was how I would fail because I didn't know how. It never occurred to me they could teach me those things. So I just said no."

The remorse didn't take long to set in. "I was so sad. I kept going to the games and watching them play. There were times I had to wipe away tears, hoping no one had seen me cry. I so wanted to be out on that field. It's a decision I still regret."

That event kicked off a lifetime of what Kerri now sees as missed opportunities. Her fear of failure kept her from succeeding at many new things. Sometimes it kept her from trying in the first place, like the singing lessons she never took or the new job she never applied for. And sometimes that fear made her quit soon after starting. She recalls a failed attempt at gymnastics. "I hadn't been in the class for long, and we were learning how to do the splits. One of the coaches said that if we couldn't get all the way down, they would push us the rest of the way. I never went back. Somehow my parents never challenged that decision. So that was the end of my gymnastics career."

One of her more memorable successes was in learning to waterski. A friend had invited her to ski. But when it was Kerri's turn, she was too afraid to even get in the water. After a few minutes of grace and ineffective coaxing, her girlfriend's father pushed her off the boat. Kerri Whitfield learned to ski that day. And the next time, she jumped off the boat by herself.

It probably wasn't until she had children of her own that Kerri decided her insecurities would no longer impact her or her growing family. She shares these stories with her son and daughter to help them have the courage to try new things. Looking back, there are three lessons she thinks she learned. "First," she explained, "I wished I'd shared my desires more openly with my parents. Maybe then they could have encouraged me to play softball. Second, I wish I'd understood then that I didn't have to be the best at everything on the first day. Everyone has to learn, even the experts. If I'd known that, I might have gone back for the second day of gymnastics class. Third, I learned that part of life is getting unexpectedly wet. Because sometimes good parenting means pushing you off the boat."

• • •

Unfortunately, you can't always rely on a parent (or a friend's parent) to push you off the boat. Usually, you have to muster courage all by yourself. Kelly Olson (whom you met in chapter 1) was lucky to learn that lesson from something that happened to her grandmother, Glenda, almost one hundred years ago. And it's been giving her courage ever since.

Glenda Cecil was born in 1908 in Parker City, Indiana. When she was still a young girl, around the age of twelve, she was invited to attend one of the biggest Christmas parties in the county. Everyone was excited to attend because word had leaked out that the hosts planned something special for the evening hors d'oeuvres: fresh oranges. That may not sound impressive to today's reader. But in the middle of an Indiana winter in 1920, it was very impressive. At the time, nobody had figured out an economical way to get fresh produce from the Southwest to the colder states during winter. It was simply unheard of to eat any crop out of season. Somehow, and surely at great expense, the party host had made arrangements to do the impossible.

Young Glenda was so excited. But her mother was raising proper young ladies, so she and her sisters received the following instructions before going to the party. The first time the basket of oranges came around, they were to pass it along without taking one. Only on the second pass were they allowed to take anything. At great pain, Glenda did as instructed. Watching that basket of ripe oranges pass by must have been extremely difficult for a twelve-year-old. Even more difficult, however, was what happened next. It never came around a second time. After the first pass, it was empty.

Glenda was heartbroken. No, it wasn't like the devastation of unrequited love. But it made just as permanent an impression on her. Enough so that sixty years later, she would tell that story to her granddaughter, Kelly. It was one of many stories Glenda told Kelly to teach her important lessons about what life was like in her day and the expectations her mother set for how young women were to behave in public. But in this case, Glenda took away a different lesson than the one her mother intended and that she wanted to impress upon young Kelly. That lesson is this: Sometimes when life presents you with an opportunity, you just have to take it, because you never know if that opportunity will come around again.

That lesson stayed with Kelly. And those moments when she's drawn upon it have turned out to be some of her greatest. One such moment was when Kelly was a junior in college. That year, she was selected to participate in an overseas study program at Birkbeck College in London, one semester abroad with twelve classmates. It was an amazing opportunity.

Near the end of the three-month program, the group had an unscheduled evening and the students were debating what to do. Kelly desperately wanted to see a live performance of *Les Miserables*. It was perhaps their last opportunity while in London, and it wasn't certain they'd get another. There were only a few cities in the world where she could see such a performance, and she didn't live near any of them. Despite her impassioned plea, none of her companions was interested. Each opted for another attraction or to simply stay home and study. Kelly was heartbroken. The thought of venturing out on foot, by herself, in the dark and cold winter of an unfamiliar city of eight million people was beyond consideration. (Was she even allowed to do such a thing?) Besides, she didn't even have a ticket. After mustering as much courage as she could, however, she decided to go it alone.

She checked her map, bundled up for the wintry weather, and set out on her adventure. She trudged two or perhaps three miles through the snow and ice to Queen's Theatre. Without an advance ticket, Kelly had to wait in line for unclaimed seats of season ticket holders. While she was waiting in the cold with dozens of other hopefuls, a rumor rushed through the line that the queen might be attending the performance that night. At first that seemed to call for excitement. And then she realized what it really meant was that season ticket holders were even more likely to show up that night. Not to see the play, but to see the queen! Her heart sank again. But she continued to wait. Slowly, the line shrank in front of her as a few people got tickets or gave up and went home. As she was close to giving up herself, the ticket master came out and announced that he had one single ticket available. "Is there anyone who wants just a single ticket?"

"Yes! Here! Here!!" she shouted, her hand shooting up like an eager college student barely able to contain a correct answer. And with that, it was hers. She took the ticket and entered the theater, her heart racing. Her eyes were wide with excitement and full of her good fortune. As the ushers directed her to her balcony seat, however, she could not believe where it was located—front row center! She had arguably been given the best seat in the house. She sat enraptured, barely daring to move for the entire performance. The queen never did show up that night, which is just as well. Because Kelly felt like she had gotten her chair.

Today, Kelly Olson describes that evening as one of the "shining moments" of her life. "It was magical." She'll never forget her tears at the climactic scenes, shed probably just as much for the heroes and heroines as they were for her own good fortune. Imagine if she hadn't been brave enough to strike out on her own that night, or to confront the dark or the distance or the weather. Or what if she hadn't had the patience to wait in that long line? She knows the answer, of course. She would have missed out.

Looking back, Kelly recognizes that many of her best memories in life were times she was alone, perhaps on a business trip, but had the courage to venture out on her own to explore her temporary surroundings: seeing the Frick art collection in New York City, visiting the DuPont gardens and Andrew Wyeth studios in Delaware, even catching her first glimpse of the Pacific Ocean.

And as she looks back at all of those moments with a smile, she hopes Glenda Cecil would be proud of her, knowing that when the basket came around, she took her orange.

• • •

Chrissy, a native New Yorker, had ideas about courage similar to Kelly's. She always thought courage was about not going along with the crowd, especially when the crowd was doing something you didn't believe in. Courage meant having the strength to walk away and follow your own compass. Until, that is, she spent some time studying in Austria. That's when she realized real courage might mean something very different. It might mean choosing to stay.

Chrissy was taking a college-level history class on the events leading up to World War II. As she describes it, "After class one day, I was sitting with some of the students in a café having a drink. Inevitably, the conversation turned to the question, 'What would you have done if you had lived in Austria right before the war?' I responded flippantly that I would have left with all the other intelligent people and moved to America. Several other people agreed with me and we concurred that we never could have put up with the Nazi incursion and hatred going on and that we probably would have left long before the war started. Everyone except one.

"One student became really angry. He shouted: 'You traitors! You idiots! It's people like you who made the atrocities possible. When Hitler was rising to power, at least half of the population did not agree with him. If they had stayed, if they had fought for what they believed in, the country would never have been hijacked and used for such evil. Shame on you!'

"Looking back, my answer would probably still be the same. Austria, and living in Austria, meant nothing to me. As people started showing signs of supporting the Nazis, I would probably have left, long before more serious choices arose. It was not my home and I did not ultimately belong there. I was just passing through.

"But his response forever changed me. Until then I prided myself on only belonging to groups I could be proud of—groups that I completely agreed with and felt wholeheartedly that I could support. Whenever someone joined the group with an agenda I didn't support, I bailed. I even left a religion because there was someone I considered fanatical in the church stating things I couldn't agree with. Later, that same church had attendance problems, trouble raising money to support its basic needs, and general problems stemming from lack of morale. I had convinced myself that I was the more ethical and devout person because I refused to budge on what I believed in. Instead, I was a coward following the path of least resistance. Had I stayed, had I voiced my opinion, perhaps others would have felt comfortable doing the same and coming to an agreement as to what they stood for. Unlike living in Austria, the church did mean something to me, and I should have stood up for what I believed in.

"In raising my children, I want them to think carefully about who they are and what they believe in. When a rotten apple joins the bin, I want them to thoughtfully consider the option to stay and fight, and not decide solely between going with the flow or leaving."

It's been said that "all that is necessary for evil to triumph is for good men to remain silent."[2] So, the next time a group you're a part of strays from what you believe in, what will you do?

• • •

The difficulty of being brave, of course, is that you have to constantly reaffirm that bravery. Otherwise, at every opportunity you risk making a different choice. So is there a way to put yourself in a position to have a better chance of staying the course? Fortunately, there is. When Spanish conquistador Hernando Cortez landed in Mexico in 1519, he famously burned his ships. With no way home, his men were more motivated to accomplish their goal, which was to conquer and colonize the interior of Mexico. Cortez knew that with such a dangerous mission, his odds of success were much greater with the complete commitment that comes from knowing that neither failure nor retreat was a viable option.

There's a lesson in Cortez's wisdom even for smaller and less gruesome objectives. I put that wisdom to the test myself as a sixteen-year-old high school junior. The result was one of the proudest moments of my young life up to that point. Here's how.

A high school track team is like any other sports team—there are a limited number of positions athletes have to compete for. In track, each team typically fields its two best runners in each event. If you're not one of the two best, you don't make the team.

I had the number two position for the mile run on our team at Conway High School. I'd been to several meets with rival schools but hadn't finished in the top three in any of them. That was important, because only the top three finishers in any race earn a ribbon and points for their team. Further, the only way to earn a letter jacket was to score at least one point in a sanctioned track meet. Halfway through the season, I was ribbonless, pointless, and still wanted desperately to earn my letter jacket.

I decided my best odds of scoring in a meet was to compete in a shorter race. I told my coach, Bob Wilson, I wanted to try my luck at the 880-yard event, a half-mile race. He agreed but explained the risk. "In our next meet, if you still want to, I'll let you run in the number two spot in the 880 in place of Matt Cooper, and he'll run your number two spot in the mile. You think about it and let me know what you decide."

He didn't have to explain further. I understood the risk. If Matt ran a better time than my best in the mile, and I failed to beat his best time in the 880, then Matt would hold the number two spot in both events. And I would essentially be off the team. As much as I wanted that letter jacket, sitting out the rest of the season was not a pleasant thought.

I considered the offer for the rest of the week. My best practice time in the 880 was several seconds slower than Matt's. I'd even had the chance to run against him in a practice meet and lost. But there's something about the adrenaline rush of a full-on competition that brings out your best performance. Matt's best recorded times were in those real competitive situations. Mine were practice. And maybe if I knew he could take my spot in the mile, I'd be even more motivated at race time.

I decided to take Coach Wilson up on his offer. In the next meet, Matt and I switched events. As fate would have it, the mile run was two hours before the 880. On the infield, I watched Matt run my race, four grueling laps around the track. In my head I battled the conflicting thoughts of wishing well for my teammate and my own selfish desire to maintain my spot on the team.

Huddled near the finish line to see the official times, I watched as Matt finished the race a good ten seconds better than my best time. Cortez was burning my ship. And Matt Cooper had just put me out of a job.

I had the next 120 minutes to muster every ounce of speed I had. Now I wasn't just fighting to earn a ribbon, but to keep a place on the team. When it was my turn to race, I knew exactly what I had to do. I had to beat Matt Cooper's best 880 time, around 2:05. But the problem was that without a huge time clock to rely on, the only way to gauge my speed was in relation to our number one half-miler, Keith Gatewood. Matt usually finished one or two seconds behind Keith. But how close would be close enough? And would this be an off day for Keith? The bottom line was that in order to be sure I'd stay on the team, I needed to beat Keith Gatewood.

I started my race with high hopes. But two-thirds of the way through, Keith was twenty yards ahead of me, and I was in about tenth place out of sixteen runners. I knew every runner would put in his final kick in the last one hundred yards of the race, the final dash at full speed down the last straightaway. In order to even get close to Keith, I would have to start my kick sooner than that, on the final curve. But even a high school geometry student knows that trying to pass anyone on the outside of a curve means you'll be running farther than everyone else. And the inside lane is taken by the runners ahead of you. So passing on the curve is a high-risk strategy. But I was already in a high-risk game, so it didn't matter.

I passed four runners from the third lane around the curve. And coming into the straightaway, Keith was just a few paces in front of me.

It's hard to explain to someone who's never run a race like this what it feels like to sprint all out for the final two hundred yards of a half-mile race. Your heart is racing at over two hundred beats per minute, at the very edge of your cardiovascular limit. Your legs start to feel numb and rubbery as they near complete muscle failure. If you kick too soon, you could literally collapse on the track before the finish line. The point is that every single second, you struggle to decide between keeping this excruciating pace or breaking stride just enough to relieve the strain on your heart, lungs, and legs.

With one hundred yards left to go, most of the runners were just starting their final kick that I was already one hundred yards into. Maintaining that pace was a battle of will between my mind and my body. But I wasn't just fighting for a ribbon. I was fighting to stay on the team! So I pressed on. And it worked.

I passed Keith at around fifty yards to go, plus two other runners just before the finish line, placing third in the race. My good friend and teammate Tim McKenna ran onto the track to meet me with a huge smile on his face. "You ran a 2:03! Coach Wilson almost choked on his whistle when he saw you passing in the third lane!"

In that meet I kept my spot on the team, earned my first ribbon, scored one point for my team, and earned my letter jacket—everything I wanted to achieve over the rest of the season, all in one race.

Both Matt and Keith were better athletes than me in high school, earning letters in both track and football. Twenty-five years later, they still are. Matt is a colonel in the U.S. Marine Corps at Camp Pendleton, California. Keith lives in Memphis, Tennessee, and by the looks of his buff pictures on Facebook, he is in the best shape of his life. But despite being outclassed by better athletes, I accomplished my mission that junior year and learned a valuable lesson about motivation. Removing your retreat option is definitely a risky strategy, but it's also a highly effective one. If you want to motivate yourself to achieve something great, even if it's great only to you, consider ways you can follow Cortez's wisdom in your situation. And then burn your ships.

• • •

While being courageous can clearly get you places in life, it will be comforting to know it's not an absolute requirement. In fact, one of the very successful people you met in chapter 2 is a self-described coward. According to Jim Bangel, "the stories of my cowardice are legion" among his family and friends. And it all started on a basketball court in New York City.

Jim was fifteen years old and had gone to play basketball at a court behind the local high school. He met up with some boys he knew and they started to play. As Jim tells the story, "A few minutes later, six really bad guys showed up and spoke to the people I was playing with. One of them said, 'I told you guys to never come to this park again. I own this place. Get out!' Well, I knew that wasn't fair. And for whatever reason, I decided to tell this guy. So of course, I end up getting in a fight with the ringleader of the group. I had to take my glasses off and square off against him. I hit him once in the stomach and he doubled over. I immediately started feeling sorry for him. But he got up and hit me back. Several times. He eventually broke my nose, and I ended up blacking out for two or three minutes right there on the court. I was a bloody mess. I had to wear a brace for my nose for a month while it healed. Not a pleasant experience in high school, having to explain to everyone how I'd gotten my nose broken losing a fight."

That experience taught Jim that typical Hollywood heroism wasn't all it was cracked up to be. "It was the first time in my life I stepped up to be brave, and look what happened to me. I was never that brave to begin with. But after that I was about as cowardly as you could possibly imagine."

But Jim still had ambitions and wanted to do well in life. So he learned to live what he calls "the life of a smart coward." He had to learn how to do risky things without taking risk, and he developed several strategies for doing that.

One of his most effective strategies was humor.

Jim recalls, "In the army, I became the funniest guy in basic training. I used humor to make the leaders like me, and then I got away with anything. Like if we were sitting on the sidewalk in front of the barracks cleaning our guns and an officer walked by. We were supposed to all stand up and salute. But it was hot and I was tired, and I didn't want to keep standing up every time someone walked by. So I would just roll over onto my back and lay down stiff as a board and salute the sky. They laughed every time, so I never had to stand up."

Later, in his working career, Jim intentionally befriended the leaders he wanted to influence. After reading Dale Carnegie's classic book *How to Win Friends and Influence People*, Jim would visit his managers and do two things: listen, and share humorous accounts of his days in the army or getting beat up on the basketball court. The more time he got to spend with them, and the more he listened, the more he learned about how the business worked and how he could help.

The last thing Jim did was to intentionally use storytelling to influence the executives. He wrote monthly memos with stories of characters with tongue-in-cheek names like Ed Zecutive and Max Profit who loosely resembled the senior leaders of the company. And through those stories, he delivered his (sometimes controversial) recommendations from the mouths of his characters. That, plus the relationships he'd developed with those senior managers, allowed him to broach topics others deemed too sacred for direct conversation.

He eventually became one of the most influential people at his company, with the ear of the most senior management. The combination of those tactics (humor, friendship, listening, and storytelling) was powerful indeed. So much so that an officer of the company once introduced him by saying, "Jim is our court jester, because he's the only one who can tell the truth to the king" (or in this case, the CEO).

What Jim had found was a way to do things most people considered brave, like standing up to the king (or CEO, or schoolyard bully), but without getting his nose broken.

SIX

Integrity

> Being honest may not get you a lot of friends. But it will always get you the right ones.
>
> —JOHN LENNON

Natalia Zinser learned the painful consequences of not telling the truth at the tender age of three. But it wasn't the sting of her father's hand when she was caught that hurt. In fact, she never got caught at all. It turns out that cost her far more dearly than if she had.

Natalia was born and raised in a suburb of Moscow, Russia. Both her parents worked. So during the summer months when she was out of school, Natalia spent her days at her grandparents' house. I'm not sure why young children are so fascinated with putting foreign objects in their nose. But they are. It seems to be a hobby for kids the world over. And three-year-old Natalia was among them. At some point that summer, she managed to lodge a single peanut an impressive distance up one of her nostrils. After a few unsuccessful attempts to remove it, Natalia knew she needed to tell her parents. But she also suspected she would get in trouble for it. So she did what most three-year-olds do when they've done something wrong. She blamed someone else. She made up an elaborate story about how the little girl who lived next door to her grandparents had actually shoved the peanut up her nose. But since the peanut wasn't visible, even to the most probing of caring parental eyes, her parents assumed she had made up the entire story and quickly forgot about it.

Two months later, while Natalia was sleeping, perhaps with her head at just the right angle, her mother noticed something lodged deep in her nose. The peanut! A quick trip to the doctor's office and a steady hand removed the peanut. But that's where the real drama started. Now her parents realized that their daughter hadn't made up the story about the peanut at all. That meant the part about the little girl next door being responsible was probably also true. Natalia's parents called her grandparents. Her grandparents then dutifully confronted the little girl and her parents. You can imagine the he-said-she-said arguments and accusations that followed. The little girl of course denied any such wrongdoing. And as you might expect, her parents staunchly defended her honor, while Natalia's parents and grandparents stood firmly behind Natalia's statements.

The talks ended in a stalemate, with no official punishment handed out on either side. But the real consequence was this: The parents of the girl next door forbade their daughter from ever playing with Natalia again. After all, what parents would want their daughter playing with another child who had lied so brazenly about their little angel? Natalia lost that playmate, for the rest of that summer and every summer thereafter. In fact, it would be more than a decade before the two girls even spoke to each other.

Trying to avoid the disappointment of her parents, or perhaps even a spanking, seemed at the time to be a worthy reward for the lie she told. But if she had known the ultimate cost of that lie—losing a friend and playmate for the rest of her childhood—even a three-year-old might have made a different decision.

• • •

Next we consider what happens when a child takes something that doesn't belong to him. In situations like that, shame is a powerful teacher. And she paid a visit to Andrew Tarvin when he was the tender age of six.

Andrew grew up in a small midwestern neighborhood. His best friend, Bud, lived in the house catty-corner to his. They played together almost every day. But despite living in the same neighborhood, it became apparent to Andrew that Bud's family was better off financially than his. His evidence for this? Bud had more toys. A *lot* more toys. In his bedroom, Bud had a giant bin the size of a garbage can stacked to the brim and overflowing with toys of all kinds. Compared to Andrew's modest toy box, it was a thing to behold.

At the time, Andrew's favorite toys were Teenage Mutant Ninja Turtle figures, based on the television show of the same name. And among the many characters, he was most enamored of Leonardo, the leader of the turtles with the jet blue bandanna. So you can imagine Andrew's disappointment when his eight-year-old brother used a black magic marker to add some artistic flare to Andrew's Leonardo figure. Even as an adult twenty-three years later, Andrew still describes the incident as having "ruined" it.

One day soon after "the marker incident," Andrew was playing at Bud's house. He noticed with now heightened envy Bud's Ninja Turtle set. Bud had the entire collection: all the main turtles, their adversaries Bebop and Rocksteady, the toy cars they rode in, the works. But what mostly caught Andrew's attention was his pristine Leonardo figure. He recalls thinking, "He has all this stuff. He'll never notice if one is missing." At the end of the day, when Bud wasn't looking, Andrew dropped Leonardo in his backpack and took it home.

The next day when his brother noticed him playing with it at home, he said, "Wow! How is it so clean now?"

Andrew hadn't anticipated any questions. That's when he realized that taking something that doesn't belong to you soon leads to other bad behavior. Now he was going to have to lie. What he quickly came up with was, "Oh, I found a really good cleaner and I cleaned it up." It was enough to satisfy an eight-year-old. But now he had a second transgression to feel guilty about.

A few days later, Andrew walked over to Bud's house to play. But before they got started, Bud's mom said to him, "Before you boys are allowed to play, we have to find Bud's Leonardo doll. We haven't seen it in two or three days."

"Oh no!" Andrew thought. "He did notice after all. Now what am I going to do?"

All three started the search. As they looked under couches and behind curtains, Andrew's mind was spinning. "What should I do now? Does she know that I took it and that it's in my bag there on the floor right now?" At this point he was surely wishing that he'd never taken it in the first place. That's when an idea occurred to him. If he "found" Leonardo, maybe he wouldn't get caught for having stolen it. So when nobody was looking, Andrew took it out of his bag and placed it on top of the toy bin. After another minute or two of faux searching, Andrew announced, "Hey Bud, here it is, right on top!" Bud rejoiced in the find and walked away happy to play.

Bud's mom waited until Bud was out of earshot. Then she looked down at Andrew and asked, "So, you were able to find the doll. That's good. Do you want me to tell Bud where it really was?"

A series of emotions struck Andrew, one after another, like waves crashing on a beach. The first were guilt and shame. "I took my best friend's doll!" he thought. It must be difficult enough for anyone, adult or child, to come to terms with having stolen something. But imagine having stolen it from your very best friend in the world.

Then the terror set in. "What if she tells Bud? He might not want to ever be friends with me. Or worse, what if she tells my mom!" He couldn't imagine a punishment appropriate for this.

"No, I don't want you to tell him." Andrew replied in a sheepish yet thoughtful manner. Bud's mom smiled and let him go play. But for the rest of the visit, Andrew was racked with regret and guilt. "I felt awful the whole time."

Later, at home, he pulled out his old Leonardo figure to play, hoping the whole ordeal would be behind him now. But life's not that kind, especially when you've wronged someone and then lied to conceal the wrong. His brother noticed the old doll and said, "Hey, why is it all marked up again?"

Now young Andrew had to lie a second time to his brother to cover up the first lie. "I got so used to it, I decided put the marks back," was what he came up with. And while that wasn't technically true, there was an important truth in it. He was more comfortable playing with his old Leonardo doll, the one that really belonged to him. Bud's pristine figure now represented his crime and transgression against his friend. He wanted nothing more to do with that one.

But even then it wasn't really over. He couldn't really be sure that Bud's mom wouldn't eventually tell. And that made the shame and guilt linger, as he wondered each day if and when the other shoe would drop. Or in this case, the other turtle. The remorse and anguish eventually faded. But not without leaving a lasting impression.

Bud's mom never did tell Bud or Andrew's mother. Andrew believes she could tell how much he was suffering in his own guilt. It might have actually been easier if she had told. Then maybe he could have had some degree of closure on the matter. What has lasted, instead, is the brutal lesson of shame and guilt that accompanies taking something that doesn't belong to you. It's not a feeling Andrew ever wants to relive.

• • •

In addition to telling the truth and keeping your hands off other people's stuff, another important component of integrity is keeping your word. "Your word is your bond," many a child has heard. But what does that really mean? Holly Getter can tell you. At the age of ten she had to stay up half the night doing math just to find out.

Holly grew up in Rockford, Illinois, in a time when much experimentation was going on in education. One such experiment in her fourth-grade class at Swan Hillman Elementary taught her how to do long division, but more important, it taught her about honoring her word.

When starting a math section on division, the teacher told the students what would be required to earn various grades on that portion of the class. To get a C they had to turn in so many pages of correct long division problems. A grade of B required more pages, and an A even more. More important, students had to choose up front what grade they wanted to earn and sign a contract with the teacher committing to complete that many pages.

Holly Getter wanted an A. So that's what she signed up for, literally. At the age of ten, it was the first time she'd ever signed her name on a contract for anything. It was a little scary, but a bit exciting at the same time.

Unfortunately for Holly, not long into the lessons it was clear she wasn't getting it. But she wasn't just a little unclear. She didn't even have a clue where to start. But she was too embarrassed to admit her lack of understanding and too afraid to ask for help. So as the due date approached, Holly hadn't completed a single page of long division problems.

The night before it was all due, Holly went to her mother in tears. Through sobbing eyes she admitted her problem and begged her mother for help, surely hoping for some kind of amnesty.

"Well," her mother began, "let me tell you what a contract is. When you sign your name on something, you're telling someone you're going to do something. That's your word. Your word needs to be something you stand by." Young Holly wondered what exactly that meant. But she didn't have to wait long to find out. Mom continued, "Tonight we're going to learn two lessons: standing by your word, and long division."

And that's exactly what they did. Holly's mom sat her down at the kitchen table and explained to her how to do long division. "Divide, multiply, subtract, and bring down. Then repeat." Over and over again they worked through that process: "Divide, multiply, subtract, and bring down." One hour, two hours, three hours . . . Holly and her mom sat working through problem after problem.

Some time after midnight, Holly complained, "Mom, I'm sooooo tired!"

"Yes, I know you're tired. I'm tired, too. But you signed a contract. This is your responsibility."

Holly's mom stayed up with her little girl till 3 a.m., until the last problem was done.

Morning came early for both. Holly hoped for a day home from school given her late night. But she wouldn't get it. Her mother knew that to learn the lesson properly, Holly needed to feel all the repercussions herself.

Today, as an elementary school teacher herself, Holly Getter shares that story with her students. She hopes to impress upon them these messages: First, math was hard for her too. But she learned it, and so can they. Second, never be afraid to ask questions. That's the only way you'll learn. If she'd been brave enough to admit she didn't understand long division, she would have learned it much earlier. Lastly, your word is binding. When you sign a contract, that's a commitment. You have to keep it, even if it means staying up till 3 a.m. doing long division.

In the end, Holly earned her A in long division. But she earned something far more important: the self-respect that comes from knowing what it means to stand by your word.

• • •

So far in this chapter, we've looked at stories used to help teach a specific lesson on integrity. But stories can also be used to help someone understand why a certain value is worthy of adopting in the first place. The following is a great example of that. And it comes from renowned sports lawyer Bob Woolf, in the book *The Greatest Sales Stories Ever Told*, about how an NBA legend picked his agent.

Larry Bird was already a basketball hero in his home state of Indiana by the time he was a senior in high school, graduating as the all-time leading scorer at Springs Valley High. By the time he was a senior at Indiana State University, he was being touted as the best college player in the nation. It was no surprise, then, in June 1978 when the notably shrewd president of the Boston Celtics, Red Auerbach, drafted Larry before his final college season, a tactic allowed by the NBA at the time. So at the young age of twenty-two, and still without a college degree, Larry Bird found himself needing to negotiate with one of the toughest NBA presidents in the league. Larry badly needed an agent! And with the prospects of a million-dollar contract, every talent agent in the sports business wanted the job.

To speed the process along, a committee of business leaders from the city of Terre Haute volunteered to help with the selection. Out of sixty-five agents on the original list, one of the lucky ones who made it to the final list of three was Bob Woolf. The final interviews were held at a country club in Terre Haute. At one end of the long rectangular table sat Bob Woolf. Along the length of the table were all the committee members. And at the other end of the table sat Larry Bird. Larry and Bob shook hands when the interview started, but Larry hardly spoke a word.

Bob knew one of the big questions from the committee would be what Larry's salary should be. He came prepared with contract details of virtually every top athlete in the country. When the conversation turned to salary, somebody asked, "What does Tommy John make?" The New York Yankees' pitcher was a Terre Haute native, and until Larry Bird came along, he was the city's biggest star athlete. A hush fell over the room, and every eye turned to Bob as they eagerly awaited his answer. But before Bob could even locate his notes, Larry spoke out: "Mr. Woolf, Tommy John happens to be a friend of mine, and I don't particularly care to know what he makes . . . or have anyone else know what he makes."

Bob was deeply impressed with the character and integrity expressed in that statement, especially coming from a twenty-two-year-old college student. And it may have helped prepare Bob for his own opportunity to exhibit character and integrity with what happened next.

After the interview, Bob returned to his hotel room. Shortly after he arrived, the phone rang. It was one of the committee members, Lou Meis. They wanted to come by to ask him one final question. Larry was coming too. When they arrived, Lou said, "Here's the situation. We've narrowed it down to you and one other agent. We have to know what your fee will be for representing Larry. The other agent gave us his number. Now we need yours."

This wasn't the first time they asked that question. But previously, Bob was able to avoid answering it. It wasn't even possible for him to approximate a fair figure this far in advance. He had no idea how long the negotiations were going to take or what the work would involve, or even how successful he would be at negotiating a top salary for Larry. All these things, he thought, should influence what his fee was. "I understand why this question is being asked," he told the committee. "But I want to work with Larry the same way I work with everyone else. At the end of the negotiations, when Larry has a contract, then we'll agree on a fee. It wouldn't be fair to my other clients if I gave special treatment to Larry to get his business."

Lou looked at Bob intently. "Do you understand the consequences?" he asked, meaning if Bob didn't give them a number, he probably wouldn't get the job. Bob nodded and said, "I'm prepared to accept the consequences."

Everyone shook hands, and the committee members left, Larry having never said a word. Bob knew he had done the right thing, but he wasn't feeling good about it. He knew he had probably just thrown away his chances at the contract.

About an hour later, there was a knock at the door. It was Lou Meis and Larry Bird. Bob was surprised to see them, but invited them in. Lou said, "Larry would like to ask you something." Since Larry had not asked a single question during all the interviews, Bob couldn't imagine what he would ask now.

"Of course," Bob responded.

"Mr. Woolf, will you represent me?" Larry asked. Despite his shock, Bob quickly answered, "I would be thrilled to."

Larry explained, "Mr. Woolf, I've heard all about how tough Red Auerbach is. And I want somebody to stand up to him the way you stood up to us. You're the kind of person I want to represent me during my negotiations."

Sometimes choosing the hard right over the easy wrong doesn't have to come at a cost. People recognize when someone stands by his convictions, and they respect him for doing so. In Bob Woolf's case, it also landed him a contract with one of the biggest NBA stars of all time. And as for Larry's choice of Bob to represent him, well, that worked out pretty well, too. Bob negotiated a five-year, $3.25 million contract with the Celtics, making Larry Bird the highest paid rookie in NBA history at the time.[1]

SEVEN

Self-Reliance

Never trouble another for what you can do yourself.

—THOMAS JEFFERSON

For the first few years of our lives, we're completely dependent on other people, particularly our parents. They feed us. They bathe us. They get us dressed in the morning and they put us to bed at night. It's a lifestyle that's easy to get used to. As a result, self-reliance is not something that comes very naturally to young people. But once they do learn it, it can become one of the most productive character traits they'll ever possess. Just ask Steve Blair.

When Steve was nine years old, he was lucky enough to live only a couple of hundred yards from Fleetridge Elementary School, where he attended fourth grade in Raytown, Missouri, about ten miles southeast of Kansas City. As an adult, he could probably hit it from his back yard with a good golf shot. But to get to school each morning as a nine-year-old, he had to follow the city streets the long way around, through several turns, and along at least one very busy thoroughfare, Norfleet Road. To a young boy who desperately wanted to ride his bike to school, that was a problem because Norfleet Road didn't have much of a shoulder and no sidewalk. So riding his bike to school wasn't an option his parents even entertained.

After he complained about his predicament at school, one of his social studies teachers asked him, "Well, Steve, what are you going to do about it?" And that turned out to be the right question.

"Maybe," he thought, "we could cut a trail through the woods between my house and school." But that required going through private property. Plus, it would only solve the problem for Steve. What about all the other kids who might want to ride their bikes to school? Steve and his teacher settled on a solution. Norfleet Road needed a sidewalk!

Steve's teacher told him the one person who could order a sidewalk built was the mayor. And once again, he asked Steve the right question. "So, Steve, what are you going to do about it?" And with that, Steve decided to write the mayor a letter. It was short and to the point. It read simply, "Dear Mayor, would you please put a sidewalk on Norfleet Road so me and the other kids can ride our bikes to school?"

At that point, Steve might have suspected his complaint had become more of a lesson in civil government from the social studies teacher than a legitimate attempt to get to ride his bike to school. So he promptly forgot about it. Then a few months later, at the end of his fourth-grade year, something happened to Steve that had never before happened in his life. He got called to the principal's office.

Over the school loudspeaker, the entire student body and faculty heard the most dreaded words any grade schooler can imagine: "Steve Blair, please come to the principal's office. Steve Blair, please come to the principal's office." Steve made the long and fearful walk to the office, all the while wondering what he could have possibly done wrong, what the consequences might be, and how he was going to explain it to his parents. When he arrived at the office, he found the principal, a strange man wearing a suit, and his mother! Steve burst into tears and sobbed uncontrollably. These were the unmistakable signs of trouble. His mother was crying too, which meant the strange man was probably there to take him to jail. In between sobs, he managed to stammer out, "Why am I here? I didn't do anything, I swear! I didn't do anything!"

The principal assured Steve he wasn't in any trouble and that he could stop crying. He handed Steve an envelope. Inside was a letter from the mayor. Steve read it out loud. "Dear Steve, Thank you for your letter. I wanted to let you know that next Monday we will begin work on your sidewalk. And I'd like for you to meet us there to have pictures taken for the newspaper."

"I'm going to be in the newspaper?" Yes. And the strange man? Well, he turned out to be a journalist, not a police officer.

Sure enough, the next week Steve met the mayor and a photographer at the construction site to have his picture taken. And his story did make it into the newspaper. More rewarding to Steve, however, was this: When the mayor said in his letter that they would begin work "on your sidewalk," he really did mean *your* sidewalk. As soon as the concrete was poured, Steve (and only Steve) was allowed to put his name and handprint in the wet cement. And from that time forward, that sidewalk would be officially known as the Steve Blair sidewalk. That brought the number of fourth graders at Fleetridge Elementary with their very own city sidewalk to a grand total of one, a very special honor indeed.

Steve rode his bike to school every day of his fifth-grade year, rain or shine. And every time he got to the point in the sidewalk that bore his name, he looked down and smiled. That sidewalk was a standing monument to a valuable lesson Steve learned that year. He learned the value of being "at cause" for something. From then on, if he had a problem, he asked himself the same question his teacher asked him that year: "What are you going to do about it?" And the two words to emphasize in that sentence are *you* and *do*. It's you that needs to do something. Don't wait for someone else to solve your problem for you. And you actually need to *do* something. Just complaining about it isn't enough.

So the next time you have a problem, find yourself complaining about something, or spot an opportunity to make the world a better place, ask yourself the same question: "What are you going to do about it?" And then do it.

• • •

If you learn the discipline of self-reliance as a youth, there's almost nothing you can't do as an adult. But of course it starts with recognizing something in need of change. In Steve's case, it was his desire to ride his bike to school and the sidewalk required to allow that. But imagine how much more impactful that self-reliance can be when your worthy objective is for the benefit of others instead of yourself. A beautiful example of that is the story of Don Schoendorfer and his personal mission.

Don and his wife, Laurie, took what would turn out to be the most fateful vacation of their lives, to—of all places—the North African country of Morocco. They left the comfort of their home in Massachusetts and flew to Spain, where they rented a car for the rest of the trip. About thirty minutes after crossing the Strait of Gibraltar by ferry at the Tangier crossing, they arrived at their first stop in the city of Tetouan. They were particularly interested in exploring the Medina, the oldest and walled-off part of town marked by streets too narrow for modern cars. As they walked among the crowd, they were shocked to see a woman, probably in her thirties, crawling across the street. Not on her hands and knees, like she was looking for something, but on her stomach, head down, dragging her torso and lifeless legs behind her. Her clothes were tattered and her legs were bleeding. But her purposeful and practiced method made it clear she hadn't just suffered an injury moments earlier. She couldn't walk, and this was simply her only means of movement. Perhaps more alarming were the multitudes of people completely unaware of her, moving around her the way a rushing stream moves around a rock in the streambed. Apparently this wasn't an unusual occurrence in Tetouan. But to Don Schoendorfer it was. That moment left an indelible stain in Don's memory, one that would resurface two decades later.

Half a working lifetime later, and at the apex of his personal spiritual journey, Don decided to shift his focus away from building his own fortune and toward giving back to humanity. He toyed with the idea of tutoring and mentoring underprivileged children. But then he decided to find a way to leverage his skills as an engineer and inventor. But what problem to tackle? That's when his thoughts returned to the disabled woman in Morocco. Why didn't she have a wheelchair?

So Don investigated and learned the stark reality. More than 130 million people in the world need a wheelchair but can't afford one. The reason? Wheelchairs are remarkably expensive. A decent one can cost from $500 to $10,000. In many parts of the world, that's several years of working income, especially for someone with disabilities. Over the prior fifteen years, charitable organizations had given away perhaps a total of 100,000 wheelchairs to those in need somewhere in the world. In other words, in fifteen years of effort, people had solved only one-tenth of 1 percent of the problem, leaving 99.9 percent still in need. Don had found his mission.

In the garage of his home in Santa Ana, California, Don went to work. His goal: design a wheelchair that could be built, delivered, and repaired anywhere in the world at a fraction of the usual cost. To do that, he decided to build it from easily accessible parts made for other purposes and produced in high volume at low cost. Instead of wheels made for wheelchairs, he settled on bicycle wheels. Bicycles are the number one means of transportation in the world. If his wheels broke down or got a puncture, they could be fixed or replaced cheaply and easily by just about anyone. For the seat, he chose the white resin stackable lawn chairs you see at every lawn and garden center. It was all held together by a simple steel frame Don designed himself. All said, Don's wheelchairs could be built and delivered just about anywhere in the world for less than $72. Don's vision, Free Wheelchair Mission, was born.

He built the first one hundred chairs by hand in his own garage. Then his first opportunity to find needy owners for them came from a medical church mission to Chennai, India, with room to bring only four chairs. One of those first four recipients was Kumadevealy, which in English means "Lotus Blossom." She was sixteen years old and had never been able to walk. She lived out her entire existence on the floor of a small room in her parents' home. She took to the chair almost immediately. The other children in the neighborhood quickly began moving stones out of the way so she could wheel herself out of the house. Her mother wept as she saw her daughter cross the threshold under her own power for the first time in her life. At that moment, Don knew he'd made the right decision.

A dozen years later, www.freewheelchairmission.org is going strong. With the help of financial donations, they've assembled and given away more than 740,000 wheelchairs to impoverished and disabled people in ninety countries around the world. Those numbers are of course encouraging to Don. But one of the most personally satisfying moments for him came in 2011 when he had the opportunity to go back to Chennai and visit Lotus Blossom. Winding his way up the alley to the same home where they'd met, he saw her out front waiting for him. But this time she wasn't lying on the floor, and she wasn't even sitting in a wheelchair. She was standing. And using nothing but the power of her own two legs, she walked over and greeted him.

In that emotion-filled visit, she explained to Don what had happened. Once she had the chair, she learned to use it to pull herself up to stand or to go to the bathroom. After several years, her legs slowly got stronger. It's ironic, really. The tool Don built to allow her to sit and roll actually helped her learn how to stand and walk.

Don's work, along with the help of the thousands who have contributed to this cause, are a testament to the power of seeing a problem and asking yourself, "Well, what are you going to do about it?"

• • •

But self-reliance doesn't have to involve your own ambitious project or noble mission. In fact, most people miss opportunities to practice self-reliance every day. And they'll never know what an enormous impact they could be having on their own lives or someone else's. Few people recognize that better than Mohit Das.

Mohit was born in India, but is now a permanent resident of Singapore. In 1999 his wife gave birth to their first child, a son they named Ritvik. The couple soon learned that Ritvik had both Down syndrome and autism. They knew at that moment that much of their life would be devoted to his care.

And as difficult as it is to raise a child with both Down and autism, things got harder. When Ritvik was five years old, he was diagnosed with leukemia, a form of cancer that affects the blood and bone marrow. Ritvik immediately started treatment that eventually included radiation and chemotherapy. And in cases like his, that treatment can last for years. It can also be frighteningly expensive for a young couple. Fortunately, Mohit had a professional job at a global company with good insurance benefits. Or at least that's what he thought.

About a month into the treatment, he got a letter from the insurance company saying that claims for Ritvik's treatment were denied because the policy didn't cover "preexisting conditions." Their logic was this: While Ritvik's leukemia wasn't preexisting, his Down syndrome was. And children with Down are more likely to develop leukemia—ten to twenty times more likely, as it turns out. So even though only one in three hundred children with Down ever develops leukemia, the cause was assumed to be the same genetic makeup that resulted in his Down. Ergo, it was preexisting.

As you can imagine, Mohit and his wife were disappointed, and they started to plan for the inevitable avalanche of medical bills. Then a few weeks later, when Mohit's boss heard about the situation, she contacted the human resources department to see if anything could be done about it. After checking the policy and appealing to the insurance carrier, the answer they got back was the same. Ritvik's condition was preexisting and would not be covered under the policy.

For the vast majority of situations like this that play out every day all over the world, that's where the story would end. Someone somewhere feels wronged and appeals the company policy. The policy wonks debate the situation and issue a decision. All that's left is for the middleman, the messenger, to deliver the bad news to the employee. "I'm sorry, your appeal was denied." Case closed.

But fortunately for Mohit, that's not where this story ended. His boss and the human resources manager still felt he was being treated unfairly. If Ritvik had not had Down, insurance would have covered 80 percent of the cost of his leukemia treatment. But since he was a special needs child, it covered none of it. So they took the matter to the leadership team, whose members discussed it. The group agreed that the insurance company's decision was unfair. But they also knew they couldn't do anything about that. So they decided on a course of action they could do something about. They decided to pay 80 percent of Ritvik's medical bills as a company expense. Each month for the next two years, Mohit filled out an expense report with hospital receipts and submitted it to his company just like he did with his normal travel expenses. And the company paid every one of them in full.

Now, notice what went on here. This isn't a story about some very wealthy and generous executives taking pity on one of their employees and paying his medical bills out of their own pockets as a charity case. That would be noble indeed. But what went on here is far more instructive. In this case, these people decided that if the company's insurance carrier wouldn't pay his bills, the company would pay them anyway as a regular cost of doing business.

I describe this as a more instructive course of action for two reasons. First, most of us don't have a big enough bank account to simply start writing personal checks every time a problem comes up. More important, in this situation, Mohit's boss and the HR manager did what self-reliant people do. When they failed to get the insurance company to do anything, they didn't just give up. They asked what they could do about it themselves: what resources did *they* have at their disposal, what decision-making space did *they* have? How easy would it have been for them to tell Mohit, "I'm sorry, we tried everything in our power. But the insurance company didn't budge." To which I would rhetorically reply, "Really? You've tried *everything* in your power? Everything? Maybe you've tried everything that somebody else can do. But what can *you* do?"

No matter what your situation is in life, you'll have far more success by developing your own self-reliance.

And fortunately, my rhetorical rant above is not a conversation Mohit ever had to have. Today, Ritvik is fourteen years old and has been in remission from leukemia for six beautiful years.

• • •

In most cases when you try to be self-reliant, people around you will encourage you. Steve Blair was encouraged by his teacher. Don Schoendorfer was encouraged by lots of people along his journey. And Mohit Das encouraged his HR manager to help him any way she could. But it's not always that way. Sometimes being self-reliant means doing something even when other people tell you it will never work. That's exactly what Emily Chang had to do as a teenager.

Emily grew up in Pittsford, New York. By her junior year in high school, she decided she wanted to be a doctor. So when she found out there was an internship available in Eastman Kodak's biohazard lab in nearby Rochester, she was immediately interested. She knew medical school would be competitive. And what better way to differentiate herself than have some real work experience in a medical-related field? It didn't even bother her that it was what she described as "a very unsexy job. I would have to harvest diseased cells and organs from mice and freeze them so they could be used in cancer research." And besides, at around $15 an hour, the pay was outstanding, certainly for a high school student.

The only real problem was that the internship was intended for college students—people a few years older, more mature, and perhaps with other work experience under their belt. Emily was just sixteen years old and had no real qualifications for the job. She recalls some adults discouraging her: "There's no way you can get that internship. It's for college students. You're still in high school. I don't know why you're even wasting your time."

Undaunted, Emily applied anyway. She filled out the application with her surely unimpressive credentials. But she also attached a passionate essay describing why she wanted the internship.

The result? "I got the job! I was so excited."

About a month into the job, she remembers being off in a corner of the lab, out of sight, when two full-time employees walked in. They obviously didn't know Emily was there, because she overheard them talking about her. She heard one of them say, "Well, sure, she's a great fit, given she's the only one who applied for the job."

That, of course, ended any mystery over how she got the internship, and perhaps tarnished a little of the luster of being selected. More important, however, consider this: Hearing that news would disappoint most people. But Emily was glad she heard it, because it taught her a valuable lesson. It reinforced how right she was to apply for the job in the first place. Imagine how foolish she would have felt if she hadn't applied and then found out the job never got filled because nobody applied. "The possibility that you're the only one brave enough," she explains, "is a great reason to try. Because you never know."

Emily credits that internship as one of the most important turning points in her life. It was the steppingstone that got her a later job in a hospital, which helped her get into a top medical school. She later switched to an MBA program and went on to a very successful career at notable companies including Procter & Gamble, Apple Computer, and the Intercontinental Hotels Group. And it all started with being bold enough to apply for a job she wasn't qualified for and that apparently nobody else wanted.

EIGHT

Grit

> Nothing in the world can take the place of persistence. Talent will not; nothing is more common than unsuccessful men with talent. Genius will not; unrewarded genius is almost a proverb. Education will not; the world is full of educated derelicts.
>
> —CALVIN COOLIDGE

The psychologist most responsible for the study of grit, Angela Duckworth, defines it as "perseverance and passion for long-term goals."[1] It's a combination of zeal and persistence even in the absence of encouraging feedback. So grit isn't just about trying hard. Anyone can try hard . . . once. Grit means continuing to try hard after you've already failed. One of the best examples of that you'll ever come across is a man you probably already know and admire.

When he was seven years old, his family was forced out of their home and off their farm. Like other boys his age, he was expected to work to help support the family.

When he was nine, his mother died.

When he was twenty-two, the company he worked for went bankrupt, and he lost his job.

At twenty-three, he ran for the state legislature in a field of thirteen candidates. He came in eighth.

At twenty-four, he borrowed money to start a business with a friend. By the end of the year, the business failed. The local sheriff seized his possessions to pay off his debt. His partner soon died, penniless, and he assumed his partner's share of the debt as well. He spent the next several years of his life paying it off.

At twenty-five, he ran for the state legislature again. This time he won.

At twenty-six, he was engaged to be married. But his fiancée died before the wedding.

The next year he plunged into a depression and suffered a nervous breakdown.

At twenty-nine, he sought to become the speaker of the state legislature. He was defeated.

At thirty-four, he campaigned for a seat in the United States Congress. He lost.

At thirty-seven, he ran for Congress again. This time he won. He went to Washington and did a good job.

At thirty-nine, when his term ended, he was out of a job again. There was a policy of serving only one term in his party.

At forty, he tried to get a job as commissioner of the General Land Office. He was rejected.

At forty-five, he campaigned for the U.S. Senate. He lost by six votes.

At forty-seven, he was one of the contenders for the vice presidential nomination at his party's national convention. He lost.

At forty-nine, he ran for the U.S. Senate a second time. And for the second time, he lost.

Two years later, at the age of fifty-one, after a lifetime of failure, disappointment, and loss, and still relatively unknown outside his home state of Illinois, Abraham Lincoln was elected the sixteenth president of the United States.

Despite being elected to a second term, he served only four years in office before meeting his final defeat at the hands of an assassin in April

1865. But during those short four years, President Lincoln successfully led the country through its greatest internal crisis (the Civil War), preserved the Union, ended slavery, and rededicated the nation to the ideals of equality, liberty, and democracy.

So the next time you think about quitting because you've already tried and failed, ask yourself this: How different would this country be if Abraham Lincoln had stopped trying after his first defeat . . . or his fifth . . . or his tenth?

• • •

If you have children who tend to give up on something if they can't master it in the first few tries, this next story is for you. It's about the same Emma Sartini you met in chapter 3.

At a very young age, Emma learned the value of practice—repeated, monotonous practice. It's the kind that's difficult for even a focused adult to endure, much less a child. And it's served her well ever since.

Emma started taking gymnastics lessons at the age of four and continued for thirteen years. If your experience with gymnastics is watching the Olympics, you're used to watching people make it look easy. But it's not. In fact, consider the very first move you're likely to see any time someone competes in the uneven bars: the kip. The kip is the standard mounting technique used by experienced gymnasts to start their routines. You'd recognize it immediately if you saw it. The gymnast jumps from the floor to grab the high bar and swings her feet up so she's hanging upside down with her legs pointing straight up. Then, in what looks like complete disregard for the laws of physics, she flips her body upright so that she's now right side up with her torso over the bar, ready to move into her routine.

Although it's considered one of the basic skills, the kip is one of the most difficult to learn. When you start learning, you can't even begin to do it. So you have to practice separate components of the move individually before putting them together. Emma began learning to kip when she was seven years old. She was daunted by such a difficult move, but her coach assured her that she could and would learn it. "If it takes a thousand tries, you'll get it. Muscle memory will take over, and you'll do it." Over the next year and a half, Emma practiced three times a week for three or four hours at a time. Not all of that time was dedicated to learning the kip, but much of it was. All told, she surely did practice that move a thousand times or more. But eventually, she got it.

Imagine that. More than a year of effort, two hundred-plus practice sessions, and well over a thousand attempts, all to learn a single maneuver that takes less than three seconds to perform. If it took that much effort to learn to ride a bicycle, there'd be a lot more kids walking to school. But the truth is that many important things in life do require that kind of repetition and practice to master. And if you don't have persistence, you'll never be any good. So developing that grit at a young age turned out to be an even more important skill for Emma later in life than learning to kip.

Case in point, after high school Emma entered the College of Design, Architecture, Art, and Planning (DAAP) at the University of Cincinnati. As an aspiring designer, one of the skills she had to learn was drawing. But it wasn't the kind of drawing you learned in grade school. As Emma explains, "In design, drawing isn't the same as art. In art you learn to draw what's in front of you: a person, or still life basket of apples. In design, you're imagining something that doesn't exist today, and drawing what it could look like." That, as it turned out, required practice—a lot of practice. Fortunately, Emma was well practiced at practicing.

In one typical class, the students were asked to imagine a chair. Any chair. And then draw it. Then imagine that chair from a different angle. Now draw it again. Now think of another chair and draw it. And again. And again. Over the course of two weeks, Emma had to draw three hundred pictures of chairs. Now imagine repeating this exercise multiple times a semester over the course of a four-year degree. By graduation, Emma had completed several thousand drawings, enough to make her gymnastics teacher proud. And, as it turns out, enough to land a great job as a designer.

Even today as a professional designer, Emma recognizes the continued value of practice. Recently promoted, she has to master the new skill of writing a design brief, a document that lays out the objective, parameters, and budget for a new project. It can take her days to craft a single page of that brief today. But her boss, with fifteen years in the field, can knock one out in an hour or two. With practice, Emma could get that proficient someday too. And she will. Because what Emma knows better than most is how to practice.

• • •

Having a long-term vision of what you want to achieve is certainly a good thing. But when that's all you think about, you can lose sight of what's happening today. That's when things start to fall apart. It's a lesson Kirk Perry learned the hard way at the age of seventeen when he was a graduating senior at Richmond High School in Richmond, Indiana.

For years, Kirk's favorite sport was wrestling, and he was very good. In fact, coming to the end of his senior season, he was ranked sixth in the state. He was looking forward to winning a berth in the state tournament and earning a college wrestling scholarship that accompanied even a decent showing there. And the only thing that stood between him and that future was the state regional tournament in Hagerstown in February. He needed to place in the top two wrestlers in his region and weight class to make it to the state meet.

Fortunately, that wasn't going to be very difficult. Kirk was the number one seed in the tournament, and he'd already beaten the number two, three, and four seeds earlier in the year. This was a slam dunk. He was already picturing himself standing on the podium with the first place medal around his neck, going to the state tourney, and enjoying a full ride to college.

The first match for the number one seed is typically the easiest. The organizers separate the top seeds early in the brackets so they have the best chance of making it to the finals. So Kirk's first match that day was against Brad. Both boys were in the 177-pound wrestling class. But at six feet two inches, Kirk was five inches taller than his opponent and had a longer reach. And while Kirk was the favorite to win the tournament, Brad wasn't even seeded. As the match started, Kirk quickly went to his signature move, the "fireman's carry." He'd beaten Brad (and most of his opponents) with that move before. But the first time he tried it, Brad blocked him. He tried again, but again Brad was able to block him. The third and fourth attempts were no different. Apparently, Brad had done his homework on Kirk. He was prepared for this match.

The bout went the full three rounds, with neither one pinning the other. But when the final buzzer sounded, Kirk was down on points, 3 to 2. His wrestling career was over. No medal. No podium. No state tournament. No college scholarship. He never wrestled again.

Reflecting on that match thirty years later, Kirk still remembers every move. "It was like one of those bad dreams where you're being chased and seem to just run in place. And when you yell out, no one can hear you. By the time I 'woke up,' the match was over."

Looking back, Kirk draws two lessons from the experience. The first and most obvious is the importance of not losing sight of what you need to do today, the task at hand. Some amount of planning and optimism for the future is good. But when it overshadows everything else, bad things happen. That lesson became clear to Kirk right away.

The second one took him decades to fully realize. After working in fast-food restaurants for a couple of years, he eventually saved up enough money to go to college. So by the time he started, he was a little older and more mature than most of the other students. And the unattractive prospect of continuing his fast-food career provided a little extra motivation to work hard at his studies. Plus, without the distraction of daily wrestling practice, he was probably able to focus more on his studies. All that, combined with the lesson he learned about not losing sight of the task at hand (what he now calls "staying focused on Friday's payroll"), has led to a stellar career. He's a former president at Procter & Gamble and currently serves as president at Google in Mountain View, California. And at the still-young age of forty-seven, he has even more amazing possibilities in his future.

That second lesson, therefore, is this: Sometimes even the biggest defeat can turn out to be a blessing in disguise. Had he won that match, he probably would have gone straight to college on a wrestling scholarship. He would have surely enjoyed another four years of his favorite sport. But his academic record and career success may have never measured up. And he almost certainly would not have met the woman who became his wife and become a father to the four beautiful kids he has now.

His great-grandfather described such blessings this way: "Everything looks like failure in the middle." And he offered this analogy: It's like childbirth. When you're in the middle of it, you're probably thinking you never want to do this again. But when it's over, and you get to look down at your newborn baby, everything seems worth it and you wouldn't want to change a thing. As Kirk describes it, "If there was ever a true blessing in a loss, it was on that wrestling mat in early February 1984 in Hagerstown, Indiana."

• • •

The opposite of having grit and persistence, of course, is giving up. And that's not always a bad thing. There are many legitimate reasons to give up on any task: you've accomplished enough of it, the cost of continuing outweighs the benefits of succeeding, or you've lost interest in the goal. But there are some bad reasons to give up as well. One of those is a demon that's haunted Shawn Spradling most of his life.

Shawn grew up in Mount Sterling, Kentucky, a city of about six thousand people in the north central part of the state, right in the heart of basketball country. At that time, school basketball teams for boys started as early as the fourth grade, and Shawn was quick to be among them. In those early grades, anyone who wanted to sign up could be on the team. But by Shawn's seventh-grade year, the teams were more selective, which meant to earn a spot he had to make it through tryouts. That made Shawn anxious. "I was really concerned I'd get cut, primarily because it would be embarrassing, and I'd have to explain that," he recalls.

Tryouts were scheduled after school every day for a week. All the boys who wanted to go out for the team played together and went through drills for the first couple of days. By the third day, the coach started making cuts. At the end of the hour, names of the players remaining on the team were placed on the board. If your name wasn't on the list, you didn't make it. Shawn made it through the first cut, and the second one. But going into the final day of tryouts, he was nervous. He knew how many spots were available on the team. And by now he knew all the other boys and what their skill levels were. So he started doing the math in his head. And he didn't like his odds. "What if I don't make it?" he asked himself. The thought of being cut weighed heavier and heavier on Shawn, and that fear eventually overwhelmed him. He started looking for an exit strategy.

So on the last day of tryouts, Shawn simply didn't show up. Instead of going to the gym after school, he got on the bus like he would have on any other normal school day and went home.

When Shawn's father got home from work, he found his son playing basketball in the driveway. When he asked him why he wasn't at basketball tryouts, Shawn told him, "I just decided I didn't want to play." Shawn thought that would be easier to say—to himself probably as much as to anyone else—than it would be to explain that "I didn't make the cut, I didn't get picked, or I wasn't good enough." But Dad saw through that immediately. Shawn described his reaction this way: "He was absolutely furious with me, that I would quit on the last day."

So there Shawn was, playing out his exit strategy, perhaps considering if he was right. Was suffering his father's disappointment indeed easier than his own embarrassment of getting cut? And if that's where his ordeal ended, he might have concluded that he was right. But it got worse.

That night, Shawn's best friend, Brady, called him and asked him why he wasn't at tryouts. Shawn practiced his rehearsed answer once again. And once again, his audience saw through it. That's when Brady told Shawn something he didn't expect to hear. "But Shawn, you'd already made the team!"

Apparently, the coach had confided in Brady that he'd been debating between Shawn and another boy named Jason. But he'd already decided to give the spot to Shawn. He just hadn't posted that decision yet. Unfortunately, since Shawn didn't show up on the last day of tryouts, he had to give the spot to Jason.

You can imagine Shawn's disappointment, both in knowing that he could have been on the team and in ending his basketball career in such a cowardly manner. Looking back, Shawn knows that wasn't to be the only time something like that happened. "I picked up a guitar a long time ago. But I couldn't play it perfectly right away. So I quit. I still have the guitar. And I still can't play it. I put a lot of pressure on myself to be perfect. If I couldn't excel at it, I didn't even try." He admits, "I've missed a lot of opportunities in life because I was too afraid to disappoint myself and other people."

One example he described was when he was a student at Cincinnati Christian University. "There was a preaching contest every year. You'd write a sermon and deliver it in front of a few of the professors. The top three finalists got to preach in chapel. It was a huge honor. At the time I felt like I was gifted to preach, and several of my friends encouraged me to do it. But here's the lie I stood behind: I told them, and myself, 'you know, I'm not a fan of preaching contests. I just don't think it's right to preach for a silly contest. It demeans the act.' But the real reason was that I was afraid I wouldn't get picked. I didn't want my name read off as 'the guy who lost.' So I never even tried it. I still regret that decision."

Shawn only turned the corner in this battle about four years ago, at the age of thirty-five. He was offered the senior pastor role at Center Pointe Christian Church in West Chester, Ohio. Instead of jumping quickly at the opportunity to take his first senior pastor role, leading a congregation of 1,100, he spent weeks debating with himself if he was good enough. Then one day, while he was still wrestling with this decision, his mother told his wife, Janelle, "I think he'll do a really good job as long as he understands it won't always be perfect." And that's when Shawn finally had a name for his demon. It was perfectionism. He faced the truth as he described it, that "perfectionism had stolen a lot of my joy in life."

Knowing he'd been unsuccessfully fighting this demon for two decades, Shawn realized he couldn't continue to fight alone. He found his solution, as he describes it, "in placing more dependence on God. I had to stop relying on my own strength and talents and wisdom."

Shawn decided to take the job and succeed or fail "according to whatever plan God had for me." He describes taking that job as "a huge victory for me over perfectionism." He admits he still struggles with it on occasion. But he finds joy in the small victories now that he knows his enemy and is no longer as afraid of failing.

By the way, Shawn has held the position of senior pastor for more than four years now. And it looks like his mom was right. Things aren't always perfect. But he is doing a great job.

NINE

Hard Work and Struggles in Life

Opportunity is missed by most because it's dressed in overalls and looks like work.

—THOMAS EDISON

"Take pride in your work" is a worthy and often-quoted piece of advice to young people. But like many such aphorisms, it's hard to really know what that means until you've seen someone in action who truly embodies it. One person who's seen that firsthand is Vikram Sarma.

Vikram grew up in the Detroit suburbs in an area he considered himself privileged to live in. The local auto company executives all had golf club memberships nearby, and that created summer work for kids like him. At the age of thirteen, he got his first job as a caddie at a local country club. He recalls it was an exciting job to get as a young teenager. "I knew I'd get to work outside for the summer, hang out with seventy other guys carrying bags, and make really good money—maybe $100 to $150 a day in cash."

Vikram's first time on the job was a Thursday night when all the new caddies got training. The next morning he was in uniform, waiting with the other boys for their assignments. While in line, he met several of the other caddies. Like Vikram, most were from upper-middle-class neighborhoods, with nicely pressed shorts and new pairs of brand-name shoes.

But one of them, Ahmad, was different. Ahmad was an African American boy from a lower-income neighborhood. He was older than Vikram, maybe seventeen or eighteen at the time. His shorts weren't as nicely pressed as those of some of the other boys, and his big toe stuck out of a hole in one of his shoes.

Before long, the first two players came in. The caddie master assigned them each a caddie for their round together. The first was Vikram, and the second was Ahmad.

As they took to the course, Vikram learned something else different about Ahmad. In the fiefdom of caddies, there are five levels of experience and expertise: Beginner, Intermediate, Captain, Honor, and the highest level, Championship. Vikram, of course, was a Beginner. But Ahmad, now in his seventh year, was a Championship caddie.

During that first round, it became clear to Vikram that he'd underestimated how hard it would be to carry thirty pounds on his shoulder while walking six miles of hills on a golf course. "By the ninth hole," he recalls, "only halfway through the round, my knee buckled. I fell and slammed my knee into the ground. And then Ahmad, without saying a word, picked up my bag and started caddying for both golfers. I was amazed. It was seamless, as if we'd rehearsed it.

"As I walked off the injury, I thanked him. And he said to me discreetly, 'Hey, at the next turn, you're going to have to put some ice on that. I'll show you where the ice machine is.'"

During the rest of the round, Vikram continued to make rookie mistakes. "At one point I accidentally left a wedge in the sand trap after I raked it. The next time my golfer needed it, I realized it wasn't there." Vikram was in no shape to go back and get it. Nor did he really know if that was the right thing to do at that point anyway. Again, without a word, Ahmad handed Vikram the bags and sprinted off to retrieve the missing club.

In another memorable mistake, Vikram was walking backwards after pacing off a distance to the hole and accidentally stepped on the ball of one of the players, smashing it into the turf. Neither player noticed Vikram's misstep, leaving him wondering what he should do. "Again, Ahmad stepped in, walked up to the player, and said, 'I'm sorry, sir. We made a mistake.' Then he explained how he could re-place the ball properly and within the rules of the game."

When the round was over, Vikram was exhausted. "I thought to myself, 'Thank God this is over!'" The players handed their cards, including a tip, to their caddies.

When the players had gone, Ahmad said to Vikram, "First round?"

"Yeah," Vikram admitted.

That's when Ahmad asked him a very simple and very important question. "What did you learn?"

Vikram gave a not-so-thoughtful answer befitting his young thirteen years of age. "I don't know. That this guy isn't a good tipper?"

And then with the same patience he'd showed all day, and again without being asked, Ahmad said, "Okay, let's take a step back and walk through the round. First, always walk three paces ahead of your player. That lets you get to the ball first and have yardage ready. It saves everyone time. Second, think of all the caddies providing an experience for the golfers. We're a team. So when you hurt your knee, it can't all be about you. It's about the customer enjoying the round. That's why I picked up your bag." Ahmad went on to diagnose the entire round, every hole and every relevant stroke—what Vikram did and what he should have done.

It was an eye-opening discussion for Vikram. Ahmad had turned the individual job of a caddie, in Vikram's mind, into a team sport. "It was like what I now know Disney thinks about all the cast members at their theme parks. I was just so blown away." But Ahmad wasn't done teaching, and Vikram wasn't done learning.

Ahmad continued, "I'm not from the best of places. But when I'm here, I have a job to do. If I do it well, it reflects well on who I am and where I come from." And that's when Vikram had his unexpected moment of clarity. That's when he realized that Ahmad took pride in his work because he had pride in himself. And he knew that each one affects the other.

The lessons he learned from Ahmad made a profound impact on Vikram. The most immediate was that he started earning bigger tips because he started taking seriously the job of learning his craft. "I started showing up early and rolling balls on the greens to see which way they would break." He went on to earn his way up to Honor caddie, and faster than most of his peers. And the habit stayed with him. "In every job I've had since, whether it was selling shoes at Athlete's Foot or doing political research in D.C., I took extra effort to learn it well. I realized if I didn't take pride in my work and really study it, I'd be doing me, my peers, and my craft a disservice."

• • •

As is true with many people, Shawn Callahan learned much about what he thinks about work from his earliest job. Only unlike most people, Shawn's first boss was a former United States Marine, and his father.

Shawn's dad served in the Vietnam War, after which he was assigned a post at the U.S. Embassy in Australia. By the time Shawn entered his teenage years, his father had a thriving business in the capital city of Canberra installing commercial kitchens in local restaurants. When on holiday from school, Shawn worked for his dad to earn extra money.

One such day, Shawn's dad dropped him off at a work site with instructions to clean all the debris from the demolition they had just completed, prior to the new kitchen going in. "I'll pop back in and check on you at lunch and see how you're doing," he told Shawn.

By the time Dad came back, Shawn had finished the bulk of his work. It was a hot day, and Shawn was tired. So he was just sitting on the floor in the foyer comfortably shoveling the last remaining bits of plaster into a waste bin. When his father walked up, he snapped at him, "What in the hell are you doing?"

"What do you mean?" Shawn asked, genuinely surprised.

"Why are you sitting on your ass?"

"Look, Dad, I'm just tidying up a few last pieces here. You should see what I've done in the other room . . ."

His dad interrupted, "I don't care what you've done. It's what you look like you're doing now that bothers me. You might have worked your tail off all morning. But at the moment it looks like you're slacking off."

What Dad knew was that the owner of the restaurant could have walked in at any minute and seen Mr. Callahan's employee sitting on his backside lazily moving some bits of plaster around instead of working diligently. Not exactly the impression he wanted his customer to have.

At first, Shawn thought he was being criticized for the work he had done. But his dad made it clear that was not the case. "I can see you've done a good job, son. But it's just as important to look like you're doing a good job. You'll leave a better impression on the people you work with and work for." Shawn concluded that it's better to work hard until the job is completely done, and then leave or take a break, or even do nothing once you're done. Any of those would be better than working halfheartedly. It would be a shame to work hard and do good work just to have the people around you conclude that you're a slacker.

It's a lesson Shawn has drawn on many times throughout his career, which has spanned three decades thus far. Today, he's a successful entrepreneur and consultant with his own thriving business. And he hasn't gotten there by sitting around on his backside.

• • •

Perhaps more important than to honor one's self or not look like you're slacking off (or even to earn money), there is actually inherent benefit in hard work and struggles. Thomas Paine articulated that concisely when he said, "That which we obtain too easily, we esteem too lightly." But how might that play out in a real-life situation? One person who knows something about that is John Chancellor.

A few years ago, a psychiatrist friend of John's borrowed some money from him and was having difficulty paying it back. At the same time, another friend of John's was struggling with a different problem, the kind that might benefit from the help of a psychiatrist. So John suggested what seemed like a great solution. He asked his psychiatrist friend if he would take his other friend as a patient, but instead of charging him, simply offset what he owed John. The psychiatrist gets his debt reduced, a troubled man gets the counseling he needs, and John gets the satisfaction of knowing he's helped both his friends. It was a brilliant idea, except for one thing: The psychiatrist refused to do it.

John was stunned, and even a bit angry. "Let me understand this," he scoffed. "You owe me a fair bit of money. My friend needs help. But you won't help my friend and offset that against what you owe me?"

The psychiatrist looked John straight in the eye and said, "Yes, you're correct. I understand and agree that I owe you. I also understand about your friend, and from what you have told me, I think I could be of real help. However, I refuse to take your friend on as a patient on that basis."

"Why?" John asked.

"For the very simple reason that I never want to enter into a relationship with a patient when I know it's doomed to fail. You see, when a patient comes to me, he has to be hurting enough that he's willing to do something about it. If the pain is enough, he'll make sacrifices; he will do whatever it takes to relieve the pain. But if it's too easy for him, he won't benefit. In this case, if he doesn't pay, the patient won't value the service and as a result won't do what it takes to benefit from it." What he meant, of course, is that in his experience, patients who don't pay for his services are unlikely to follow his advice or take whatever medications he prescribes. In this case, the psychiatrist would get his debt reduced. But his patient would be no better off. And that didn't seem to be a fair arrangement.

John's anger slowly subsided as the wisdom of these words sank in. We tend to value things based on what we have to give up to obtain them. If something comes too easy, if the cost is too low, we place little or no value on it.

John's conclusion from this is as useful to a child as it is to a parent. He summarized it this way: "Don't rob people of the benefits that come from solving their own problems by trying to solve their problems for them." However difficult it may be, sometimes as a parent we need to heed that advice and not solve all our children's problems. And for the children, this story may help them understand why we can't (and shouldn't) always come to their rescue.

• • •

But it's not just work or physical struggles that bestow benefits. Wrestling with mental, emotional, and even spiritual struggles leave us better, too. One person who knows that well is Dorinda Phillips.

When Dorinda graduated from Aston University in Birmingham, England, she moved to Mainz, Germany, to start her career. Within two months of arriving in Mainz, she met a man—an amazing, caring, wonderful man. And she realized that for the first time in her life she was truly in love. It quickly became clear to her that she'd found her partner in life. As they approached a year into their relationship, Dorinda was growing even stronger in her feelings. Unfortunately, he began to have second thoughts. Why? Dorinda says of herself at that time, "I was shy, lacked confidence, and wasn't comfortable talking in group situations. That might have made me seem cold and distant to him and his very large, outgoing family."

By the end of the year, it all fell apart. As Dorinda recounts it, "He left me, and I was absolutely devastated. It was the first time I'd ever felt such pain. For the first two weeks I cried all day, except when I was at work. I still didn't know that many other people in Germany. Then I remember one day sitting down on the couch in my flat and thinking, 'Okay, you have a choice. You can either go home to England and the comfort of family and friends. Or you can stay here and change what it is you don't like about yourself. But you cannot go on like this.'"

While she did feel that her lack of confidence led to the breakup, her motivation to change that about herself wasn't an attempt to woo back her lost love. It was something she had never liked about herself. This was simply her wakeup call. "I told myself, 'This is it. I do not want to go home. I'm going to stay here and change this about me. I want to be more confident.'"

Dorinda started reading a book called *Assertiveness at Work* by Ken and Kate Back. "It was the start of a complete change in my life. The next nine months were amazing. I started going out more often and put myself in situations I would normally have been uncomfortable in. I talked to people I didn't know. I invited people to go out with me instead of waiting to be invited. And I looked for new and courageous things to do. I even took up belly dancing!"

Dorinda admits she still cried herself to sleep for three more months following her breakup. But her confidence grew every day. And then, out of the blue, her ex-boyfriend's mother called. "And this is a woman I had been terrified of, the matriarch of the family, and she asked me if I wanted to come on a vacation with the family. And I thought, 'Wow! Now that would be a test of my newfound confidence.' So I did it." Fortunately, perhaps, her ex-boyfriend did not attend, but the rest of the family did. And she "had the most amazing time. I talked to them so much more and more easily than I had before. I disagreed with them without hesitation. And I came back with this incredible high."

The whole ordeal showed Dorinda that she could learn to change anything she wanted. As she explained, "It was all just a question of learning, and there were people out there who could help." And that turned out to be a powerful realization, which ultimately led to discovering her purpose and passion in life—helping people learn the skills they want for greater happiness and success. She's devoted her career to it ever since. She started by creating more effective global training programs at the company she worked for. Then later she left to start her own company that focused on improving the impact of learning, which she appropriately called Maximizing Learning.

Looking back, Dorinda counts the relationship, the breakup, and what came from it as one of the best things that ever happened to her. Without the pain of breaking up, she likely wouldn't have had the impetus to make such a bold change in herself. Dorinda needed this struggle. In her case, it helped her become the successful, confident woman she is today.

• • •

As we've learned so far in this chapter, hard work and struggles are good for us. But that doesn't mean what looks like an unpleasant chore has to remain that. Work is what we make of it. We can leave it the ineffective burden it was when we found it. Or we can make it into something beautiful, effective, and even enjoyable. Just ask Cindy Beckman.

When Cindy was in high school, one of her least memorable teachers was . . . well, she can't actually remember his name, but he taught economics. She describes his teaching style as "read the book, take the test, read the book, take the test." Not exactly inspired teaching. Despite that, Cindy knew by the time she graduated that she wanted to be a high school teacher herself. Her passion area was history. So after high school, she entered the history department at the University of Central Arkansas, where she earned bachelor's and master's degrees.

After graduating, she landed her first job teaching social studies to sixth and seventh graders at nearby Conway Middle School. Not where she wanted to be. But it was a start. Then in January, Cindy got her big break. One of the teachers at the high school quit, and Cindy had done her student teaching under him a year earlier. So she was offered the job to replace him. The course she would have to teach, in an ironic twist of fate, was economics. And teaching the class turned out to be no more interesting than taking it had been earlier. She managed to get through it the first year. But she knew there had to be a way to make it better.

The next year at a teacher's conference, Cindy learned about a program called Junior Achievement (JA). It was a nonprofit organization that provided more experiential learning opportunities for students in finance, economics, and entrepreneurship. It sounded like just the thing she needed to spice up her economics curriculum. After getting permission from her department chair, Cindy leaned into JA's economic offerings full force. She had her students participate in stock market simulation games to teach them how the markets work. They participated in a computer simulation program to evaluate their management choices and see the impact their decisions had on the company's profits.

But the most exciting thing she did with her students was to start a company. Not another game or simulation: They actually started their own business. To raise money, the students sold shares of stock in the new company. And they elected a president and hired student officers to run it. Local business leaders volunteered to train the young executives in their new roles and responsibilities.

They chose school spirit wear for their new company product: T-shirts and hoodies with the school logo and graduating seniors' names on them. The students designed the T-shirts themselves, ordered the materials, sold the product, fulfilled their delivery, and did all the accounting. Eventually, they created a marketing program that reached across the whole school district, selling almost nine hundred T-shirts in one semester. And to make sure she nurtured their hearts as well as their minds, Cindy inspired her students to contribute their profits to a local charity. The program was a remarkable success, both educationally and financially.

A few years later, Cindy got an opportunity to spread her impact even farther. That year she spent two weeks at Khujand Technical University in Tajikistan, part of the former Soviet Union. To help them celebrate their tenth year of independence, she took her JA materials and curriculum to teach Tajik college students the concepts of free enterprise.

Without realizing it, Cindy was actually enjoying teaching economics. In fact, now she found it exciting. And that excitement got passed along to her students. Eventually, driven by the enthusiasm of her students and the success of her curriculum, Cindy got the school to make her one-semester economics course a full-year offering.

Cindy's success, and that of her students, continued to grow. In 2001, she was recognized among her peers all across the country for her efforts and was named the National Junior Achievement Teacher of the Year.[1] More rewarding for Cindy, however, is seeing the impact the experience has had on her former students. "I'm so proud because I still see some of them and they tell me they remember that company experience so many years later. And seeing what they've done with their lives, I can tell it made a difference."

Cindy continues to teach economics to this day, and she still loves it. That's amazing when you think it all started with a class she didn't like taking and certainly didn't want to teach. She made it into something better for her students and for herself. She found a way to turn that hard work dressed up in overalls into a lifetime of enjoyment and learning.

TEN

Self-Confidence

What other people think of you is none of your business.

—UNKNOWN

People who lack self-confidence don't lack confidence. They just gain it from a source other than themselves. Usually that means from other people. But the constant need for other people's approval to support your own confidence can lead to all kinds of bad decisions in life. One person who learned that lesson early was Sarah Milligan.

When Sarah was eight years old, she thought her big brother hung the moon. At the mature age of ten, he was bigger, taller, and faster than her. "And he was fearless," she reminisces fondly. Like a western explorer, "he could go out into the woods and return hours later with an animal or some other fascinating discovery" she would have never been able to find on her own. And with no other siblings or cousins in her small-town home of McAlester, Oklahoma, he was the most obvious actor to play the role of her hero. "I did just about everything I could to get him to spend time with me," she explains.

But like most older brothers, he usually had better things to do than play with his little sister. But one day, while visiting their grandparents' farm just outside Buffalo Valley, her brother actually invited Sarah to go out with him into the pasture. She recalls being so flattered that he asked her to go. Of course, she quickly accepted.

In short order, she and her big brother (with his rifle in hand) struck out on their adventure. They walked until they came across a thicket of small bushes. It was a big enough area to be home to all kinds of interesting things, but small enough that they could walk around it in two or three minutes' time. "Okay, Sarah, you run around to the other side and make as much noise as you can," he said.

So she ran a wide circle around the thicket, stomping and whooping, just excited to be part of this excursion. A few seconds into her ruckus making, she heard the thunderous "boom" of his gun. Although they hadn't talked much about what her job was, she understood it was complete and ran back around to see if she had done it well. There her brother stood, with a wry grin, his rifle lowered, staring into the high grass at the lifeless body of a small rabbit she had just helped flush out.

Sarah's heart sank. Perhaps it should have been obvious to her that this outing wasn't just a hike in the fields. It was a hunting expedition. Her brother had just killed a living thing. And she helped him do it.

Looking back, Sarah remembers being so angry at her brother, but not for killing the rabbit. He often returned from the woods with birds, squirrels, and other small animals, and that had never bothered her before. She was angry at him for getting her to participate in it. More important, she was disappointed in herself. She had looked past all the obvious signs of what was happening and was a willing participant. After all, what did she think he intended to do with his gun anyway? And what did she think she was scaring out of the thicket right into his crosshairs? She was so focused on the thrill of being included in her big brother's adventure that she looked past all of that. She didn't take the time to think about whether she really wanted to help kill something. And that's what disappointed her most. "It became a turning point in my life. 'Never again will I let this happen,' I thought. 'Never again will I blindly agree to something just to get someone else to like me.'"

Like most people, Sarah faced many similar situations in life growing up. In high school, for example, just about everyone faces decisions when out with their friends about whether they're going to drink with them, or smoke, or stay out late. Each time Sarah faced those types of situations, she asked herself, "Am I doing this for me? Or am I doing this to make someone else like me?" If the answer was "it's for someone else," Sarah's mind returned to the rabbit in the field. And she remembers the sickening feeling in the pit of her stomach she felt that day. Not just the feeling of sadness for the rabbit, but the loss of self she suffered from being so beholden to what someone else thought of her. And while she didn't always make the right choices growing up, she recognized this gut feeling as a sign to stand back and evaluate why she was doing something.

It's a great question for young people (or old people, for that matter) to ask themselves. Any time you're in a situation where you feel pressure to do something you're not certain you should do, ask yourself, "Am I doing this for me? Or am I doing it to make someone else like me?" Answer honestly, and act accordingly, and no rabbits will get hurt. More important, neither will you.

• • •

An even more common barrier to self-confidence than wanting others to like you is just being too concerned with what other people think. That's a lesson Richard Feynman learned while standing at his wife's hospital bed.

Feynman was a Nobel Prize–winning physicist known in scientific circles almost as much for his sarcastic wit and bongo playing as he was for his brilliant science. Publicly, he was a bold character remembered for his defining role in the investigation of the 1986 space shuttle *Challenger* disaster. Characteristic of Feynman, he refused to go along with the prescribed inquiry arranged for him and the other investigators. His unapproved conversations with NASA engineers led to the correct conclusion that the cause of the shuttle disaster was a rubber O-ring on the fuel line. During the panel hearing—unannounced—Feynman flamboyantly illustrated his theory by pulling O-ring material out of his glass of ice water and throwing it on the dais, shattering it in front of hundreds of journalists and television cameras. Apparently, the temperature the morning of takeoff was well below any previous shuttle launch. Too cold, in fact, for the rubber O-ring to maintain its flexibility, causing it to shatter under pressure.

Was Feynman just born a brave soul? Probably. But there was at least one defining moment that shaped his life and his science by building on an already courageous character.

In the early 1940s, Feynman was working at Los Alamos National Labs on the Manhattan Project, the top-secret government effort to build the atomic bomb. His wife, Arline, whom he had recently married, was undergoing treatment for tuberculosis in nearby Albuquerque, New Mexico. Feynman would hitchhike to the hospital on weekends to visit her.[1]

Arline knew Richard was frustrated at his own inability to comfort her or heal her terminal illness. So one weekend when he arrived, she presented him with an eighteen-inch charcoal grill she'd ordered through the mail. She desperately wanted a home-cooked meal over the hospital fare, and she asked him to cook her a steak.

Always the pragmatist, Feynman protested, "How the hell can we use it in the room, here, with all the smoke and everything?"

Arline suggested he just take it out on the lawn in front of the hospital. But the hospital was located right on Route 66, one of the busiest highways in the country at the time. Richard again protested that with all the automobile and pedestrian traffic, he couldn't just fire up a grill and start cooking steaks. People would think he was crazy!

"What do you care what other people think?" Arline asked.

Those words struck a profound chord with Richard. Not only did he cook Arline the steak she asked for, he did so every weekend thereafter.

Feynman must have realized the wisdom in her words. Why *should* he care what other people think? He cared about Arline! Her comfort and happiness was more important.

Being overly concerned about what other people think can sap your self-confidence and paralyze you with indecision. His wife's words helped Richard Feynman realize that. And they can help you too. If you find your young person becoming too worried about what other people think, share this story and ask your youngster, "What do you care what other people think?"

• • •

Looking for a simple and sure-fire way to build confidence in your young person? Arrange for her to do something she's already good at. It worked every year for Dr. Art Shriberg.

Dr. Shriberg has been a member of the faculty or staff of Xavier University in Ohio for thirty years. In that time he's worked with literally thousands of students from dozens of countries around the world. Over the years, one of the things he noticed is that the foreign students, far from home and with a first language other than English, often entered the program more timid and with less confidence than the local American students. In some classes, participation and group projects made up a meaningful part of their grades and learning. So that put them at a disadvantage.

Dr. Shriberg's solution? A soccer match. Each year while he was vice president for student development, he arranged for the students to play soccer ("football" to the rest of the world) as part of new student orientation. He explained his reasoning this way. "The international students were invariably better than the Americans at soccer. Those early victories on the soccer field gave them confidence and helped them win friends and respect. I noticed they consistently did better in their studies afterwards."

It's really a simple concept. A sure way to build confidence in a new environment is to do at least one thing you're already good at. It builds your own confidence while at the same time building the confidence others have in you.

ELEVEN

Self-Discipline: Money and Delayed Gratification

Man's greatest invention is compound interest.

—ATTRIBUTED TO ALBERT EINSTEIN

To many people, making wise decisions about what to spend and how to save are tedious and unpleasant chores. They're often lumped together with balancing the checkbook and choosing between complicated investment options on the list of things we don't really understand and would rather not spend our time doing. So they're often neglected. But it doesn't have to be that complicated, according to someone who should know: Pledger Monk.

Pledger has spent a lifetime studying, managing, and teaching prudent finance and investment. He holds a bachelor's degree in economics as well as an MBA from the Wharton School at the University of Pennsylvania and has spent the past twenty years as a financial adviser at one of the most prestigious investment banking firms in the world. So it should be no surprise that he's well versed in the most modern and sophisticated financial theories and investment vehicles. But what might be surprising is that when asked what are the most important concepts about money that people need to learn, he offers two deceptively simple ideas. And the first is one you think you understand. But you don't.

As Pledger explains, "I believe one of the most important concepts in investing and finance is one that's not talked about enough. In fact, it's supposedly well understood. Even finance professors in school assume all their students understand this principle like the back of their hand. But in my experience, they don't. The concept is this: compound interest or exponential growth. Everything in our financial system works on a compound basis. If you understand it, it can work for you to your benefit with incredible force and power. If you don't understand it, it can move you with equal force in the opposite direction."

And most people simply do not understand the magnitude of that force. Pledger believes this is because we're taught from an early age to understand mathematics in a linear fashion: two plus three, three times four, five minus one. "We can do those problems quickly off the top of our head," he explains. "But if we're asked to answer an exponential question, our minds just shut down. If I asked you what's six to the fifth power, or three to the one-fourth power, most of us couldn't even wager a guess. And if I asked what four is to the negative eighth power, you wouldn't have a clue."

So when Pledger teaches courses on investing at his local university, he introduces this topic with a couple of insightful examples. He first asks the class, "If I were to give you a penny every day in January, how much money would you have at the end of the month?" Just about everyone quickly answers "thirty-one cents." "Correct," he tells them. "Now what if I gave you one penny on the first day, but two pennies on the second day? Then I doubled it to four pennies on the third day, and doubled it again to eight pennies on the fourth day, and so on until the end of the month. Now how much money would you have?"

Most of the guesses he gets are in the $10 to $20 range. "Sometimes I'll get a few guesses around $100, and occasionally someone will throw out a really big number. But no matter how big it is, it's never even close to being big enough." And he can say that confidently, because the correct answer is 2.1 billion pennies. Yeah, that's billion with a "b." More than 21 million dollars' worth of pennies.[1] "You could all retire very nicely at the end of the month."

Next, he asks them to consider a piece of paper. "Now fold it in half. Then fold it again, and again. Now imagine folding it forty-five times." That last statement usually gets a good laugh, because most people realize you couldn't actually fold a sheet of paper more than six or seven times since it would get too bulky. But he asks them to just humor him. "How thick would it be?" he asks.

"Just to get us in the ball park, do you think it would be thicker than a good dictionary?" Some people think so. "Would it stack higher than this desk?" That turns out to be too thick for most guesses. "Higher than the ceiling?" And that's usually where the rest of the class drops out. "The correct answer," he tells them, "is that it would be thick enough to stack from here to the moon!" He's right, and perhaps even much farther depending on what kind of paper you're folding. If the 2.1 billion penny example didn't work, this more visual example usually brings the lesson home. And that lesson is the uncommonsensical nature of exponential growth.

When his students are all sufficiently impressed with its power, that's when he explains to them that every time they choose to buy something, or pay off a debt, or save and invest their money, they're making an important decision. They're choosing whether to let the power of compound growth work for them or against them. True, these examples are deliberately extreme to make a point. Nobody will pay you 100 percent interest compounded daily or extract that kind of penalty for a late payment on your mortgage. But the difference between investing money at an 8 to 10 percent annual return versus buying something on a credit card that charges 15 percent annual interest is still quite big. That's a 25 percent annual difference!

Before we see how compounding plays out with money, let's turn to the second deceptively simple concept Pledger espouses. And it didn't come from any of his graduate studies in finance, or the dozens of books he's read on the subject, or even his professional work or certifications. He heard it twenty years ago from his pastor at church. One Sunday his pastor said, "My experience watching people going through life tells me this. The single best indicator of whether they will be financially secure, have a low level of stress, and maintain a healthy marriage is if they follow the

'80/10/10 principle.' And that principle simply states that you should live on 80 percent of your income, give 10 percent to your church or charity, and save the remaining 10 percent."

In his two and a half decades of working, studying, and teaching in his field, Pledger has never heard a simpler framework for guiding people to live within their means. Most of the courses he's taken and books he's read teach sophisticated methods to invest the 10 percent (or whatever amount) one saves. But like the compound interest concept above, most just assume that everyone knows that in order to invest money, you have to save it first. And his observation (along with his pastor's) is that a significantly large percentage of people fail to do that. "As a result," he explains, "when they have a flat tire, or a tree limb falls on their house, or they have an unexpected medical problem, they're unprepared for it. So it causes stress and often trouble in their marriage."

Once Pledger's students understand these two basic concepts, then he's ready to bring them both together with a story of two hypothetical recent college graduates. We'll call them Jack and Kate. Let's assume both are twenty-one years old. And to make the math easy, we'll assume each earns $48,000 a year for their entire working career, which is a little below the median household income in the United States.[2]

Kate understands both the compound interest and 80/10/10 principles well and puts them to use for her benefit. She saves $4,800 a year ($400 a month) and invests it wisely every year, earning an 8 percent return until she retires at the age of sixty-seven.

Jack, on the other hand, understands neither. Like many people, he spends more money than he makes every month by using credit cards to buy things he can't afford. We'll assume that he spends all the money he makes each month, plus an additional $400 a month on his credit card, for the first four years after college. With a typical 15 percent interest rate on credit cards,[3] Jack is now almost $24,000 in debt, not an unusual amount for people in the United States with a history of bad financial decisions.[4] Let's then assume that Jack wises up and realizes he can't continue down this path. Instead of spending more than he earns, he makes major changes in his spending and manages to save $200 a month for the next four years that he can use to start to pay down his credit cards. That helps.

But since $200 isn't even enough to cover the interest, his total debt continues to grow.

By the time Jack gets to the age of twenty-nine, let's assume he finally manages to start saving $400 a month, just like Kate has been doing for eight years now. Except with Kate, that $400 a month is getting invested and growing for her. For Jack, he's using it to pay off his credit cards, which he owes close to $30,000 on now! That $400 a month is right around the minimum monthly payment, enough to cover all the interest and reduce the principal of the debt just a little each month. At that rate, it takes Jack twenty years to pay off those credit cards he spent only four years running up. And in that time, he's paid more than $100,000 to his credit card company because of the $19,000 worth of stuff he bought back in his early twenties. Now he's forty-nine years old and is back to a net worth of zero, exactly where he and Kate started twenty-eight years ago.

Jack and Kate continue to save $400 a month until they reach the standard retirement age of sixty-seven. And with Kate's smart 80/10/10 living, that $400 a month she put away for forty-seven years added up to a total of $225,000 saved. But because of the magic of compound interest, she actually has more than $2 million in her retirement account! Kate retires comfortably and confidently.

Jack, on the other hand, only has about $200,000 in his retirement account, only one-tenth as much as Kate. Said another way, Kate has ten times as much money saved for retirement as Jack. And while his $200,000 may sound like a lot of money, with all the inflation between college graduation and retirement, that money won't last long, and soon he'll be completely broke again.

What if Jack wanted to keep working past sixty-seven to save up as much money as Kate? How long would that take? It would take another twenty-eight years! He would have to work until he's ninety-five years old to save up the $2.2 million Kate had at sixty-seven.

Think about that. Here we have two people the same age with the same income. And for most of their adult lives (starting at age twenty-nine), they both saved exactly the same amount of money, $400 a month. It was only the first four years that Jack was spending on credit cards while Kate wasn't. And then for another four years he saved, but not quite as much as Kate. Those early eight years cost Jack $2 million, or twenty-eight years of his life, whichever way you want to look at it.

And what did Jack get for that $2 million he gave up? He probably got a fancier car and a slightly larger apartment between the ages of twenty-one and twenty-five. Certainly not worth $2 million or twenty-eight years of extra work in his life. But people make those kinds of decisions all the time. The reason is they don't realize the enormous cost it will have on them forty-five years later. Once you understand Pledger's two principles and the story of Jack and Kate, you're in a much better position to choose. Will you be a Jack? Or will you be a Kate?

• • •

The key to saving that $400 a month like Kate instead of spending it like Jack is learning to be happy without constantly having more stuff. And in a wealthy, Western culture, that might seem an impossible task. That explains why it took several trips to a less wealthy place for Ami Desai to really get it.

Ami was born in New York, a first-generation natural-born American citizen. Her parents were born in India and immigrated to the United States after getting married. During her first few years of life, Ami spent half the year living in New York and half the year in her aunt and uncle's home in Bombay visiting family. Even after she started going to school, Ami and her mother traveled to Bombay for a few weeks every year or two until Ami graduated from high school.

The home her aunt and uncle lived in wasn't just the home they lived in at the time. It was the home her mother and uncle had grown up in, and the one her grandmother had grown up in, and her great-grandmother had grown up in. But if you're picturing a fancy suburban estate the family owned, think again. It was a two-bedroom apartment they'd been renting for generations. In addition to the two small bedrooms, it had an eating area with a simple table and a cabinet against the wall for dishes, and a kitchen about five feet by five feet with a refrigerator, sink, and pot burner. And there was one bathroom with a sink and a hole in the ground for a toilet. By Western standards, it would be considered severely impoverished. But by local standards, it was quite normal.

Ami fondly remembers visiting Bombay. During those visits, that simple two-bedroom apartment housed six people: her aunt and uncle, mother, grandmother, sister, and Ami. During the day, she would go shopping with her mother and buy all sorts of exotic things with their Western-size bank accounts, large by local standards, though quite modest back home.

At the end of one season's visit, Ami recalls vividly her uncle feeling some pressure to give her a gift before she left to go home. Then he gave her, with some fanfare, a tiny gold-plated clock. "I remember they were so excited and proud to give it to me. But I also remember feeling guilty taking it. I knew they didn't have much money. And we had so much." But that wasn't the only reason Ami felt awkward accepting this gift. The other reason was that while they clearly wanted to be generous, she realized they probably thought what Ami needed to be happy was a gift. In short, they thought that for her to be happy, she needed more stuff.

That's when it dawned on her, still at a young age, that more stuff wasn't necessary for happiness. And she didn't have to look far to see examples. Her aunt and uncle and grandmother living there were very happy people, and they had next to nothing. So she started watching how they spent their time and noticed some differences. "In the U.S., what seemed to make people happy was buying a new TV, or some other material possession. But my aunt and uncle seemed so happy just going to the market to buy their daily food, or picking up a visitor at the train station. When we got home, my grandma would cook the most wonderful meal for us. Then we would all go out and play together. Friends and family were always stopping by to visit. And we'd have tea and biscuits and talk with each of them every time. Back home in New York you'd need an invitation before showing up at someone's house to visit. It would be rude to do otherwise. But in Bombay, it happened every day because you had dozens of friends who lived in the same building. We were never by ourselves and never bored. It was like an adventure every day."

How did that trip affect Ami's perceptions of money and material possessions? She explains, "I remember being upset just before leaving for that Bombay trip because my mom wouldn't buy me the Keds sneakers with the blue dot that was all the rage at school. But by the time I returned home, somehow it didn't seem all that important. The cheaper pair she got me at Walmart suddenly seemed just fine."

Not everyone can afford the time and expense of a trip halfway around the world to learn the lesson Ami learned in Bombay. But you can start by sharing her story with your young person. Then talk about ways to spend your time that doesn't involve buying lots of stuff. You'll be well on your way to saving that $400 a month.

• • •

Not everyone is lucky enough to learn that lesson as early as Ami, or as cheaply. Most of us learn it later in life, when it's much more costly. A particularly instructive example of that is what happened to a guy we'll call Jun-seo.

Jun-seo was born in South Korea and grew up in the home of his adoptive parents in Brussels, Belgium. His father was a lover of fine automobiles. He always drove nice cars and attended high-performance car rallies—a real car aficionado. So Jun-seo grew up with a taste for fine cars himself. Having his own fancy sports car was a goal he set for himself at a young age.

But buying nice cars is expensive, so he knew he needed to earn a lot of money. At sixteen, and an amateur DJ, he started his own business creating custom mix tapes of popular music. This was before the days of digital music and MP3 players when anyone could do that themselves. After a couple of years doing that, he started importing hi-fi stereo equipment from Germany and selling it in France, where the demand was higher. Both these ventures worked and paid him quite well. All that work, however, took away time that he could have spent with his friends. But it was worth it to him at the time.

Plus, Jun-seo found he liked having money. He even described himself as becoming "somewhat materialistic" at the time. So his focus continued to be on earning money. Over the next several years, Jun-seo accumulated enough to buy the car of his dreams. It was a red 1990 Mazda Miata, first edition—the hardtop version, loaded with options. "It was beautiful," he remembers fondly. He bought it used with only 36,000 miles for about 11,000 euros. He was proud to drive it and even prouder to have someone ride in it with him.

Such was the case one day, about three months after he bought it. It was January, and the streets were slippery. "I had never replaced the original tires. And I was driving a bit crazy," he admits, "really trying to show off the car and what it could do. I remember taking a fast corner and the nice controlled skid turned into an uncontrollable spin. The car spun around completely once before hitting the curb and flipping upside-down, sliding to a stop on the roof."

Miraculously, Jun-seo and his friend walked away from the crash without any serious injuries. But the car was totaled. "I didn't have insurance at the time, so I had to sell the car. I think I got about 2,000 euros for it." So he had lost 9,000 euros that he'd been saving up for seven years, just to drive his fancy red sports car for three months.

Looking back, Jun-seo learned several lessons from that experience. Of course, he should have replaced the worn tires on the car. And he shouldn't have driven it so fast and out of control. More important, however, was this. He thinks he should have never set such a shallow and materialistic goal in the first place. Today he believes it ended up costing much more than money. "I think it cost me friendships as well." In hindsight, he knows he had good friends before the age of sixteen, before he had any of that money. And he's had many strong friendships again after the age of twenty-three, when he wrecked his car. But in between?

"I lost many of the friends I had. And I was too much of a materialistic show-off focused on earning money for the car to make any new ones. I was a really different person during that time. In fact, a girlfriend I had in college told me, 'If I had known you at that point in your life, you wouldn't be with me now.'"

It's ironic really. Many people want to have fancy cars because they think it will attract friends. But at least in Jun-seo's case, it seems to have done the opposite.

• • •

Of course, it's okay to have material possessions as long as the pursuit of them doesn't consume your whole self. So let's turn our attention to one of the most common ways young people come to possess things in the Western world—in the form of Christmas presents.

Richard Pascoe grew up in the small village of Blunsdon in the southwest of England. When he was seven years old, he recalls doing something most honest people will admit to doing at least once or twice in their childhood. He was trying to find his presents before Christmas.

He recalls stealthily walking around the house in a determined search. Then, opening up one particular cupboard, he saw an open plastic bag with something inside. One peek at the unwrapped package with a picture of the toy on the front, and he knew he'd found one! But in his long and not-very-well-thought-out search, he hadn't given any consideration to how he would feel after finding his presents. He just knew he wanted to know what they were. And the long wait till Christmas was excruciating.

He recalls being surprised at his own reaction. "It was an instantaneous moment of excitement and accomplishment and satisfaction, followed by several hours of remorse. All of a sudden, my discovery that should have made me so happy came with all this complexity." Richard described the cascade of feelings that followed his elation. "Now I know what I'm going to get. So the surprise is all ruined. The anticipation is gone. But I can't actually hold it in my hands and play with it either. That's even more frustrating than not knowing! Plus, now I've got to pretend and look as if this was a surprise when I do open it. But Mom and Dad will probably find out anyway. And then they'll be disappointed in me. Worst of all," Richard wonders, "wouldn't I have spoiled the pleasure my parents should enjoy seeing me open my presents for the first time? I ended up really regretting looking for that present in the first place."

Looking back, he's not sure he would have articulated all those thoughts and emotions the same way. But he definitely felt and struggled with them, regardless of the descriptors you put on them. And it's definitely affected how he thinks about presents, surprises, and the value of delayed gratification. "Ever since then, if I'm in a situation where there's a surprise coming and I have a chance to know ahead of time, I say, 'No, I think I'll wait.' Because I know it'll be that much sweeter."

In fact, today Richard has two children of his own, Genevieve (age seven) and Bill (age six). He shared this story with both of them just a few weeks prior to Bill's birthday in December. "Bill had already been talking about what he might get, and even speculating on where we might have the presents hidden. But after hearing the story, I could tell he was thinking much more about the downsides of going on the present hunt I went on about his age. And I honestly don't think he did."

Nothing can guarantee your kids won't find their presents before they should, except of course not getting them any. But a story like Richard's can help them really understand why they might be much happier to wait.

• • •

When running for president in the year 2000, George W. Bush was asked by the press to explain his immature behavior in his twenties and thirties. He responded simply, "When I was young and irresponsible, I was young and irresponsible." Most of us would like to forget at least some of what we said or did. If you decide to run for president, you can bet you'll be reminded of it—often. But even if you're not running for the highest office in the land, many of us have built-in memory retrieval devices that live in our homes and listen to our every word: our children. If you're not careful, an unwelcome reminder can be hurled at you at the most inopportune time. That's exactly what happened to Mark.

When Mark was still in his twenties, he'd been married with children long enough to lose some of his "young and irresponsible" habits, but apparently not all of them. One Sunday afternoon, around Halloween, Mark walked into his local grocery store with his two-year-old son, Andrew. He remembers seeing lots of people in line at the checkout, still dressed in their Sunday best after coming from church.

As Mark tells the story, "It's important to know that Andrew was verbal early as a child. And loud. So imagine me strapping Andrew into a shopping cart and pushing off to do my shopping. Well, as we passed the checkout aisles, Andrew apparently got an eyeful of all the display cases of Halloween candy. All of a sudden, I heard him yell out to me, 'Dad, I want some fucking candy!'

"I could not believe what I heard. And for some foolish reason, I leaned over and said, 'What did you say?'

"Well, he's two, so of course he assumed I didn't hear him properly. So he reached out with his little hands, grabbed me on both sides of the face, looked me right in the eyes, and said, even louder, 'I saaaaid . . . I want some fucking candy!'"

At that point, Mark could feel all the eyes in the grocery store on him. A quick and embarrassed look up confirmed a dozen Sunday churchgoers glaring, not at the two-year-old but at Mark. Two-year-olds don't learn that word on their own. Mark knew it, and they knew it. He quickly wheeled Andrew to the back of the store, away from the convicting stares. He said, "Son, that's a really bad word. And I promise I will not say it around you again. And you don't need to say it either."

There are several lessons to be learned from this story. The one that landed it in this chapter is the importance of patience and the ability to delay the gratification of Halloween candy until, well, Halloween. It doesn't make anyone look good rolling through the grocery store demanding some candy when in a few days you'll have a bucketful.

Second, Mark articulates the lesson for him as a parent this way. "Kids will show you the worst part of yourself." That event largely ended Mark's use of that word and a few other words. "I'm not saying when I hit my thumb with a hammer, I don't squeak out a bad word. But it radically changed my language around Andrew."

But I think there's one more lesson for the child in this case, no matter what age. That is, when you behave poorly, it's not just a bad reflection on you. It reflects badly on your parents as well for not raising you better. So even if your "young and irresponsible" behavior doesn't embarrass *you*, think about how it makes your parents feel. Think about the many convicting eyes that fall on them whenever you cross the line. When you realize your behavior comes back to haunt not just you, but others in your family, you might be more careful what you say and do, even if you're not planning to run for president.

TWELVE

Health

Just because you're not sick doesn't mean you're healthy.

—AUTHOR UNKNOWN

If you don't have your health, nothing else in life seems to matter much. So fixing whatever health issue ails us becomes painfully impossible to ignore. But when we do have our health—or at least think we do—it's often easy to neglect it and take it for granted. But that's when the seeds of destruction are usually sown. One person who knows that well is David Casterline.

March 23, 2013, was a big day for David. He'd been looking forward to the race for some time. But today was the day. The Kal-Haven Trail runs 33.5 miles along the former route of the Kalamazoo and South Haven Railroad in southwest Michigan. It's a beautiful path through woods, small towns, and farmland. David and his relay team of four co-workers would collectively run the entire distance, with his segment being the final five miles of the race.

David's in good shape compared to most fifty-two-year-olds, and very active. He's not too experienced of a runner, but he did run a 5K race the year before. So he was confident he'd do okay.

It was cold that morning. Snow and ice from the night before was turning to mud as the sun got higher. That made the run even more challenging. When it was David's turn, he found most of his leg was uphill, even the final sprint to the end. But he attacked it like a champ and finished his leg in just over forty minutes, an impressive time for an experienced runner, much less a novice.

He crossed the finish line feeling a bit lightheaded. That's typical for someone running a longer distance and a faster pace than he's used to. He even stumbled into a pole when he wasn't looking where he was going. It wasn't too embarrassing, though. It's a little hard to focus when you've just run five miles uphill and you're still trying to catch your breath.

Half an hour later, he met up with his team at a local restaurant to celebrate their accomplishment. In addition to finishing a 33.5-mile race, they and the other 572 runners that day raised more than $9,000 for a local charity, a great cause for celebration.

At lunch somebody noticed that David didn't look very good. His lips were still blue from the cold, even though they were inside now. "Are you still dizzy, David?" they asked.

"Yeah. A little."

"Sick to your stomach? Breathing a little fast?"

"Yeah, those too."

"David, you're dehydrated. Those are the classic signs. You didn't get enough liquid on your run. Drink some water. Better yet, have some Gatorade."

It was a typical mistake for a rookie runner to make: Not hydrating enough before, during, and after the race. Now he was paying the price. But he was catching up with fluids now, so he assumed he'd feel better soon. What he was too embarrassed to say at the time was that he was really feeling the effects of the race in the muscles of his arms and chest. He'd prepared for a strenuous leg workout. But he didn't expect that all the pumping of his arms during the sprint at the end would take so much out of him. Now he was cramping a little.

After lunch, some of his friends were kind enough to drive David home, even though he was feeling better by then. On the way they called David's wife, Val, just to let her know he wasn't feeling well and they were bringing him home. They described his symptoms. But David talked to her and assured her that he was fine. Already feeling better. "Next time I'll train better for the race. And drink more water."

When they hung up, Val called their sons, Matt and Chris. Both were ninety miles away at college studying medicine. Was Val worrying unnecessarily? She just needed someone to tell her that David was going to be fine. In separate phone calls, Val relayed everything she'd been told to both boys. Both came to the same conclusion and told their mother the same thing.

When David got home a few minutes later, Val met him at the door. "David, you need to go to the hospital. You're having a heart attack."

He was afraid she'd say that. It's typical for the people who love us most to overreact to the smallest things. Now he was going to have to calm her down, and he really didn't have the energy.

"No, no, Val. I'm fine. Really. Look at me . . . I'm fine."

Val got her boys back on the phone and talking directly to David. "If he won't listen to me, maybe he'll listen to them," she thought.

For several minutes both boys tried to convince their father to go to the hospital. And with the same pride and stubbornness most men would show in the same situation, he resisted. But two things stand clear in his memory today from that phone call. First, there was the stark distinction of being told that just because he was *feeling* better didn't mean he was *getting* better. In fact, one of them said, "You didn't *have* a heart attack, Dad. You're *having* a heart attack right now! It's still happening." The second thing he recalls is either a promise or a threat, depending on how you look at it. They said, "Dad, if you don't get in the car right now and go to the hospital, we're driving home and taking you ourselves, whether you're willing to or not." At twenty-one and twenty-three years old, both boys were very capable of delivering on that threat, and David knew it. So whether it was to avoid a messy confrontation or just to appease his loving family, David let his wife drive him to the local hospital.

A few tests later and the doctors confirmed, "Mr. Casterline, you've had a major heart event. We're sending you to Borgess Hospital in Kalamazoo. They have better facilities for this."

"Can this really be happening to me?" David thought. "I feel much better now. Why is everyone making such a big deal out of this?" So he asked the doctor, "Do I need to stay here tonight? Or can I sleep at home and go to Borgess tomorrow?"

"No, David. You don't understand. You're going right now. The ambulance is pulling around front as we speak."

Thirty minutes later at Borgess, David was rapidly assessed and treated. We'll skip all the details of that here. But at approximately 1 a.m., when the danger had passed and the treatment was bringing David's vital signs back to safe levels, the doctor stopped by to talk. David told him of the valiant efforts his wife and boys went through to get him to come in. And that's when the severity of his situation became clear for the first time. The doctor said, "David, if they hadn't gotten you to come in, by morning you would not be alive."

Those words hung in the air for a somber moment. David could not believe how close he had come to not going to the hospital, how close he had come to losing everything. He clearly owed his wife a debt of gratitude. As for his boys, who had become the parents in this situation, he could not be more grateful and proud at the same time.

Thanks to good teachers and public health and safety campaigns, these days just about everyone knows the symptoms of a heart attack: pain or discomfort in the chest or arms, shortness of breath, lightheadedness, and nausea. But there are problems with that description. First, lots of medical problems cause some of the same symptoms, like dehydration. But the other problem is this: If you were having those symptoms yourself, you probably wouldn't think of them in such terse, clinical terms. "Oh my, I'm having 'shortness of breath' and 'nausea.'" You're probably not thinking in words at all. You're thinking in feelings. And what you're feeling at that moment is that you're having trouble catching your breath and feel like you might throw up.

The other thing you're feeling is a desperate need to convince yourself (and anyone else who will listen) that you're just fine. Having a heart attack is embarrassing. Only "old and out-of-shape people" have heart attacks, right? Not me. I'm too healthy for that. That's just what David thought too.

Recognizing the symptoms of a heart attack—the covert, confusing, and embarrassing way they happen in the real world of a busy workday or tennis match or road race—can save your life or someone you love. Read this story to your kids and make sure they know they have license to send you to the hospital if they see these symptoms in you. Like David, you'll be glad you did.

• • •

Now let's turn our attention to a couple of health issues that are even more common and just as serious. And we'll start with a beautiful woman in Mexico.

If you were to meet Fadia Perez today, you would describe her as nothing short of stunning. She is tall and lean, with high cheekbones, a figure that most women would envy, shiny jet-black hair, and a magazine-quality smile. Not surprisingly, she's been encouraged many times in the past decade to pursue a modeling career, and she even considered it seriously once or twice. But it wasn't always that way for Fadia. She was born in Mexico City, where she lived with her mother, grandmother, and younger sister. Like her mother before her, she struggled with her weight as a child.

By the age of twelve, she weighed sixty pounds more than she does now at the age of thirty-six. And that led to an understandably difficult childhood. She explains, "At the time, I had been a fat kid as long as I could remember. I was never comfortable with myself. My mom made me wear these cheesy dresses, because they were the only ones I could fit into. I had stretch marks on my legs, so I was embarrassed to go swimming. I had to wear long shorts instead of a swimsuit. And the other kids would call me names like 'meatball.' In sports, I wasn't just the last one picked. I wasn't picked at all. The teacher usually had to place me on a team. Then the other kids would say, 'Awww, not the fat girl! We're going to lose for sure now!' I usually ended up just playing with my sister.

"My mother always taught me to pray for what I wanted. So every night I would pray, 'Oh God, please, please, please, make me slim.' When I woke up, I'd keep my eyes closed and pray again, 'Please let me be slim now.' Then I would open my eyes and pull down the sheets and cry when I saw that I was still fat."

One day Fadia's mother had seen enough. She said to her daughter, "I don't want you to suffer like me. The teenage years are worse. I'm going to take you to the doctor. You're going on a serious diet." And she did. For the next six months, there was no candy or milkshakes. She followed a sensible diet and exercised. How did she like it? "I hated it," she admitted. "And at the time I hated my mother for making me do it." It must have been difficult not to be able to eat the same foods as the other kids at school. And to not enjoy candy at all seemed cruel to her at the time.

But by the end of six months, Fadia had lost fifty pounds. For the first time in her life, at the age of thirteen, she felt pretty. Instead of baggy dresses, she got to wear cute tops and slim jeans, and she looked and felt good in them. And she didn't have to suffer any more "fat girl" comments at school. She liked who she was for the first time. As a result, Fadia learned the value of discipline and sticking to a plan. She learned that achieving a worthy goal requires hard work. And instead of being resentful of her mother for making her go through it, she was grateful and has thanked her many times in the years since.

Unfortunately, Fadia's newfound body and healthy body image didn't last.

The following year was a tough one for Fadia's family. Her mother lost her job and money was tight. As much as a parent tries to hide such things from her children, it still creates stress. Perhaps because of this, or perhaps for no reason at all, Fadia started feeling fat again. Only she wasn't. "I looked at myself in the mirror and saw a fat image of me. I saw a big belly and big hips. I felt ugly. None of my clothes seemed to fit right anymore. I was getting more insecure." So even though she was now eating a healthy diet, she started cutting back on her food. First she cut out tortillas, then beans. And when Grandma was making dinner, Fadia would say, "Just give me half a portion, please."

But once she noticed Fadia's weight falling, Grandma would say, "You're getting too skinny. I'm giving you a full portion." And that's when Fadia started lying about what she ate. "I would tell my mom that I had breakfast when I hadn't. And I started hiding food in my clothes or in plastic bags or flushing it down the toilet. I became mentally obsessed with the next meal. All day long I would think about how to hide my food. I would think, 'Tonight Grandma is making tacos, and that's difficult to hide, because it has a hard shell with a shape.'"

Despite growing taller since achieving her healthy weight, Fadia lost another twenty pounds in three months. Her eating and weight loss were so unhealthy she started losing her hair and growing weak. And her menstrual periods stopped entirely. For about a month her mother left town to look for a new job, leaving Grandma in charge. When Mom returned and saw how much her daughter had changed, it frightened her. Fadia's tongue was white, her hair was thin, and her skin was pale. Mom took Fadia to the doctor immediately to find out what was wrong. He asked if she was eating properly, and of course she and her mother assured him that she was. So the doctor checked for parasites in her stomach and intestines, but found none. That led him to an even more dire hypothesis: cancer.

Her mother was devastated. How could this have happened to her sweet fourteen-year-old baby girl?

Fadia watched her mother's reaction to the news and took stock of her own condition. She soon came to the conclusion that she couldn't keep doing this to herself or to her mother. She decided to start eating again. But that turned out to be easier to say than to do. As Fadia explained, "When you don't eat for that long, it's hard to eat normal again. I had to wean myself off of pitching food."

By then the tests had ruled out cancer, and the doctors settled on anemia as the culprit. So Fadia had to suffer painful iron injections daily and beef liver drops on her food, which she describes as "the most disgusting thing you could ever eat." So that gave Fadia even more incentive to eat properly again.

It took her a year to regain that twenty pounds. But she did. At sixteen she was back to a healthy weight, which she's maintained for the two decades since. Out of guilt and shame, she never did tell her mother about her intentional weight loss and hiding her food. But in her mid-twenties she read a magazine article about anorexia and realized that's exactly what she had had. She thought she had been alone with her problem.

Looking back, Fadia has been on both ends of the spectrum of weight problems that plague many young people today. But her story has many lessons for kids facing similar issues. First, while it might not work for everyone, with the discipline of a reasonable diet and exercise, the problem of being overweight can usually be managed. Second, regarding anorexia, having an incorrect and unhealthy body image is not uncommon. Both children and their parents should be aware of the signs: rapid weight decline, fear of gaining weight, distorted body image, and in extreme cases hair loss, weakness, and irregular periods in girls. But as she did with her excess weight, Fadia learned to overcome her anorexia. She insists that "no matter how bad and out of control your life can be (and mine was), you can always change it. But you must realize that you are the only one who can change it. Once you do that, you control the food. The food no longer controls you."

THIRTEEN

Positive Mental Attitude

> Most folks are about as happy as they make up their minds to be.
>
> —ABRAHAM LINCOLN

Finding out a hurricane is about to bear down on your hometown isn't the kind of thing most people get excited about, especially when they're eight years old. But then, most people aren't like Jayson Zoller.

Jayson grew up in a town in central Florida called Winter Haven, where his father ran the local hardware store. The store was open six days a week, so his dad had to work a lot of hours. "You had to hustle to make a living in that business," Jayson recalls. But he also says, "Some of my best memories growing up were during hurricane season." And it was because of that hardware store.

Starting at around the age of eight, Jayson remembers being shaken out of bed in the early hours when a storm was brewing. The whole family would drive to the store together in the pitch black. "Then we'd spend the day working as fast as we could because there was a line of people out the door trying to stock up on batteries and flashlights or whatever else they needed to weather the storm."

In the spirit of full disclosure, that extra business did mean more money for his family. In fact, Jayson describes the time after hurricane season as something like Christmas for a hardware store owner's family. But there were two more important things going on for Jayson. First, there was a clear sense of purpose and duty in these emergencies. "My parents could have done what most people did during these storms: board up the windows, lock the doors, and hunker down till it was over. But we stayed open because we knew that was part of our role in the community. If we locked our doors, people couldn't get what they needed to feel safe."

Second, those crisis situations made for serious family bonding time, the kind you can't orchestrate with a card game or afternoon matinee. Mom, Dad, Jayson, and his little sister all worked hard together to serve a common purpose. It turned something dire and ominous into something exciting and playful.

As an adult, Jayson realized that sense of duty, purpose, excitement, and bonding wasn't unique to the hardware store business. Any crisis or challenge can provide those same rewards. Today, any time something difficult pops up at work, he harks back to his days in Florida. Instead of retreating, he rallies a team and attacks the problem with the same attitude of purpose, duty, and excitement he enjoyed during hurricane season in Winter Haven. And he knew he'd come out of it at the other end with even stronger relationships with the people he works with.

And that, I think, is the most important point. Crises crop up all the time in life. You can choose to look at them as things to dread and board up the windows against. Or you can choose to look at them as opportunities to help those around you weather the storm and a chance to bond with the family, friends, or coworkers who stand beside you. As with adopting any positive mental attitude, the choice is yours.

• • •

In fact, just as choice is the single most important factor in adopting a positive mental attitude, it's also the most important component of being happy. Happiness is not something that happens to you. It's something you choose to be. That fact isn't really a secret anyone's been keeping from you. But it takes a surprisingly long time for most people to realize it, if they ever do. Jeremy McInnis learned that powerful lesson at the young age of twenty. And ironically, he learned it from a boy half his age and halfway around the world.

After high school, Jeremy served in the U.S. Army National Guard's 1313th Engineer Company in Indianapolis, Indiana. In May 2012, his unit was deployed to Israel for search and extraction support during a period of heavy Palestinian conflict. That meant when a bomb blew up and collapsed a building, Jeremy's job was to go in and pull out victims trapped inside.

One of the first such occurrences after they arrived was in a five-story apartment building in Jerusalem. The 1313th was the first extraction team on the scene. Jeremy described the work this way: "These things turn into something that's not a building anymore, but not just a pile of rubble either. We used jackhammers to cut our way in until we found a tunnel to move through. Then we put up braces to maintain what little structure was left so we could get out the way we came in. We knew there was fifty thousand pounds of reinforced concrete over our heads ready to come down any minute."

About six hours into the work, they found a room with a partially collapsed roof. In it was a barely conscious eleven-year-old boy just visible underneath his mother and father. His parents had obviously covered him with their own bodies as the building collapsed, which saved his life. But it cost them their own.

After medical treatment, the boy was taken to an orphanage only a few blocks from where Jeremy's unit was stationed. Each day for the next four or five days, Jeremy saw him playing in the yard with the other children. Jeremy recalls, "He was smiling, and laughing, and . . . happy. I thought 'How on earth can that be?' This kid just lost *everything*!" So at his next opportunity, Jeremy stopped to talk to the boy and find out. He asked him how he could be so happy and smiling all the time after what happened.

"He responded in impressive but broken English, and in a heavy Israeli accent, 'Because the sky is blue.'" That didn't make sense to Jeremy, and it must have showed. The boy invited Jeremy to sit down and then continued, "It's something my father taught me repeatedly for as long as

I can remember. 'Because the sky is blue' can be a reason for anyone to do anything, any time."

What he meant, Jeremy explained, is "it's like saying 'because it's Thursday,' or 'because I'm left-handed,' or even 'just because.'" In other words, I don't really have a reason. Nor do I need one. It's just how I choose to be.

That eleven-year-old boy had just lost his mother and father and every worldly possession they owned. And yet he was happy and smiling simply because that's the way he chose to be. That's the secret Jeremy learned. Happiness isn't something that happens to you. It's a decision you make. It may be the most important legacy that boy carries with him from his father. And now Jeremy carries it. If you met Jeremy today and asked why he's happy, he'll be glad to tell you. It's because the sky is blue.

• • •

That lesson isn't true just in a war zone. It's true everywhere. In fact, if you had to pick the unhappiest place to work in a modern hospital, you'd be hard pressed to suggest a better candidate than oncology, the cancer ward. Yet that's where my sister, Bobba Rhine, took her first job after finishing nursing school. Even for the survivors, cancer treatment can be a gruesome affair. And imagine how hard it must be for the nurse who has to administer that treatment. On top of that, patients who didn't survive often stayed just long enough for a nurse to develop a genuine, caring relationship with them. And then that nurse has to watch her patient (and now friend) die, a process that gets repeated dozens of times a year. Not a place for the faint of heart.

So in oncology, the patients could rightly be expected to have short tempers and long faces and make for the most unpleasant of company. As you might expect, then, the more experienced nurses opt for other departments. So it shouldn't be too surprising that when Bobba got her first job offer as a nurse, it was for oncology. So that's where she started.

To be sure, her first year had its share of tears. But it didn't seem to be the disagreeable place she expected. In fact, her patients were more peaceful, kind, and appreciative than their circumstances would seem to warrant. "Imagine," Bobba explains, "if you knew you had two or three months to live. Suddenly it wouldn't matter if there was a wrinkle in the bed, or the room was cold, or if your eggs were runny. It matters if your grandkids get to come visit, or if the nurse has a few minutes to look at your pictures or read a letter from home."

But she only came to really appreciate that outlook when she was later placed in a nursing pool and assigned to other departments on a rotating basis. "On other floors you could have people in for short stays or even outpatient visits, people who were otherwise quite healthy and would be home in a few days or maybe just a few hours. And yet they were the crabbiest people you could ever meet. I would think to myself, 'Shut up! You don't have anything to complain about. So you have an ingrown toenail. You go spend one day in the cancer ward and tell me you have problems.' I couldn't wait to get back to oncology."

Every other ward of the hospital is filled with people who come in knowing they're going to leave eventually. Some of them are just pissed off at the inconvenience of having to be there for a few hours. But in oncology, some of them are terminal and know they're not getting better. So being there is not the burden that's keeping them from enjoying life.

The lesson is that your happiness is not a function of your circumstances. It's a function of your outlook on life. In other words, happiness is a choice. Those cancer patients are arguably in the worst circumstances imaginable. Yet they're the happiest people in the hospital. If your children are habitually irritable, or have a generally unpleasant demeanor, and blame it on their terrible lot in life, share this story with them. Invite them to spend one day on Bobba's cancer ward, and then tell you they have problems.

• • •

So choosing to have a positive attitude helps us be happy. Is that all it can do? Fortunately not. The possibilities are almost endless with a great attitude. The next three examples show you how it can help you learn, stop worrying so much, and even share your great attitude and happiness with others. Let's start with learning.

It's amazing how two people can sit through the exact same experience and have completely different impressions about it. When that happens, there's usually something interesting to be learned in the reason why, if you bothered to look. Dorinda Phillips looked.

Dorinda is the organizational learning expert you met in chapter 9. Early in her career in Germany, she attended a three-hour corporate training course on statistics. And she happened to be sitting next to someone who was already quite knowledgeable about statistics. As she recalls it, "To be honest, the training was awful. As an effective learning expert, I couldn't help but get more and more agitated during the training. The trainer was droning on and on while the class was falling asleep. And nobody had a clue what the business impact of all this was. I felt bad for the trainer and worse for the class." The trainer happened to work in Dorinda's department, so she somehow felt a small degree of responsibility and embarrassment for this unfolding disaster.

"When the class was over," she explains, "I turned to the man next to me and asked, 'Well, what did you think?' fully expecting, of course, for him to tell me it could have been so much better. But he didn't. What he said was, 'I learned one thing I didn't know, and I can already see how I can use it tomorrow. And I'm really happy about that. It's going to be very helpful.' And I remember thinking, 'How did he not see how awful this was? Could he not tell that most people weren't getting anything out of this?' And that's when it hit me. I realized that he wasn't judging the course, or trying to find all the things wrong with it, or even trying to determine what 'everyone else' was or wasn't getting out of it like I was. He was looking at it from a mindset of 'what can I take out of this that's useful to me? What can I learn?' It was definitely a big 'Aha' moment for me."

Yes, Dorinda still wanted to make that training more effective. But she was mostly struck with the unbelievable power of finding the good in things versus finding the negatives. That man's positive mental attitude allowed him to find value in the course that Dorinda, and perhaps many other people, could not. He attended the same course as everyone else. But his attitude made it useful to him instead of a waste of time.

How often do children sit through a school lesson thinking mostly about how boring it is? How often do adolescents or adults spend their time trashing the last book they read instead of focusing on the few things they did get out of it and how they're going to leverage it in their life? What a difference a good attitude can make.

• • •

Brazilian writer Paulo Coelho once said, "Everything will be okay in the end. If it isn't okay, it isn't the end." It's become one of my favorite inspirational quotes, for a number of reasons. I'm enamored with the reassuring persistence it promises when offered by someone committed to helping his or her fellow human beings. It's as if to say, "I will not quit on you until everything is okay." But I also love the positive attitude it engenders with the confidence that things really will turn out okay. Worry has to be one of the biggest wastes of time known to humanity. And it's one we all spend too much of our time invested in. When you have an impending sense that something bad is going to happen, planning a corrective course of action is good. Preparing yourself mentally or physically to respond is good. But empty, stressful, unproductive worry serves no purpose.

I've not seen a study of this question, but I'd love to know: Of all the times human beings worry about something, what percent of the time does it turn out to be the awful, doomsday scenario we imagined it would be? My guess is that number is exceedingly small. Most of the time the worry was probably for nothing. And even when something bad does happen, my guess is that more often than not we find some way to deal with the situation in a positive, productive manner. So even if that empty worry did serve a productive purpose, my guess is that only rarely would we have needed it. A case in point is the following account of what happened in the former Soviet state of Belarus in June 1995.

John Ray was traveling by train from Belarus to Poland. At the time, one of the many hangovers from the Soviet era was that the train tracks used in Russian states were narrower than those in Western Europe. So when his train came to the border with Poland, instead of switching trains, the train switched wheels. The train pulled into a huge building where a crane lifted each car a few feet off the tracks. Station workers then uncoupled the undercarriage of the train car that held the wheel assembly. They pulled that carriage out and replaced it with a new one that fit the Western-style train tracks. All this happened while the passengers were still on the train.

While all that was going on outside the train, on the inside, one of the other hangover Soviet-era practices was transpiring. That's when the border patrol agents did their jobs. It was customary at the time for international travelers to need a significant amount of paperwork to enter or leave a Soviet state. You needed passports, visas, documentation of how much money you entered with, the purpose of your visit, destination, proof of hotel accommodations while in the country, etc. It was quite an ordeal. But John had all that paperwork already since he had used it to get into Belarus several days earlier. Leaving should be no problem.

They arrived at the Polish border around one o'clock in the morning. John remembers hearing the knocks getting louder as they got closer to his cabin. He could hear muffled English words in a thick, Russian accent. Knock, knock, knock. "Byelorussian border patrol. Papers please." When they were about three doors down, he started to wake up enough to find his paperwork. But he couldn't put his hands on it right away.

Two doors down: knock, knock, knock. "Byelorussian border patrol. Papers please." John still couldn't find his papers. Now he was starting to sweat.

One door down: knock, knock, knock. "Byelorussian border patrol. Papers please."

"What I was thinking then was 'Oh, crap!' This was still not long after the Berlin Wall came down and the Soviet Union dissolved. Everything was still very Soviet and I could imagine getting thrown in jail and forgotten."

Now they're at John's cabin door: knock, knock, knock. "Byelorussian border patrol. Papers please." John opened the door and handed them the only travel document he could find: his passport. The officer flipped it open to examine it. He looked puzzled, pointed to something on it, and said something to his partner in Russian. The other officer agreed, and the first officer turned to John and said, in his deep and very serious Russian accent, "John Ray. Come with us."

This was definitely not good. It was like something out of a bad movie with a bad ending John wanted no part of. John quickly woke his travel partner and asked him to come with him. He thought a witness would at least provide some protection. The four men walked down the corridor to the border patrol officer's cabin. Once inside, John and his companion were instructed to sit down. One officer sat in a chair on the other side of a desk. The other officer stood behind them, blocking the door. More bad movie endings started racing through John's head. This cannot be good.

One officer reached under the desk, pulled out a briefcase, and placed it on the desk, opening it in a way that prevented John from seeing what was inside. He pulled out a bottle and four glasses, placing them all on the desk in front of them. Was this some strange version of Russian roulette with poison in place of a chambered bullet? John's heart was racing.

The officer poured what appeared to be vodka into all four glasses, picked up one of them, and held it up. Then he looked John right in the eyes. "John Ray," he said in his still very serious tones, "happy birthday." And with that, he smiled for the first time.

John's shoulders relaxed. He took a deep breath. He then realized that what the officer had been pointing to on his passport was his date of birth, which it had become as of approximately one hour earlier: June 10.

The four men enjoyed their drinks in celebration of another year of life for John Ray. Then the two travelers stood to leave without any further requests for their "papers." As they walked out, John looked back at one of the officers, who offered a campy signoff by saying, "Byelorussian border patrol," followed quickly by a cheesy grin and two thumbs up.

Everything was, indeed, okay in the end. It just didn't seem that way until it really, really was the end. The next time you find yourself needlessly worrying about something that may or may not happen in the future, remember John's story. And then relax. Odds are, what's waiting for you in the end is nothing more threatening than a shot of Byelorussian vodka.

• • •

To end this chapter, we turn to one of the most wonderful things about a positive mental attitude: that it's contagious. So while the previous stories highlight the impact a great attitude can have on the person who holds it, this last story shows what a powerful impact it can have on the people around him.

When he was in his early thirties, Daniel Dorr decided to climb a mountain. But not just any mountain. He wanted to climb Mount Kilimanjaro, the tallest mountain in Africa at 19,341 feet above sea level. After all, he was in the prime of his life, with a successful career, living in the heart of Silicon Valley, and newly engaged to be married. What else would you do to top all that?

After months of planning and preparation, Dan left for his great adventure. He flew into Nairobi with his gear, crossed Kenya by bus, then finally arrived in Moshi, Tanzania, at the base of Mount Kilimanjaro, and checked into his hotel. By breakfast the next morning, he had spent forty-eight hours on the African continent, meeting, conversing, and traveling with local people from two countries, three cities, and countless small towns. And that was long enough for him to realize things were not as he expected.

Like most Americans, Dan's image of the people of Africa was shaped by the television commercials he'd seen his whole life that depicted them as desperately poor, starving, miserable, and in dire need of assistance. ("Just one dollar a day can feed this girl . . .") And to be sure, most of the people he met were poor by Western standards. What surprised him, however, was this: "They were happy—happy with each other and themselves. And they were stunning. They stood tall, smiled, and exuded pride and energy. They weren't the sad, miserable people I saw on TV." But Dan was only beginning to learn how wrong his misconception had been, and he had no idea yet how that would impact him over the next ten days.

After breakfast, Dan and seven other climbers went with their guide to the base of the mountain where dozens of local men were waiting. These were the porters. Their job was to carry the climbers' gear up the mountain ahead of them, set up their tents, prepare their food, and carry everything back down after reaching the peak. Dan described them as "dressed in disheveled clothing. In fact, anywhere in the developed world, you would mistake them for being homeless." But like all the other people he'd met so far, they seemed quite happy.

As instructed, Dan laid his backpack with the others from his group, while their guide selected and assigned porters to carry the loads. He watched as each person's pack got picked up, one at a time, while his still lay off in the corner, untouched. So he started to get a little concerned. "That's when this little guy named Mik, who stood maybe five feet two inches tall, walks over and looks at my pack." Now at six foot four, Dan was equipped with a tall pack that might have been nearly as tall as Mik's whole body. "So Mik takes one look at my pack and walks away. I thought he was giving up on it. So I got more concerned. Then a minute later, he comes walking back over with someone else's pack. He lays it on top of mine, straps the two of them together, and picks up the new bundle and places it on top of his head! So you have to imagine this little man barely over five feet tall with about six feet or more of equipment balanced horizontally on his head.

"Now I knew my pack weighed almost thirty pounds, so the other one must have also. Plus he had a small pack of his own gear on his back that must have weighed around fifteen pounds. So there he stood with probably seventy-five pounds of gear, and he takes off walking up the trail wearing only flip-flops on his feet. I couldn't believe it. The first day of the climb was through the rain forest, across a slippery, muddy ground covered with protruding tree roots and vines. I had $50 trekking poles and the latest $120 full-grain upper leather boots. Plus I was only carrying a ten-pound daypack on my back. And without that equipment, I would have fallen a dozen times. This guy was carrying sixty pounds on his head and wearing flip-flops! I couldn't think of a worse job to have."

By that evening, the group made it to ten thousand feet. The air was thinner and it was much colder. But when he arrived at the campsite for the night, Dan's tent was already set up and waiting for him. And another porter brought over hot tea with popcorn and cookies. "It was the most civilized camping I'd ever done."

The next day, Dan packed his gear, left his bag for Mik, and headed up the mountain to get an early start. Day two was much steeper and rockier. He found he had to focus a lot more on what he was doing. Then, about three hours into the day's hiking, Dan recalls, "I looked over and there's Mik. He'd caught up to me with the same sixty pounds of gear on his head. And I was feeling like I needed to apologize to him for the horrible conditions he had to work in. Then he looks over at me as he's passing and says with the biggest smile on his face, 'Polle, polle,' which I'd come to learn in Swahili means basically 'relax, take it easy.'" Dan smiled back, his burden lighter somehow.

That evening, one of the other climbers taught Dan a little Swahili he'd picked up. The phrase was "Haraka, haraka, hiena barraca," which meant "There is no blessing for being first." Apparently in the Tanzanian culture, there's no value seen in rushing around to get somewhere. Dan soon found an opportunity to use his new phrase. The next day, when Mik passed him again, once again he wore an enormous smile. And once again, he said to Dan, "Polle, polle" as he passed. Dan, using his best diction, smiled and responded, "Haraka, haraka, hiena barraca." Well, that sent Mik into an uncontrollable fit of laughter. Dan watched as the six feet of packs on his head teetered back and forth with each bellow. Both men enjoyed the moment and continued their journey with a smile.

Over the next five days, the climb got increasingly difficult and the conditions increasingly unpleasant. The temperatures could swing from seventy degrees to below freezing in a matter of a few hours. Thick, cold, wet clouds surrounded the climbers as they hiked up to ten miles a day uphill. But the altitude was the worst. At 19,000 feet, there's only half the oxygen available in each breath compared to at sea level.[1] That not only makes the climb twice as hard on your heart and lungs, but it leaves many people with severe headaches and nausea. So as you might expect, Dan's outlook and demeanor grew progressively serious, focused, stoic, and at his worse moments, defeatist.

Yet in every interaction, Mik was the same gleeful person he had been on the first day. "I didn't understand how he could be that way. His job was to carry sixty pounds of someone else's stuff up a mountain every day.

Yet he always had a smile and a great attitude. It had an enormous impact on me and my attitude. No matter how bad I was feeling, no matter how tired I was, when Mik passed me with a smile, it absolutely made my whole day and gave me the strength to keep going. It made me realize, if this guy can keep a positive attitude climbing this mountain with my stuff on his head, why can't I?"

Even today, when he finds himself struggling with anything in life, Dan just thinks back to Mik and his contagious attitude and smile. "He probably has no idea how big of an impact he had on me that week on the mountain. And he certainly has no idea what a positive influence he's been on me since."[2]

A positive attitude can bring joy to those around you, help a friend take on the day, or even motivate a stranger to the top of a mountain.

A great attitude is contagious. Infect someone.

FOURTEEN

Dealing with Loss

The most beautiful people I've known are those who have known trials, have known struggles, have known loss, and have found their way out of the depths.

—ELISABETH KÜBLER-ROSS

People lose things every day—a set of keys, a matching sock, or the homework they can't find on their computer—all minor daily frustrations. Not the kind of loss most people need help dealing with. The kind we need help with is the kind of loss that stops your heart, the kind that forever alters the course of your life, that brings you to your knees, or that tries your soul. On October 20, 1991, that's exactly what happened to a woman we'll call Debbie.

Debbie was twenty-one years old and a senior at the University of California at Berkeley. She lived in a beautiful house in Berkeley's Oakland Hills area with a lovely view of the Bay Area off the back deck. That made for a more inspiring study spot than the converted storage closet that served as her bedroom. She worked three jobs to afford her rent and tuition, and she carried a full schedule of classes. And for the past three months she'd been dating a handsome post-doc student from Switzerland we'll call Rafael. Her life was definitely running at full speed. But she was very happy, and it was only going to get better. She had an ambitious life planned out in five-year installments, starting with completing her degree in archaeology the following May. Then she would be off to graduate school and eventually earn a Ph.D. and become a professor. But that was all still seven months away. She had one semester of school and a nearly completed thesis paper to finish first.

Then, one Sunday morning in October, she got up early to attend a conference outside the city. She and a friend left at 6:30 and drove south across the San Francisco–Oakland Bay Bridge to the all-day event. It gave them plenty to talk about on their return trip home at the end of the day. So driving back that evening, they left the radio off. If they'd had it on, what they saw next might not have seemed so strange. As they approached San Francisco, they saw a thick, black cloud hanging over the entire Bay Area.

"It was unbelievable," Debbie recalls. "It looked like San Francisco was turning into Los Angeles with all its smog. So we decided to drive around and use the Golden Gate Bridge instead. My mom and stepfather owned a restaurant in the city, and we were hungry, so we stopped there to eat on the way home. By then it was probably eight or nine o'clock at night. And these were before the days of cell phones, so we'd been out of touch for an entire day. As soon as we walked in, the staff at the restaurant ran up and said, 'Oh my God, you're alive! Where have you been all day?'"

Debbie and her friend must have looked as confused as they sounded when they responded, "What are you talking about?"

"Don't you know what's happening? All of Berkeley is on fire!"

She immediately went to the bar next door to see a news report on TV. That's when she learned the fire not only passed through her neighborhood but appeared to have started there. "All I remember thinking is, 'I've got to get to Berkeley.'"

They got back in her friend's car and drove the rest of the way to Berkeley. Her reaction when they got there? "It was in complete chaos, like something out of Dante's *Inferno*. Nobody knew where to go. There were firemen and police everywhere, people screaming and running in all directions, and cars abandoned in the middle of the street. It was like a scene from a horror movie. And then somehow, in the middle of this chaos, I ran into Rafael. He was supposed to be at a triathlon that day. But when he heard about the fire, he came to look for me. My housemates didn't know where I was all day either. Everyone thought I had died in the fire."

And that wouldn't have been an unreasonable assumption. Later called the "Oakland Hills firestorm of 1991," the blaze ultimately killed 25 people and injured 150 others. More than 1,500 acres were destroyed, including almost 3,500 homes and apartment units. The total economic loss was estimated at $1.5 billion.[1] And while Debbie's share of that $1.5 billion was quite small, it was everything she owned in the world, except for the clothes on her back and $300 in her bank account. She lost all of her family pictures, the rest of her clothing, the artwork she'd traded her time modeling for, her grandmother's jewelry, her computer, her car, and, importantly, her senior thesis she'd spent months working on. She stood there in shock, assessing her loss. It was devastating.

She doesn't even remember where she slept that night. But she does remember whom she spent it with. And she remembers what they did. She and Rafael consoled each other the way young lovers do. And as it turned out, among all the loss, fate saw to it that Debbie gained something wonderful on the very night she lost everything else: a son. Usually a very conscientious woman, she had unprotected sex for perhaps the only time in her life. Two weeks later, Debbie found out she was pregnant.

"I've always been an advocate of a woman's right to choose," she explains. "So if you'd asked me earlier what I would do if at twenty-one I end up with an unplanned pregnancy, I'd have told you I'd have an abortion. But I didn't. And I never even considered it. As soon as I found out I was pregnant, everything changed. All of my priorities shifted." Debbie married Rafael and moved back with him to Switzerland at the end of the semester, where her son Andy was born.

She ended up returning to Berkeley when Andy was eighteen months old to complete both her bachelor's and master's degrees before returning to Switzerland. So she got some degree of closure on that part of her life. But having a new child, a husband, and an exciting new life in a different country just after the fire provided Debbie an opportunity to compare two things not many of us get to see so closely juxtaposed in time and place: the role and importance of people and relationships in your life versus the things in your life. As Debbie explains, "It took me a while to fully appreciate the lessons from that time. But it did teach me a few things. First, you can try to plan your life out. But you can't control everything. Life is the combination of things that happen to us and how we choose to respond to them. Second, I learned that stuff isn't important. People are. Everything I lost in that fire, that was just stuff. What I gained was far more valuable."

The third lesson Debbie learned was that if you do find yourself losing most or all of the "stuff" in your life, it's okay. "Don't fret over lost stuff or things you can't change. Embrace them. Life has a way of working out. More beautiful and meaningful things may come from it," just like they did for her.

But even if you're not as fortunate as Debbie to gain a new family at the moment you lose your things, you will gain a similar perspective. Because having everything you own destroyed leaves you with only the people and relationships in your life to hold on to. That's when you'll learn how very important they are. You'll realize that you're much better off losing the things in your life and keeping the people than keeping all your stuff and losing even one person you love.

That unfortunate scenario is the one we turn to next.

• • •

When I was fourteen years old, my mother was diagnosed with an advanced case of pneumonia. For four months, her doctors tried every medicine and treatment known to cure it, none of which had any effect. Then they realized why. She didn't have pneumonia. She had lung cancer. They'd been misled by the strangely uniform and checkered pattern on the X-rays. By the time they had a proper diagnosis, it had progressed beyond their ability to treat it successfully. They gave her six months to live.

At the still young age of forty-seven, and with five children, three of whom still lived at home, she searched for any way she could to ease the burden she knew the loss of a mother would have on her kids. One of the things she found came from an unlikely place: a poem.

Her mother (my grandmother) had been an accomplished poet and therefore had a circle of friends who were also poets. When my grandmother passed away, one of those colleagues wrote to my mother to console her. In the handwritten letter, she included a poem she had composed that she thought might help. Apparently it did. Because thirteen years later, my mother still had the letter. And facing her own imminent death, she took it out and read it to each of us. Below is that poem.

One Dark Branch
by Marie Erwin Ward

I have at last returned . . .
I have come back from alien lands that burned
With hate; back to this tree.
I dreamed her sweeping fronds were over me
Through nights and days, rest-yearned.

I ease my tortured way
To sit beneath the pepper tree and sway
My mind with her green lace
To calm my broken spirit, lift my face
And learn once more to pray.

This tree lives not to grieve
Because of one dark branch where green sprays weave.
One useless bough a grief?
She crowns her loss with crimson fruit and leaf . . .
I touch my empty sleeve.

After reading the poem to us, my mother shared the author's explanation: A soldier has returned from war. He comes home and sits under the pepper tree he used to sit under to think. His quiet time under the tree helps calm him from the horrors of war he has seen. And it is there that he relearns the healing power of prayer.

He looks up and sees "one dark branch" on the tree, a dead limb. He notices the tree does not give up and die because of the loss of one branch. Instead, it just makes that many more leaves and fruit on the other branches to fill the empty space. The last line is "I touch my empty sleeve." This soldier, like the tree, has also lost a limb (his arm) in the war. What he learns from the tree is that because he no longer has his arm, the other parts of his body and mind should strengthen to accommodate the loss. He must become a more stable and mature person to persevere with this handicap. Our mother explained to us that God gives extra grace to people like that to help them, such as blind people whose sense of hearing becomes more acute to compensate for their loss of sight.

The way she related this to us was by showing us how the same thing applies to families that lose members. When someone dies, the other members of the family must grow, strengthen, and mature to compensate for that loss. The family must grow new love and wisdom, just as the tree grew new leaves and fruit.

The poem was her dying gift to us. But it was also her expectation. It was her expectation for how we were to respond as a family after she was gone. When the situation calls for it with someone you love, it can be your gift as well.

• • •

So what exactly does it look like for a family to grow, strengthen, and mature following the loss of a loved one? That's a great question to ask Andrew Nemiccolo.

When Andrew was a sophomore at Colby College in Waterville, Maine, he decided to spend his junior year studying abroad. Since he was pursuing a degree in East Asian Studies, a year studying in Japan seemed the perfect fit. So Andrew selected Doshisha University in Kyoto. And since learning conversational Japanese was part of the objective, instead of a traditional dorm room with other foreign students, Andrew was assigned to live with a host family nearby to immerse himself in the language and culture.

He arrived in September, at the beginning of the semester. His host family consisted of a father, a mother, a college-aged brother, a sister in high school, and a younger brother in elementary school. Andrew was quickly accepted by his host family and felt relatively at home.

But by December, it was clear that his host father wasn't feeling well. And by January it was clear why. He was diagnosed with throat and stomach cancer, both of which were progressing quickly. He soon found himself unable to continue with his normal duties as father and as the head of the family winery that employed about a hundred people. One of those duties was to take his youngest child to Australia for a one-week study abroad program with a host family. That duty now fell to Andrew, who eagerly picked it up. He spent eight days going to and from Hawkesbury, in New South Wales, Australia, with his new little brother.

By the time Andrew returned, the father was in a hospital in Osaka and going downhill fast. In March there were family members in his room with him around the clock for his last few days. It was during that time at the hospital that Andrew's host mother really started to seem like a mom to him. "On one of those days she said, 'Son, you need to go home and eat. I left some food out for you. You know how to work the stove and where everything is in the kitchen.' At that moment I felt like a member of the family."

At the final moments, the entire family was by the father's side: mother, eldest brother, sister, youngest brother, and Andrew, along with many aunts, uncles, and cousins. He described it as "sad and terrible and beautiful, as much as the death of a loved one can be. I remember every moment of it. Watching the heart rate monitor sounding out the last few beeps . . . and then the silence; the wails of sorrow from my host mom, calling out his name; the gut-wrenching feeling of sorrow and loss in the room; exchanging hugs with the family, as one of them. I was sad, yet honored to be there and be treated like family, not just some random college student from the States."

A month later, Andrew's thoughts were turning to the end of the semester and his inevitable journey home. That's when his host mother said something to him he didn't expect to hear. She said, "I've been thinking about this. It's been a difficult time this year. Having you here has been good for us. I want you to stay." Andrew can only assume his sense of humor provided some levity and lightness in such a heavy time. But regardless of the reason, the family wanted him to stay. He was one of them now. So he agreed to stay for the rest of the summer.

He got a job working at a restaurant and picked up some students to teach English to during the morning hours. The rest of the family, meanwhile, started filling in the void left by their father as the head of the company business. Mom stepped in as interim CEO, eventually earning many awards as one of the few female heads of a midsize company in Kyoto. And the rest of the family all chipped in as well. Everyone had a role to play. And Andrew remembers fondly the many conversations over dinner that summer as they reminisced about their father.

Andrew returned to Colby College in September for his senior year. But he's continued to stay in touch with his Japanese family ever since. Each New Year's Day for the past twenty-two years, Andrew calls the family in Kyoto. And he's found many occasions to return to visit in person. He visited several times during a Thomas J. Watson Fellowship grant that enables graduating seniors to pursue a year of independent study outside the United States. A decade later, Andrew returned for his host sister's wedding, bringing with him his own growing family, including his son, Noah, and daughter, Grace, ages five and three at the time.

And his Japanese family even came to the United States to visit Andrew occasionally. "They all came to my wedding in Kansas City, and my host brother came to visit us by himself a couple of years later. We were still just like family."

Imagine instead if Andrew's study abroad year had not been marred by the untimely death of his host father. He still would have learned much of the Japanese language and culture. And it's of course possible that he could have developed strong ties to the family. But is there any doubt that the loss of their father brought them all together closer as a family? Andrew wouldn't have been invited to stay for an additional three months. He would have never been needed to take his host brother on an international trip to Australia. He would not have had occasion to cry with them, to mourn, or to hug them as tightly. And they would not have had occasion to work together as closely to maintain the family business, and each other, in their father's absence. And they certainly would have had less need to accept a new member into their family to fill some of the void left by that one dark branch. Indeed, it's much less likely that he would still be in touch with them all these years later.

Marie Erwin Ward would be proud. This family definitely crowned their loss "with crimson fruit and leaf." Andrew Nemiccolo is honored to be one of those pieces of fruit.

PART 2

HOW YOU TREAT OTHER PEOPLE

FIFTEEN

Kindness

Teaching a child not to step on a caterpillar is as valuable to the child as it is to the caterpillar.

—BRADLEY MILLAR

Like thousands of people in cities all over the world, Kristin Pedemonti[1] spends much of her time on the sidewalk holding a sign. And like many, her sign is cardboard with handwritten letters in faded black marker. It's a familiar scene. Most people walk by without even noticing her. Others see her and her sign but choose to walk past. But the ones who do stop approach with a smile and have their lives changed for the better. Some just for the day. Some for a lifetime.

Why? Because Kristin's sign isn't asking for spare change, nor does it say "Will work for food." In fact, it doesn't ask for anything at all. It offers to give something, free of charge, with no strings attached. Kristin's sign simply reads "Free Hugs." And that's exactly what she gives. Free hugs, to anyone and everyone who wants one.

But it's not just Kristin's sign that will surprise you. She isn't who you expected either. Her offer to give free hugs isn't a clever ploy to solicit donations. Kristin's not homeless. In fact, she's a successful actress and cause-focused storyteller who speaks to audiences all over the world. So why does she give away free hugs? To bring more joy into people's lives.

Nothing more. Studies show humans need four hugs a day to maintain a healthy mental and emotional state. You don't have to look far to see that too many of us aren't getting our daily minimum. Kristin's personal mission is to change that.

If you've ever been free-hugged by Kristin, you know what a real hug feels like. She doesn't hug you like a stranger, timidly leaning in with one arm from a respectable distance. Kristin's hugs are full on: both arms and a tight squeeze, and she doesn't stop hugging you until you stop hugging her. That can be fifteen seconds or more, which is an eternity for a hug. After the first two or three seconds, the uncertainty and awkwardness of hugging a stranger fades. Your muscles relax. Your shoulders fall slightly, and you give in to the hug. A warm, happy feeling comes over you that lasts the rest of the day.

On a busy street corner, Kristin can bring a smile to the hearts of hundreds of people in a single hour. Watching her in action is inspiring. People who stop for a hug leave with a huge grin and a zeal in their stride. But even the ones who just pass through are affected. Some find amusement in her sign and laugh. Others stop and watch, amazed at the humanity of what's going on in front of them.

The most powerful free hug Kristin ever gave was to a small boy in Paris. The boy and his mother watched her for several minutes as she stood with her sign. They eventually went on their way. But a few minutes later, the boy came running back to her, leaped into her arms, and gave her an unabashed koala bear hug as only a small child can do. The mother came trailing behind, with tears in her eyes. As Kristin put the boy down, she apologized and asked if she had done something wrong. "Oh, no," the mother said. She explained that her son was severely autistic and rarely hugged even his own parents. Getting him to accept and express love was a lifelong challenge. Somehow Kristin had helped him take a new step.

Today, Kristin organizes Free Hug events wherever she happens to be, whether it's New York City; Belfast, Ireland; or Jonesborough, Tennessee. It's not unusual for passersby to quickly fashion their own signs and join the cause. And hugs aren't the only thing Kristin gives away to strangers. She's been known to pull out a bottle of soapy water and blow bubbles to soothe a crying baby on a crowded subway, or don a pair of wings on her back as she walks down the street, or ride a tricycle in Central Park with a superhero costume on—all things to bring joy to everyday moments, for herself and for others. She explains, "It goes so much deeper than hugs. The hugs are a gateway to connecting with others." Kristin now travels the world making those connections and collecting true stories of potential and overcoming adversity. "If you're brave enough to take a chance," she concludes, "there are no strangers."

Being a source of joy doesn't take any special skills. And it doesn't have to cost a lot of money. All it takes is the will to do it and the guts to share a moment with a stranger. Of course, hugging strangers isn't for everyone or for everywhere. It's probably not a good idea for unaccompanied children, or in a dark secluded alley. But with some common sense, just about anyone can give away free hugs. Or blow bubbles. Or ride a trike in a superhero costume. Or whatever it is you want to do to bring joy to those around you. You pick. Just pick something.

And the next time you see someone on the streets holding a cardboard sign, give it a read. Whether you end up putting spare change in a tin cup or getting a free hug, the life you change might just be your own.

• • •

Being kind to strangers is a good start. But far more impactful is being kind to the people we know and see every day. In fact, if you were to ask someone who's been on the receiving end of unkindness, odds are it didn't come from a stranger. It came from a classmate, a coworker, or a friend. Just ask Scott Mautz.

Scott was born with muscular dystrophy, a degenerative disease that attacks the skeletal muscles. This was complicated by a noticeable case of scoliosis, or curvature of the back, which often accompanies MD.

Today, in his forties, he still walks a little funny. He describes his gait as "looking like I've been riding a horse for two days." But when he was a child it was a much more debilitating condition. He wore a full body brace including a collar around the neck and thick spinal support down his back. His nickname at school was "Mr. Twister" because of the awkward gyrations he had to go through with every step.

Not surprisingly, he wasn't athletic enough to play varsity sports at his high school in Syracuse, New York. But he still wanted to be part of the team and hang out with the athletes and the "cool kids" one way or another. So he volunteered to be the team manager. That meant he got the towels, carried the water, and corralled the equipment. Combined with an impeccable sense of humor, this kept him in the good graces (and in the company) of the popular crowd.

But the natural cruelty of teenagers and his humblingly visible disability were too much for that to last. Eventually, his luck ran out. "One day at lunch," he said, "somebody decided it was uncool to be friends with me." Within a matter of minutes, everyone at the table turned on him. "I was suddenly conscious that I was a bit of a freak and that I wasn't welcome there anymore."

Words are probably inadequate to describe the sobering moment Scott was to face next. He knew what he had to do. "I had to stand up, pick up my tray, and leave." Tray in hand, he desperately scanned the cafeteria for an empty seat and a welcoming gaze. He found only one, the one everyone else would know as the "nerd" table. There were no athletes there. Most of the kids were either overweight or underweight, spent their time playing Dungeons & Dragons, and had terrible acne. But since sitting anywhere was more appealing than sitting alone, Scott started off in their direction. In that one cathartic moment he crossed physical as well as social and emotional thresholds. He felt every eye on him as he took the long walk of shame, "twisting" past all the boys he looked up to and the girls he had crushes on. The entire scene is seared in Scott's memory: the color of his tray, what he had for lunch, the looks on the faces as he moved to the only table that would accept him.

Scott recalls the awkwardness of having to sit down and make friends with the very people he had participated in teasing with his former friends until only moments before. He remembers openly mocking and teasing one boy in particular only a few weeks earlier. "But they accepted me. They never asked me why I was sitting there. Never said one word about it. They just took me in." And about the boy he had teased? "I remember thinking, 'This is the coolest kid in school!'"

How did this humbling experience impact Scott? "It changed me forever. I was never that unkind to anyone again. And I'm sure it shaped much of who I am as an adult."

As a child or an adult, the lesson I take from Scott's story is this: Resolve to be kind to everyone you meet, because none of us are ever that far from the nerd table.

To help you make use of this and other stories in this book, it might help to know that at the end of our interview I asked Scott if he'd ever shared that story with his daughter. "No," he responded. "I'm waiting for her to do something mean like that so I'll have an opportunity to use this story."

"Really," I responded. "What are you waiting for? Do you want her to learn this lesson after she's already hurt someone? Or before?"

• • •

In Scott's case, fate saw to it that he learned his lesson by turning the tables on him. Life has a way of doing that to us. But it doesn't always happen that way. Often, as a parent, we need a way to intervene to help our children learn a lesson as important as this. One way to do that is to share stories like Scott's. A very different way is to do what Kelly Hymas did for his son, Chad. Both terrifying and insightful at the same time, it became one of the unexpected moments of clarity Chad holds most dear more than two decades later.

Chad was a senior at West Jordan High School in Salt Lake City, Utah, and the captain of the basketball team. The night before a big game, the entire team came to Chad's house for dinner. While Mom and Dad were upstairs cooking, the boys were downstairs listening to music and talking about the game—what they knew of their opponents and what plays they might use. It was their way to both hold a strategy session and get pumped up for the game.

At one point in the evening, the conversation turned to a girl at school. That might not seem unusual in a group of teenage boys. But they weren't talking about just any girl. It was a very special girl we'll call Jenny. And the things they had to say about her were, to say the least, unkind. What's more, the instigator of those unkind words was the captain of the team, Chad Hymas.

Jenny was a very smart young lady. She had a lovely smile that she always wore and long dark hair. But she also had a number of visible disabilities. Jenny was confined to a wheelchair and was blind in both eyes. She was missing one arm, and her other arm and hand had limited functionality. When she ate she wore a pink bib to protect her clothes from the inevitable spill. She also had difficulty with speech, so she carried a computer that could speak for her when she typed out words on an oversized and simplified keyboard. Any one of these challenges could make adequate fodder for cruel teenage jokes. So you can imagine what kind of ridicule her collection of them brought out on that night.

A few minutes later, Chad's father knocked on the door and walked in without saying a word. He shut off the music and then dropped to his knees. That got the attention of all twelve varsity players. He then said, "I can't believe what I've heard for the last twenty minutes. But it's not your fault. I'm mostly disappointed in your captain." After considering that for a few seconds, he continued, "Actually, it's not even my son's fault. It's my fault. I raised him. I owe you all an apology." And with that, he left the room.

It was an awkward and uncomfortable moment for everyone. Understandably, all the boys left quickly. Nobody asked them to leave. But the combination of guilt and embarrassment had obviously spoiled the evening's fun. The next morning at school, nobody talked about it. They mostly wanted to pretend it never happened, which they were having some degree of success with until the lunch hour. That's when Chad's father unexpectedly walked into the school cafeteria.

He found the table where his son was eating with the rest of the team. He walked up and said, "It's good to see you today, son."

Chad sat in silence, too afraid to respond, and nervous about what his father could possibly have in mind. Then Dad continued, "Son, where's the girl?"

Chad pleaded, "Dad, please don't embarrass me. I'm really sorry for what I said last night."

Undaunted, his father replied calmly, "I'm here to teach you how to stand up. And I need you and the team to follow me right now."

Tentatively, the whole table of boys stood up. Chad pointed to the lonely table in the middle of the room where Jenny was eating lunch by herself. As Chad describes what happened next, "Dad went over and gently touched her arm to announce their presence. Jenny started to shake. But it was clear she wasn't shaking out of fear, because at the same time she let out a very telling sound that's difficult to explain. It's a noise I've since come to learn some people make that's an indication of joy and gratitude. She was actually nervous with excitement that someone, anyone, wanted to be next to her and to talk to her.

"Well, by that time it seemed half the cafeteria was watching us. So we sat down at her table, and Dad said to her, 'My name is Kelly. I need you to meet my oldest son and all of his friends who play on the basketball team.' Jenny continued to shake with excitement. Then Dad started asking her questions so that we could all get to know her better. It took probably thirty minutes to get through only four questions, since it took a while for her to type out her answers." But it was worth the time. Because the questions he asked, and the answers she gave, taught them more than they could have imagined four simple questions were capable of.

The first question Mr. Hymas asked was, "Who's your best friend?"

Jenny responded, "My mother, Stacy." The time it took Jenny to respond to each question gave the boys a painfully long moment to reflect on the significance of her answers. So it probably wasn't lost on them how unusual it must be for a teenage girl to count her mother as her best friend and what that might suggest about her social life at school.

The second question was, "What does your dad do for a living?"

Jenny's chillingly simple response came back. "I don't know who my father is."

The third question he asked was, "How long have you been in a wheelchair?"

Jenny answered, "My whole life."

For a group of boys who spend every day running and jumping up and down on a basketball court, this was a sobering answer. But even it paled in comparison to the fourth and final question and answer.

Mr. Hymas asked, "What is it you dream of and love to do the most?"

Jenny responded, "I like listening to the girls cheer at the basketball games."

Consider that for a moment. What Jenny loves to do the most is listen to the girls cheering for the very boys who the night before had spoken so poorly of her. If any of those boys hadn't felt some degree of shame yet, they all certainly felt it now.

Over the next week, the talk in the school rightfully centered on Jenny: who she was as a person and how everyone (not just the basketball team) treated her.

On the eighth day, Jenny was elected captain of the cheerleading squad. She was outfitted with a skirt, joined the rest of the squad court-side, and learned to twirl circles in her wheelchair. As the captain, it was Jenny's job to call each and every one of the cheers the girls performed. And that must have been quite a sight. Her story made the local news, which was quickly picked up in syndication and reprinted in newspapers across the country. Soon, people who usually didn't come to basketball games were showing up, not to watch the game but to watch Jenny.

For the rest of her high school career, Jenny still sat at the same table for lunch. But it was no longer empty. As Chad describes it, "They couldn't make a table big enough for everyone who wanted to sit with Jenny after that."

Looking back, Kelly Hymas could have responded to what he heard downstairs that night any number of ways. He could have just let it slide, thinking it's just how teenage boys are. Or he could have quietly confronted Chad when the evening was over and the team was gone. The following day, I'm sure he had other things he needed to be doing in the middle of the workday. But in both cases, he took the time and the risk to make a point to his son in a way he will never forget.

Would you do the same?[2]

• • •

So far in this chapter we've talked only of kindness to our fellow human beings. But most of us also share some level of compassion for the other species we share our planet with. Apparently the degree to which we extend that compassion can be influenced at an early age by the stories we hear. A prime example of that comes from Anand Jayaraman in his youth growing up in India.

When Anand was only four or five years old, he often visited his maternal grandfather in India's port city of Kochi. On one such visit, Anand was outside in the yard playing. He'd found a row of ants marching across a long plank of wood. As his grandfather walked by, he saw Anand banging on the plank with a stone, knocking the ants to the ground. So he said to him, "You shouldn't do that. Those ants didn't do anything to harm you."

He must have known the boy didn't fully understand, so he went on to describe the ants and what they must be doing in more human terms. He engaged Anand in a story about the ants that went something like this: "Those ants are just on their way home from work. They've been out collecting grass and leaves to take home for their families to eat. And it's probably a long way home for them." Then, kneeling down, he pointed to one ant now on the ground. "That one there. He might have a wife and children at home waiting for him. He's probably hungry and just wants to get home to have dinner himself. But now it will take him much longer to get there because you've knocked him off his path. That is, if he ever gets home. He might be lost now and never find his way home. Then he'll never see his family again."

The story had a profound impact on Anand. It taught him to empathize with living things he wouldn't normally have empathy for. And he's returned to that story many times over his life. In fact, when he was in college, recalling that story of the ants moved him to adopt a completely vegetarian diet for a period of time.

Today, Anand has a family of his own, including two daughters, Meghna and Meha. When Meghna was about four years old, Anand and his wife served fish for dinner one evening. Meghna tasted it, liked it, and ate the whole serving. But reflecting back on the meal after dinner, she asked, "Was that a real fish or was it a cartoon fish like Nemo?" Anand told her it was a real fish. Then he told her his grandfather's story of the ants. Over the next few weeks, without being pushed by her parents, Meghna chose to not eat any more meat. Anand himself still goes through periods when he eats meat and periods when he doesn't. So he doesn't push her one way or the other and leaves the choice strictly up to his children. But today, both Meghna and Meha have great respect and compassion for other living creatures, and so far both have also chosen to be vegetarian, largely, he believes, as a result of his grandfather's story of the wayward ant.

Regardless of your views on eating meat, helping young people see and feel the impact their behavior has on other living things is a worthwhile effort. A story like this, or one you make up in a similar situation, can help them understand that on a more tangible and personal level. As in this case, it may impact your family for generations to come.

• • •

Now let's turn our attention to a particular form of kindness: charity. Learning to be generous with what we have is difficult for most people. By nature we're selfish. Our instincts drive us to find food, shelter, and clothing—not for other people, but for ourselves. Nurturing compassion and generosity for others means demonstrating it through your own behavior, but also celebrating it when you see it in your young person or in others. The first story below is a great example.

At one point in her career, Kim Dedeker lived in Caracas, Venezuela, with her husband and five-year-old son, Bryan. As an executive on foreign assignment with a U.S. company, Kim was quite wealthy by local standards. Per capita income in Venezuela is about $13,000 a year, with 30 percent of the population living on less than $2 a day.[3] In addition to being a poor country, it's also a dangerous one. Caracas has the second highest homicide rate of any large city in the world.[4] Accepting the assignment there was a difficult but deliberate choice. Kim believes it's only by taking such risks that some of life's greatest rewards are possible. One of the most touching examples of that for her happened in Caracas on the way to the toy store.

Bryan had been saving his money for months to buy one of the wildly popular Teenage Mutant Ninja Turtle figures to add to his collection. He'd finally accumulated the required 800 bolivars, about twenty U.S. dollars. Kim strapped Bryan into the back seat of their car and started the drive to the toy store for the much-anticipated purchase. Unlike a drive to a toy store in the United States, however, there is no way to drive across Caracas without coming face to face with the harsh reality of local life. Poverty is all around you. But it was the danger that was on Kim's mind as they ventured outside their compound of largely U.S. expatriate homes and apartments. Kidnappings and carjackings were not unusual. As a result, it's common practice to not even come to a stop at an intersection if you can avoid it, and you certainly don't roll down your windows.

En route to the toy store, Kim came to an intersection and had to stop for a red light with oncoming traffic. She noticed a woman on the corner whose appearance led Kim to assume was homeless or at least severely impoverished. She was holding a baby of about eighteen months, and standing beside her was a young boy about the same age as Bryan. The two mothers made eye contact with each other, one destitute and one well off, both surely considering for that brief instant in time what life might be like for the other.

While Kim was still waiting for the light to turn green, the boy outside began walking toward the car. As any protective mother would, Kim turned her immediate concern to her own safety and that of her son. Is this how the many unfortunate incidents in Caracas start, with a child providing distraction? But the mothers had not been the only ones who'd made eye contact. The boy saw Bryan in the back seat as well, and it was his window he was approaching. Before Kim could react, Bryan rolled down his window. The two boys were face to face with each other, separated by only a few inches of space, but separated even further by language and the harsh contrast of their economic realities. Without exchanging a single word, Bryan reached into his pocket, pulled out his 800 bolivars, and handed it to the other boy through the window. The traffic light turned green, and Kim cautiously continued through the intersection.

The next few minutes passed quietly with both driver and passenger processing what had just happened. Kim finally broke the silence by asking, "What are you feeling right now?"

Thoughtfully, Bryan responded, "I'm feeling really good, Mom, because I think that little boy needed that money a lot more than I needed another Teenage Mutant Ninja Turtle."

As you can imagine, Kim was marveling at the selflessness her five-year-old had just shown. She debated in her head what to do when they arrived at the toy store. Should she reward her son's generosity by buying him the toy anyway? Or should she afford him the full experience of giving by feeling the loss required to be truly benevolent? When they arrived, they found the exact figure Bryan was after, a rare one imported from the United States, unlikely to be there on a future trip. That made Kim's decision even harder. Bryan looked at the price tag on the figure and said to his mom, "It's 810 bolivars."

"You're right," Kim responded, "You almost had enough."

"But I don't have any now," he said, just fully realizing the impact of his decision in the car a few minutes earlier.

Having made her decision, Kim offered, "I could buy it for you, if you want."

After a thoughtful pause, Bryan said, "No. I don't think I want it today."

"Are you sure? I don't mind getting it for you."

"Yeah, I know," Bryan answered. "But I can probably get that turtle anytime I want, either because I'll save my money or because you can afford to buy it for me. It just doesn't feel important now."

Of course, you probably can't give money to every needy person who crosses your path. In some cases that might not even be a good idea for you or for them. And that's a great conversation to have with your young person after sharing this story. When should you—and should you not—give to those less fortunate? But for most of us, the problem is not curtailing our boundless generosity from the many worthy causes we can't afford to support. For most, it's generating the empathy for those worthy causes to begin with, seeing how truly blessed we are relative to the rest of the world, and coming to the realization (like Bryan did) that we can probably have that shiny bauble some other day, and that for now it just doesn't seem that important.

• • •

Giving some of what you have to those less fortunate is one way to think about charity. But what if you don't have anything? Does that mean you can't be charitable? Of course not. A beautiful example of that comes from Noemi Abrinica. You met her son, Marvin, in chapter 4.

When Marvin was growing up in Cleveland, Ohio, his family wasn't the wealthiest among his friends. But he does remember his mother, Noemi, being very generous to others with one particular thing: food. She threw amazing holiday parties for the other Filipino families nearby. She helped them celebrate with egg rolls and Filipino noodles and other traditional dishes. "And she would always make more than anyone could possibly eat. So inevitably, my mom would package these take-home plates. So everyone left with even more food."

He remembers asking her, "Mom, why do you cook all this food? It seems like such a waste." And in response, Noemi Abrinica told him this story.

When she was a little girl growing up in Manila, her family was very poor. But her parents made sure that every day she was fed well when she left for school. Not every child in her school, however, was as fortunate. The whole country was still recovering from World War II, and poverty was widespread. "There was always at least one child in class," she explained, "who hadn't eaten that day." It broke Noemi's heart to see them suffering in silence. After a time, she could no longer bear to see other children starving right in front of her. So she decided to do something about it.

Noemi lived next to a rice field. At the end of the growing season, the farmers harvested their crops. But the reaping methods were never 100 percent efficient, so the fields were always left with a scattering of rice. After school each day, Noemi took a five-gallon plastic bucket out to glean the remaining rice from the field. When her bucket was full, she took it to the local market to sell it for a few pesos. And with that money, she bought some food and brought it to school to feed whoever hadn't eaten that day. Then after school, she did it again. And again. And again.

And so to Noemi, being poor didn't mean you had nothing to give. It just meant you had to be a little more creative and perhaps work a little harder to do it. And for the rest of her life, that compassion and love and charity has continued to show up in the form of food.

Her story helped Marvin understand why she always made too much food at her parties. And it surely taught him something much more important about charity.

So, what are you doing after school today?

SIXTEEN

Patience

A man who is a master of patience is master of everything else.

—GEORGE SAVILE

Not too long ago, "ropes" courses were all the rage in the United States. These are the outdoor adventure programs where participants climb through trees on a series of ropes and ladders. Companies often send their leadership teams to these programs to learn about teamwork. So learning the value of patience was not what Dave Orewiler expected from his nine-day course outside Asheville, North Carolina. But that's exactly what he got.

Dave was a human resources executive from Long Island, New York, at the time "in between successes," as he politely put it. Not being with a corporate team, Dave was put in a diverse group of a dozen others who were also not part of a larger company. Among them was a teacher, a nurse, a small business owner, and a retiree, who ranged in age from the early twenties to nearly sixty.

In addition to the ropes courses, the program also included hiking, camping, rappelling down mountain slopes, and canoeing. And it was in the three-day canoeing portion of the program that Dave learned the most worthy of lessons.

Each participant was paired with another for the two-person canoes. And while the course wasn't designed as a race, there's a natural tendency to make a competition out of it and learn how teams work together and compete most effectively. So while he would never say it, Dave was probably disappointed when he found out his assigned partner was an extremely thin woman in her forties with limited upper body strength and a deformity in one arm that kept it bent at the elbow.

After making it successfully through most of the canoe trip, they quickly approached the most difficult part of the river: the rapids. As Dave recounts the adventure, "Riding the rapids had a certain degree of thrill to it, but also some danger. If you don't do it right, you can find yourself upside down very quickly. Our coach taught us how to put our oars straight down into the water and stabilize the boat without paddling until we made it safely through the rough water.

"Several of the faster boats had already made it through. When it was our turn, I reminded my partner to keep her oar straight and upright in the water. However, once we shoved off, her fear overtook her and she clutched her oar waist-high above the boat. We quickly lost balance and tipped over. The next attempt yielded the same result. After the third spill, the cold water took its toll and I admit that my patience was waning. The others in the group waited downstream, cheering us on. Quietly embarrassed, I thought to myself, 'We've got to make it this time.' What I wanted to say was, 'Why don't you get out and I'll take it in myself.' But I bit my lip and reminded my partner one more time to keep her oar in the water to help stabilize the canoe."

The pair sped down the river again, taking the rapids head on, but this time with both oars in the water, straight up, and without paddling. After a few turbulent bumps and an acceleration that took their breath away, they found themselves safely on the other side of the rapids, welcomed by a round of cheers and applause from the other canoers.

A few months later, after returning home and landing a new job, Dave received a letter in the mail from his canoe partner. During the trip she had shared her struggles with her disability, and part of how she responded to it was by developing a propensity for competitive bicycling. But the letter explained even more. For her, enrollment in the ropes course was an investment in self-confidence, to help her get to the next level of cycling. And apparently Dave had played an unwitting role in that. Before the ropes course, she considered trying out to compete as a cyclist in the Paralympic Games, but had decided against it. In her letter, she explained that Dave's patience helped her regain her confidence. "Thank you for being such a patient teacher," she wrote.

She went on to explain that after returning from the trip, she decided to try out, and she made the team. She closed the letter with words that forever changed the way Dave thought about the value of showing someone patience: "I won the silver medal."

Dave's patience had paid off for her. And after reading her letter, he knew it had paid off for him too.

• • •

One of the simplest ways we can show patience is by listening. It's also probably the most common and frequent opportunity we have to show patience with others during everyday conversations. And despite how deceptively simple it is to do, at least in concept, it can be unimaginably impactful. Someone who learned that lesson firsthand is Michael McGlinn.

When Michael was a rising sophomore at the University of Notre Dame in South Bend, Indiana, he was an offensive lineman on the football team during head coach Lou Holtz's nine-year streak of bowl game appearances. At around three hundred pounds, he played second string to All-American lineman Lindsay Knapp, who was in line to graduate the following year. After red-shirting his first year, Michael had three years to play as a starting lineman on one of the best college teams in the country, under arguably one of the best football coaches in history.

August meant two-a-day practices for the team. But it also meant summer housing. All scholarship athletes move into one athletic dorm for the summer and don't return to their regular dorms until they open for the next academic year. At least, that's what they're supposed to do. But Michael and his friend Pete made other arrangements. A graduate student offered them her apartment for the summer since she would be at home and wouldn't need it. The boys got a more adventuresome place to live off-campus for the summer, and she got her apartment guarded by two of Notre Dame's most capable young men. It seemed like a good deal for both, until, that is, she returned to campus unexpectedly a few days early.

Michael and Pete had already moved some of their things into the academic dorms for the fall semester. But they assumed they had a few more days to clean up the apartment to get ready for its rightful owner to return. When she arrived, she was shocked at the scene. None of the lights or appliances were working. Apparently, the boys had forgotten to pay the electric bill. But she could see well enough to find a hole in one of the doors about the size of an offensive lineman's fist, dirty dishes strewn about the sink and kitchen, and wet clothes in the washing machine already beginning to mildew. As Michael described it, "It must have looked like we'd been having parties there all summer even though we hadn't. Just a couple of cavemen living in a girl's apartment." But no matter how you look at it, Michael admits, they hadn't been good stewards of the home and belongings they were entrusted with.

By that evening, the grad student and her mother had tracked Michael and Pete down to the football field. The final practice of the day was just winding down and the boys were all gathering around Coach Holtz. Getting the attention of the assistant coaches, the women made their complaint. Finding out two of their players hadn't been living in the athletic dorms as expected was bad enough. But finding out how they'd trashed this young woman's apartment was infuriating to at least some of the coaches.

Practice came to an abrupt stop as the coaches called Michael and Pete to the front. Both boys were admonished in front of the grad student, her mother, the other coaches, and the entire football team. But not admonished the way a kindergarten teacher might chastise a five-year-old for not raising his or her hand. And not even the way any normal adult would admonish a teenager for bad behavior. After all, these were football coaches. If you've seen the way football coaches yell and scream on the field at their players just for the way they're playing, then you can imagine the loud and angry tirade that might erupt if they're embarrassed by a surprise visit from an irate parent and her daughter.

"It was brutal," Michael recalls. "One of the coaches just went nuts! And especially at me." It seems Michael had a reputation for being more level-headed and responsible than their typical player. He was an accomplished singer and musician as much as he was an athlete. So he took the brunt of the coaches' outrage. Too much, he thought. He'd seen worse infractions from other players met with a much less vitriolic and personal response. And none were quite as public as this one.

Michael was embarrassed and angry at how it was handled. The coaches ended the discussion by saying, "You guys need to go get the rest of your stuff out of the apartment. We'll deal with you later." But Michael didn't give them that chance. When it came time for practice the next morning, Michael wasn't there. Before long, one of the graduate assistants called Michael in his dorm to find out why he wasn't at practice. And that's when Michael told him, "I'm not coming back. I quit." Michael admits that as a nineteen-year-old, he didn't have the emotional tools to deal with the situation. "And it showed in poor decisions like that one."

Sometime that day he called his parents and told them what happened. He was completely honest about how poorly they'd left the apartment. But he also shared how unfairly harsh he thought the reaction was and that as a result he decided to quit the team. He always wanted to pursue music and art in college anyway, and football made it hard to do that well.

His parents' response? "At first they were speechless, perhaps for the first time in my life. They couldn't believe I actually quit the team. They raised me to thoughtfully consider every opportunity life presented me, and once I committed to one, to not quit. So they made it clear they were upset with me, and understandably so."

Michael got off the phone more agitated than when he got on, and he probably spent the majority of his day stewing over it. But then that evening he got a phone call he wasn't expecting. It was from his uncle, Gary Hense. He'd somehow tracked him down in the new dorm at a new phone number. Michael said hello and recognized his uncle's voice. Gary said simply, "How are you doing, Michael?"

Michael proceeded to tell him the entire saga: every painful detail about how he'd felt unfairly treated and picked on and embarrassed, everything up to and including his quitting the team. And what Gary did while Michael unloaded his woeful tale was just listen. As Michael remembers it, "He didn't judge me. He didn't tell me I was right or wrong, or tell me what to do, or how I should feel. He didn't remind me of my responsibility and the commitment I had made. He simply listened."

At the end of Michael's tale, Gary said, "That sounds tough. I love you. If you need anything, call me. I'm here for you." And with that, the call was over. But as soon as he hung up the phone, Michael could tell something amazing had happened.

"I felt this enormous weight off my shoulders. Somehow I was able to release everything that was bothering me in that one call. The next morning I woke up and felt remarkably better. And I knew what I had to do. I went into Lou Holtz's office and I sat down. I said, 'Coach, I'm sorry. I made a mistake. I'd like to ask permission to be allowed back on the team.' I didn't make any excuses or try to explain my behavior."

Coach Holtz looked Michael right in the eyes, smiled, and said, "Absolutely. I just need you to do one thing. I need you to apologize to your team."

Michael was elated. When practice started, he walked out on the field to stretch with the team. He marveled at how just twenty-four hours before there wasn't a place on the planet he wanted to be less, and now no place he wanted to be more. When they finished stretching, Coach Holtz addressed the team, saying, "Someone on the team needs to say something."

Michael turned to face the group and said, "Hey, listen guys. I'm sorry for quitting the team." Then, referencing a nickname he'd been given his freshman year by the senior players, he said, "I just want to be good ol' 'Cheese' again." After that moment, it was never spoken of again. But it became a defining moment of Michael's football career. Notre Dame went on to win the Sugar Bowl that year against third-ranked Florida, and two Cotton Bowl games against Texas A&M his junior and senior years.

But if asked what his unexpected moment of clarity was that year, he won't tell you anything about football, or bowl games, or Notre Dame. He'll tell you about his uncle Gary and the phone call that made all the difference. "He preached to me without words. His nonjudgmental presence was the most powerful sermon I ever experienced. It defined my development of sensitivity and mercy today as a husband and a father." And to think Gary did all that—made an enormously positive, memorable, and lifelong impact on Michael McGlinn—by doing nothing more than just listening.

• • •

So listening is a powerful tool. But even when we do listen, most of us listen with the intent of responding, not with the intent of understanding. In other words, we're thinking about the next thing we're going to say. That's not listening. Sometimes really listening means more than being quiet while other people talk. You have to be looking for the meaning in what the other person is saying and doing.

A wonderful tool to help you do that is asking questions. In fact, I would submit that asking good questions is less a form of talking than it is a form of listening. A lovely example of how to do that well comes from Dan Ball, a brand narrative designer in London.

Dan was having lunch at one of his favorite pubs in Greenwich with a good friend, a struggling illustrator who lives with his grandmother. As Dan describes him, "If you want to find him, you'd probably be disturbing him at whatever time you call. He locks himself away in his home studio and works strange hours on satirical pieces of art." So he obviously has a high degree of passion for what he does.

During lunch, the topic of work inevitably came up, and Dan eagerly shared what he was working on. "I spent a good deal of time sharing the projects I was most excited about. And he was very happy to join in and ask questions along the way. But when I turned the conversation to him and asked how his projects were coming along, all he said was, 'I've been working on a new technique to add more texture to my illustrations.' And he left it at that."

Here we arrive at a critical point in the conversation. Dan could have filled the silence by returning to one of his projects. And that's what many of us would do, return to our favorite topic—ourselves. But that would be talking, not listening. To get his friend to do the talking, Dan knew his best tool was to ask a probing question. A good listener, then, might ask his friend to say more about this new technique: "How exactly does the technique work?" or "What kind of texture does it add?" or "How did you discover it?"

But a *great* listener can ask an even more probing question. And Dan, it turns out, is a great listener. Dan noticed that recently when he asked about his friend's work, the answers have gotten shorter and shorter. So he responded, "Why do you rush through telling me about achievements that I know are important to you?" And he immediately knew that he'd asked the right question.

"His eyes moved from me and the conversation to something in the distance, and then back again. And his lips started to quiver as if what I said hit a chord. No longer holding back, he told me, 'Well, living with my Nan . . . she doesn't quite understand what I do or why I even do it. So when I get a new client or work with someone of interest or I win an award, I have to share it really quickly. If I don't, she just looks confused and loses interest. I guess I've gotten in the habit of doing that now.'" And that, of course, took the conversation in an entirely new and probably more important direction for the two men.

Dan believes asking the right questions is a powerful listening tool. But, as he explains, "You can only ask the right questions if you're truly listening to what the person is saying." So the two feed off one another. "And truly listening," he continues, "doesn't just mean listening to the words that are coming out. It's observing their body language as well. When they get agitated or show some flecks of emotion, that's when you see some little tics in their behavior. I think that's what truly listening is. It's seeing people's tics and asking questions about them."

If listening is something you or the young person in your life struggle with (and who doesn't), try asking more questions in the conversations you have every day. You'll be amazed how quickly you'll lose interest in your own favorite topic (you!) and how much more fascinating and important the people you talk to will become.

SEVENTEEN

Fairness and Justice

Being good is easy, what is difficult is being just.

—VICTOR HUGO

Every culture has a code of conduct by which behavior is measured. Some is written in our laws, and we often learn of those expectations in formal schooling. But much is left for subtler forms of influence. We generally learn those on our own through the reaction our behavior elicits from others and how we feel about their actions toward us. In his 1902 publication *The Seven Cardinal Virtues*,[1] Reverend James Stalker describes three schools of justice we use to regulate our behavior: justice of the law, justice of public opinion, and justice of conscience. Interestingly, he describes them in that order as having an increasing degree of strength and impact.

Laws govern only a small fraction of our daily behavior, and sometimes with questionable priorities. As Stalker eloquently explains, "The law often strains at a gnat while it swallows a camel." His example is that if someone were to "defraud his neighbor of a shilling, the law would lay hold of him and set its whole machinery of police, judges, lawyers and prisons in motion for his punishment. But the same person might, by the arts of temptation carried on for years, make his neighbor's son a drunkard, or his daughter still worse, and yet escape altogether the notice of the law. That is to say, you may not touch your neighbor's purse, but you may break his heart with impunity as far as the law of the land is concerned."

That's where the stricter justice of public opinion comes into play. It fills in those gaping holes left by the law. That same man above who escapes legal scrutiny would certainly suffer being thought a rogue and a reprobate by his friends and neighbors. "He is not fined or imprisoned. But society frowns on him, he loses his character, and the doors through which access is obtained to the pleasures and honors of life are shut in his face." In other words, it might be hard for him to find a local company willing to hire him. And he certainly won't be welcome in the nearby country club or invited to Thanksgiving dinner with the neighbors.

The last and most powerful justice is conscience. It plugs the remaining holes left by both law and public opinion. It works because even the slightest unfair act, which may be unregulated by law and unseen by public opinion, cannot escape the notice of even the most hardened conscience. Deep inside, we all know the difference between right and wrong. And while none of these three justices can prevent all undesirable behavior, it is this last one that probably prevents most unkind acts from ever being considered in the first place.

These last two justices, though lacking any legal authority, clearly make society a more habitable place. But they can, at times, be at odds with one another. Which means we're left to consider each and decide what is the right thing to do. Which route is the more just or fair? An interesting example of this is what happens to Bradley every year on July 4th.

Independence Day in the United States is traditionally celebrated with fireworks, commemorating the country's declaration of independence from the British in 1776. But fireworks can be dangerous to their users and potential fire hazards, and the noise and smoke they cause could be a nuisance to neighbors. Because of this, today many kinds of fireworks are legally banned inside city limits. But to many, the enforcement of such a ban on even the most harmless firecrackers and bottle rockets would be a bit like enforcing a complete stop at a stop sign in the middle of the night with no traffic for miles in any direction. It would be overkill. Which is why many police officers look the other way on that one night a year when revelers might shoot off a few "illegal" fireworks. And with two young children growing up in the city who look forward to July 4th every year, Bradley was one of those once-a-year revelers.

In fact, most neighborhoods have at least one resident who can be counted on for a few small fireworks each year. The other families tend to congregate in that family's front yard each Independence Day around dusk just to see the show. But in Bradley's neighborhood, there was at least one person who didn't approve. A curmudgeonly old man in his seventies, Mr. Pease drove around the neighborhood each July 4th admonishing anyone with so much as a firecracker. His reason? "The noise frightens my dog." And when his pleas didn't have the desired effect, Mr. Pease called the police.

During Mr. Pease's visit one year to complain, Bradley picked up his five-year-old son and introduced him. "I'd like you to meet my son. Mr. Pease, when you were his age, did you get to see fireworks on July 4th?"

"Yes, I suppose I did."

"I did too. And they are wonderful memories. I want my son to grow old with those same wonderful memories you and I enjoy. I understand the fireworks bother your dog. But I wonder if on this one night of the year, for about an hour, you might just take your dog on a walk in the park across town? Or perhaps just go for a drive in your car, all knowing that for the next 364 nights, you won't hear a peep out of us. And neither will your dog. What do you say?"

Well? What would you do if you were Mr. Pease? Would Bradley's appeal convince you to drop your complaint? And what if you were Bradley? Don't you care about Mr. Pease's dog? And aren't you a little concerned about somebody getting hurt? Or perhaps one of those bottle rockets going off target and starting a fire in someone's backyard? And you do realize that it's against the law, don't you?

So I'll leave it to you to discuss. What do the justices of law, public opinion, and your own conscience have to say about this case? And then ask yourself, what would you do?

• • •

So far in this chapter we've talked about justice. Now let's turn our attention to fairness and the single greatest tool we have to bring it about: compromise.

On December 16, 1961, something beautiful happened in Caracas, Venezuela. Twenty-one-year-old Aquiles Sanchez married the woman of his dreams, nineteen-year-old Carmen Rodriguez. Six days later, just three days before Christmas Day, they had their first fight.

On that day the young couple moved into a small studio apartment and began setting up Christmas decorations. That's when they discovered that the Christmas traditions held most dear in both their families were at odds with one another. In Carmen's family, the Christmas tree was the most important symbol of the season. Christmas revolved around the tree: the family all together decorating it, placing presents underneath it, and spending time around it. In Aquiles's family, the nativity scene was the ultimate symbol of Christmas. After all, Christmas is a celebration of Christ's birth. And with little money between them, and even less space in their tiny apartment, Carmen and Aquiles simply could not have both. They would have to choose.

Attempts to persuade each other to the other's side turned to bickering. Bickering quickly turned to resentment. Then the couple did something it takes most couples years to learn. They decided to look for a third option. In other words, they decided to compromise.

They spread out a set of old magazines on the kitchen table to look for ideas. Eventually, one picture caught Aquiles's eye. It was a Christmas ornament that looked like both a Christmas tree and a nativity scene. It was basically a two-foot-tall triangular frame wrapped in evergreen branches, so it essentially resembled a short Christmas tree. In the center of the frame, however, was a nicely sculpted figure of Mary, Joseph, and the baby Jesus. It wasn't a perfect Christmas tree. And it wasn't a perfect nativity scene. But together, it was perfect.

Aquiles built a triangular frame from wood. Carmen picked up some fallen evergreen branches from the floor of a Christmas tree vendor. And she found small porcelain images of Mary, Joseph, and baby Jesus for the center of the triangle. Then together they decorated the frame with the branches, ribbons, balls, a few lights, and even a star on top. They couldn't rightly call it a Christmas "tree" or a "nativity scene." So they decided to call it their "little Christmas Triangle." With still a few days before the 25th, a Sanchez Christmas tradition was born.

Every year for the past fifty-three years, Aquiles and Carmen have put up their Christmas Triangle. And during the years they had small children at home, the day the Christmas Triangle was set up and decorated was the most cherished day of the season. Aquiles and Carmen would tell the story of how the Triangle was born, first to their children, and years later to their grandchildren. So year after year, generations of the Sanchez family learned and relearned the value of compromise.

They learned that compromise isn't something that happens by accident. It's an intentional thing, a choice. As long as you're fighting for whatever it is you want, you won't make any progress finding a compromise. It was only when Aquiles and Carmen dropped their attempt to win the argument, and picked up some magazines to find a solution they would both be happy with, that any real compromise happened. So any time a conflict arose in the Sanchez house, they asked themselves, "What's the 'little Triangle' solution?" Usually they found one. They just had to look for it.

On the day each of their children got married, Aquiles and Carmen gave each his or her own Christmas Triangle to keep the tradition alive. Their youngest son, Hector, and his new bride, Milagros, put that tradition to use within days of getting that wedding gift—on their honeymoon.

The couple spent their honeymoon in Las Vegas in October. An avid baseball fan, Hector wanted nothing more than to watch the World Series on TV. There were even a couple of Venezuelan players on the teams that year he really wanted to see do well. But for Milagros, wasting three hours in an amazing city watching baseball on television was the furthest thing from her mind. "We're in Vegas! I don't want to miss anything here. I want to see all the sights!" Like Hector's parents thirty-six years earlier, he and his new bride were about to have their first fight only a few days into their marriage.

The couple quickly asked themselves, "What's the 'little Triangle' solution here?" After a few minutes of thought, they came up with this creative solution: In just about every restaurant, bar, and casino, there is a TV where the game would be playing live. "Let's bar-, hotel-, and restaurant-hop our way around Las Vegas. We'll stop for a short while in each place and watch a little of the game. Then move on." From the Bellagio, to Rio, to the New York-New York hotel, they took in all the must-see attractions. And at each one, Hector got to see a little of the game. His wife even commented when the night was over, "That's the baseball game I have enjoyed the most. It was like a scavenger hunt!"

The spirit of compromise in the little Christmas Triangle had served them well and has continued to do so over their sixteen years of marriage. And it can serve you well, too, even if you don't have one of your own. When conflict arises in your life, ask yourself, "What's the 'little Christmas Triangle' solution here?"

• • •

For our last lesson in this chapter, let's turn to one of the most widely shared aphorisms across time and cultures—the Golden Rule: Treat other people as you would have them treat you. Its simplicity is only outshined by the truth and wisdom it contains. But, like all maxims, it still pales in comparison to the effectiveness of a good story to communicate a message that will be heeded. A centuries-old but perhaps less well-known example of that is found in the thirteenth-century French folktale called "La Couverture partagée" (The shared covering).

There once was a family with three generations living under one roof. The time came when the grandfather was unable to work to help support himself or the household, and he became a burden on his son and grandchildren. His son told him that he must move out. But to protect the old man from the cold, he instructed the eldest grandchild to find a nice warm blanket for the old man to take with him. The child quickly returned with the nicest, warmest blanket in the house, but only half of it. And the father noticed that it had been quickly and crudely torn in two. He asked his son, "Why have you kept the other half of the blanket?" The child responded, "Why it's for you, of course, father, when it's your time to go."

As parents, it's easy to forget that our children learn much more from what we do than from what we say. Let this story remind us all to not only teach our children the lessons contained in this book, but to live them out ourselves. If we treat others fairly, they will treat us that way. Our children will see that and do likewise.

EIGHTEEN

Humility

Pride. That's my favorite.

—THE DEVIL (Al Pacino's character in the movie *The Devil's Advocate*)

To understand humility, it's often easiest to start with its opposite: pride. In his book *The Seven Deadly Sins*, Reverend James Stalker defines pride as "the inordinate assertion of self."[1] In other words, pride is an inflated sense of our own importance or status or accomplishments. When we're prideful, we hold ourselves in such high esteem it's difficult to recognize the value and importance of the people around us. "It's all about me!" we think. Letting go of that self-focus and adopting a more humble attitude can drastically improve the enjoyment in your life and the lives of the people you care about. It's a lesson I hadn't learned well until one Thanksgiving Day, eight years into my marriage.

My wife, Lisa, and I were hosting dinner at our house with a few guests, including my sister Val and Lisa's mother, Jeannie. And as cliché as it may be, before the meal had even been served, I had already had enough of my mother-in-law's company. Out on the back patio, I complained to my sister about how I thought Jeannie had made too much of a production of how she had to be the one to cut the turkey because it had to be done just so. I explained how I thought she was a little too proud of her electric carving knife, how she had to cut exactly the right sized pieces, and how one just couldn't appreciate the meal without a properly cut bird.

While I blathered on with my nitpicking, my sister smiled with a knowing look on her face. Then she told me she recalled having a similar frustration a decade earlier with our grandfather, Ping. In Ping's later years, Val had become his full-time caregiver. She told me about how he tried to micromanage her every move. "He told me exactly how to set the thermostat, and which way to put the mail in the mailbox so the mailman would be sure to see it. I was a grown woman! Did he think I hadn't picked up mail at my own house for the past twenty years? Did he think I hadn't figured out how to set a thermostat yet?"

At that point, I assumed my sister was just commiserating with me. But I soon realized she was actually teaching me a valuable lesson in humility.

Continuing her story, she explained that she ended up so frustrated with Ping that her patience became short and her temper even shorter. Then she started thinking about him and how his life had been up until just a few years earlier. His working career began when he had to drop out of school in the fourth grade to help support his family, and it ended some eight decades later when he retired at the age of eighty-nine. He worked hard his whole life, was one of the most generous men either of us has ever known, and by then was in his nineties and in the final few years of life.

What Val realized was that he had spent the past several decades as a leader in his industry, at times managing large teams of people. He was accustomed to telling people how to do their jobs more effectively. "Then all of a sudden he wasn't in charge of anyone, except for me." Her conclusion from this soul searching was this: "It's late in the game for him. He's close to the end. I don't need to try to change him. I need to change me. He just wants to feel useful like he did for so many years. And my pride was getting in the way of that. It's not going to hurt me to have him give me more instructions than I need. But it will make him feel useful again."

That's when Val turned the analogy to my problem. Jeannie had just retired a few months earlier from her own forty-two-year career. As a single parent, she was used to providing for a family. But now her only child was all grown up and married and had a family of her own. For years, Jeannie was the one who cooked the turkey and hosted Thanksgiving dinner. Now she was a guest waiting to be served. The only thing she wanted was to feel useful again and maybe get a little acknowledgment for her contribution. Who was I to begrudge her that very small and understandable desire? All it would take on my part was a little less pride and a little more humility for the woman who raised the mother of my children.

Indeed. It was an eye-opening realization and the beginning of the better half of our Thanksgiving Day that year. More important, it was also the beginning of a much-improved relationship with my mother-in-law.

• • •

But pride doesn't just make us ugly and unappreciative. It can literally get in the way of accomplishing our goals. Jayson Zoller, whom you met in chapter 13, learned that at the young age of ten.

Jayson had been a member of his church choir for as long as he could remember. But in the fourth grade, he got his first big solo opportunity in a major production the church had planned. Not just a single solo line or phrase, mind you. He was asked to sing an entire song, solo! It would be very challenging, and he was incredibly excited about it. For the rest of the show, his only role would be to sing along with the rest of the choir in the group performances, with the slight exception of a single solo line he had in the second-to-last song. All that would be a piece of cake.

He practiced for weeks leading up to the big performance. When it came time for his big solo, he nailed it! He recalls, "It was the best I'd ever performed it. I remembered all the words and hit all the tough notes." When he finished, the crowd stood and applauded. "I was beaming! So happy, and so proud.

"The show went on and eventually we came to the second-to-last song, to my one-line solo. I started to sing it, but I got tongue-tied, and I sang the wrong words. But rather than just muddling through it, for some reason I stopped singing and just blurted out, 'Blah!'" The crowd couldn't contain themselves. They erupted in hysterical laughter. It was so disruptive the pianist stopped playing and the entire show came to a screeching halt. "It was humiliating," Jayson remembers all too vividly.

In reflecting on his thoughts at the time, he said, "I couldn't believe that in a matter of minutes, I went from feeling unconquerable and on top of the world to being the cause of this disaster. And it was all over that simple one-liner."

Jayson had been so proud of his big solo performance he couldn't stop thinking about it. And it's hard to think about your next performance when you're still reliving the last one. He realized that being proud of your accomplishments is fine. But when that pride becomes so consuming that it's distracting you from your next task, you know you've let it go too far.

• • •

Most of us want to be liked and admired by other people. So in social settings we find ourselves constantly returning to our favorite topic: us. We try to impress anyone who will listen with our job, accomplishments, how much we know, or the neighborhood we live in. And while that may work some of the time, usually it just results in us coming across as the kind of arrogant, self-absorbed know-it-all nobody likes or wants to spend time with. Ironically, the best way to make people like you and want to spend more time with you isn't by proudly sharing everything impressive about you. It's by humbly sharing only a little. Consider as evidence the following scene from a dinner party in Washington, D.C., in the summer of 2012.

Pete Leibman, author of the book *I Got My Dream Job and So Can You*, attended the party, hosted by a friend of his. After some initial mingling, each person was asked to describe him- or herself to the group in less than sixty seconds. Pete was fascinated with what he saw his fellow partygoers do with their one minute. He noticed most people seemed to fall into one of four types, each of which he named appropriately.

The first group he named Self-Absorbed Sally/Stanley. He recalls one member of this group who "missed the majority of the event because she showed up over one hour late. During the second round of introductions, she started off by saying how busy she is because she runs two businesses."

That left Pete thinking, "Yeah, we're all busy. Whining about it doesn't impress me." But more off-putting to Pete was what she did while everyone else was speaking. "She scanned through her cell phone, apparently checking and replying to emails or text messages. When other people are talking, you should be listening, especially if you showed up more than one hour late."

The next group he called Rambling Ron/Rhonda. The request to introduce themselves in sixty seconds or less came in the original invitation. At the event, the host assigned a timekeeper with a stopwatch to keep everyone on pace. But despite all that effort, as Pete describes it, "almost half of the room still needed a warning to stop talking. One person in particular must have gone on for at least three or four minutes, despite several cues from the person with the stopwatch that time was up. Even worse, after he spoke for four minutes, I still had no clue what he did for work."

Group three was Conceited Connor/Connie. "One person in this group stuck to her allotted sixty seconds. However, she spoke 100 mph in order to highlight every professional achievement in her life. She rattled off the complete name for each of her four books. She dropped the names of five 'major' clients, and she also felt it necessary to tell everyone her life motto, some cheesy catch phrase that had something to do with being your best. Yuck. There's no faster way to turn people off than to brag about how great you are or to lecture people you just met on how they should live their lives."

The final group he called Humble Harry/Harriett. And he described one interesting person in this group like this: "He began his remarks by saying that he would rather give up his allotted time to hear more about a prior woman's background. Everyone smiled. Then he briefly and humbly mentioned that he was a documentary filmmaker and that he loves his job because he gets to spend it with some of the most amazing people in some of the most beautiful places in the world. No bravado. No name dropping. No 'elevator pitch.' No need to ask him to stop rambling. Just a regular guy who was humble, self-deprecating, concise, and who clearly had been listening to the other people in the room."

So which one of these people do you like the most and would want to spend time with? More important, when you're at your next dinner party, which of these people will you be?

• • •

Sometimes even all the sense in the world can't talk someone into trading a little pride for some humility. That's often the case with teenagers. Many a teen has thought his parents or teachers quite foolish, only to be amazed in his mid-twenties to see how much smarter those grownups had become in the previous decade. For those cases, sometimes an alternative strategy helps. And it's as simple as it is genius. Just ask Brooke Davis.

Brooke had the third highest GPA her junior year at a private school in Columbus, Ohio. She was also her class president. A bright, ambitious, and well-rounded African American young woman, she was exactly the kind of student you'd expect to find in the National Honor Society. So when it came time that year for Honor Society nominations, Brooke assumed she was a shoo-in. Much to her surprise and disappointment, however, she wasn't even nominated by her teachers.

Looking back, Brooke speculates as to the reason why. "It came down to my attitude and how I was perceived. My academics and extracurriculars were good. But I talked a lot when I shouldn't have. And I was sometimes disrespectful to my teachers, especially when I was getting disciplined." In fact, she recalls that she and one particular teacher "went at it all year. I disagreed with him in class very publicly. And I always had to have the last word."

Brooke carried some resentment over that decision for a few weeks, right up to the end of the academic year. The last day of school, Brooke was the last person to walk out of one of her classes when the assistant principal walked by. He'd always been a big supporter of hers, so when he stopped to chat she took the opportunity to commiserate with him a bit. "I was complaining about not getting into the Honor Society and about how misunderstood I was. Basically, I was blaming everyone else instead of myself. And he just looked at me and said, 'Brooke, you're going to have to learn how to play the game. You're not going to get anywhere fighting against the system.'"

That was the simple part. Now here's the genius part, the reason why that was all he had to say. Brooke was convinced she was right in her resentment at being overlooked for the Honor Society. And she couldn't and wouldn't accept any responsibility for her own behavior and the pride underlying it. But she was also bold enough not to pass up a challenge like that. She was smart enough to play, and win, any game she set her mind to, and that assistant principal knew it. So instead of telling her what she'd probably heard from her parents and teachers already, he simply told her it was all a big game and if she learned how to play it well enough, she'd win.

Brooke immediately changed her behavior at school. "I chilled out and completely changed my attitude. I showed more humility, was less proud, and I was nicer to my teachers. And I didn't always have to win every argument. By the middle of my senior year, I had turned it all around and come full circle." As evidence, one of her teachers came to her and said, "You've completely changed your attitude, Brooke. Who you are now would be an excellent fit for the Honor Society."

The beauty of it was that by the time Brooke realized that it wasn't all a game—that being kind and humble are worthy character traits for anyone to possess—it was too late. She'd already adopted them for the purpose of winning the game. Now they were hers to keep.

That assistant principal knew Brooke well. He knew she was too young to accept her own role and responsibility for not being in the Honor Society and too ambitious to turn down a challenge to succeed anyway. But he also knew that regardless of how he got her to change, she would like the person she had become and wouldn't want to go back. And he was right. Brooke went on to finish high school and college with high marks, landed a great job at a prestigious company, and is now working on a master's degree. More important, she's a wonderful human being, worthy of being on anyone's honor society rolls.

If your young person, like many others, is having trouble seeing the inherent wisdom of adopting a more humble attitude, you might employ a similar strategy and invite her to play a little game.

NINETEEN

Respect for Others

> Hating people is like burning down your own house to get rid of a rat.
>
> —HARRY EMERSON FOSDICK

The importance of showing respect and tolerance for other people is an easy thing to say. But it's a surprisingly difficult thing to do. That's because there's often a formidable degree of pressure from our peers to do exactly the opposite. In that sense, it often takes courage and creativity to show others the degree of respect they deserve. One person who learned that at a young age was Ed Tanguay.

When Ed was a five- or six-year-old boy growing up in Monument, Colorado, he noticed that his was the only house in the neighborhood painted red. All the other houses were either brown or green. When he asked his dad why, his father said very matter of factly, "Because when we moved in, the Homeowners Association told us we could only paint it brown or green. So, naturally, I painted it red."

Apparently, Mr. Tanguay wasn't much of a rule follower, at least not with rules he considers unworthy. So you shouldn't be too surprised at how he responded on another occasion when he received a more unsettling directive from the HOA.

When Ed's older brother Mark was fourteen, he visited their aunt and uncle, who were on assignment in the Peace Corps in the Marshall Islands, very close to the equator in the western Pacific Ocean. Just prior to returning home, he called his parents to ask if he could bring home a guest for a while. He'd befriended a local boy named Torlick who had never been to the United States. Mom and Dad agreed, and both Mark and Torlick arrived home in Colorado a short time later.

As it turned out, Torlick liked to play basketball. So one day when Mark, his dad, and Torlick were playing basketball, a member of the same Homeowners Association stopped and had a chat with Dad. The man told him it was okay to have Torlick as a houseguest for a while. But if the boy wanted to play basketball, "it would be best if he didn't do so between 5 and 6 p.m., when everyone would be driving by on their way home from work." You see, because he was a native of the Marshall Islands, Torlick's skin was many shades darker than everyone else's in this very Caucasian Colorado suburb. "We wouldn't want anyone to get the wrong idea about this neighborhood," the man explained.

Since he was still a young boy, Ed wasn't privy to most of the conversation, just the part his father shared with him. What Ed does recall vividly, however, was that every day for the next few months, his father came home from work and yelled down the hallway, "Torlick! It's five o'clock—time to play basketball!"

Everyone is aware of great civil rights leaders like Martin Luther King Jr. or Nelson Mandela or Gandhi. But you don't have to be a larger-than-life civil rights hero to practice your own form of civil disobedience. Just take a page out of Mr. Tanguay's playbook and do the right thing.

• • •

Part of dealing with issues of race and prejudice in a healthy manner starts with recognizing that we all have deep-seated preconceived notions about others. Some we're conscious of and know how we got them, and others we're not. But both can and do affect how we view and interact with other people. A university professor we'll call Karen learned that the hard way when she had to face her own preconceived notions. But in her case, that preconceived notion walked into her class one day with a bomb strapped to his chest.

Karen is the department chair of women's studies at a large midwestern university. One fall, already a week into the semester, a man of Middle Eastern descent walked into her office. We'll call him Saeed. Saeed was in his late twenties, had just arrived in the country, and was asking permission to enroll in Karen's Introduction to Women's Studies class. Typically, 75 percent of the students in that course are female. And she'd never had a man from the Middle East take the course before. Looking back, she admits her first thought was, "This is going to be a tough semester. He's going to challenge everything I say. And it's certainly going to be awkward when I talk about how women aren't allowed to drive in some Middle Eastern countries." She could already picture him rolling his eyes when she discussed modern views about women that would contradict conventional wisdom where he's from.

Despite those misgivings, she approved his late entrance for the course. And as soon as he left her office, she started having pangs of guilt over her quiet reservations. "I hated myself for it almost immediately. Honestly, I just met this man. I had no evidence to make those kinds of assumptions."

As early as the next week of classes, she began to get a picture of what Saeed was like as a student. And it was nothing like what she expected. "He was respectful, interested, engaged, and very bright. He even brought me a copy of the Qur'an with all the passages about women highlighted to help me understand women's issues in his culture. And there wasn't a single day he didn't talk to me after class about how it was relevant to his culture and what he was trying to accomplish." And what he was trying to accomplish was even more impressive than his in-class behavior. Saeed had arrived in the United States with his wife, who was getting a master's degree and had plans to continue toward a Ph.D. The two wanted to return to their home country when their studies were complete to provide an example of what an educated Muslim woman can accomplish and to show that it's possible to be both a good Muslim woman and educated. He was taking this class to help him prepare for that journey.

Karen's perception of Saeed had taken a radical turn for the better in a short eight weeks. She really had been too quick to judge him. He was truly the ideal student. Or so she thought, until one morning he walked into her class with a bomb strapped to his chest.

Despite the bulky jacket covered in explosives, the combat fatigues instead of pressed pants, and the uncharacteristic countenance on his face, she of course recognized Saeed immediately. But what on earth was behind this? What would cause her erstwhile ideal student to turn into a terrorist overnight? Or was it worse? Was the entire eight weeks of class all a ruse and this was Saeed's real plan all along? She didn't have to wait long to find out. It turned out that the cause of this sudden change in behavior in Saeed was the same thing that caused Karen to presume he'd be such a burdensome student. In fact, the cause of his decision to strap a bomb to his chest wasn't something inside Saeed. It was something inside Karen. And she realized that the moment she bolted upright in bed in a cold sweat to find that the bomb scare was nothing but a nightmare.

Karen relaxed. There was no bomb and her student was no bomber. He was the fine upstanding student she had come to know and appreciate over the first half of the semester. But then she had to ask herself, "Why would I have had such a dream? For the prior two months he'd shown me nothing to give me the impression he would do anything of the sort." Quite the opposite. He was one of her favorite students.

She concluded two things from this. First, while there was absolutely no association in her conscious mind between suicide bombers and Saeed, clearly in her subconscious mind there was. Second, she concluded we're probably all susceptible to making judgments about people based on stereotypes and deep-seated preconceived notions. Of all people to have had this experience, she is a professor of not just women's studies, but also courses on race, class, and gender. She teaches awareness of these issues for a living! She of all people should be as free from such biases as possible. Yet twice in two months she suffered one bout of conscious-biased thoughts of Saeed and one disturbing subconscious one. And if you're honest with yourselves, some of you reading this will admit that somewhere two paragraphs ago, you thought to yourself, "See! She was right to begin with. She should have never let this guy into her class!"

"You have to be vigilant," Karen advises. "When you see it creep into your consciousness, confront it. None of us are immune."

• • •

Being vigilant against bigotry based on ethnicity is only one form of prejudice we have to be on guard against. Another is based on the abilities each of us is born with, as the following story illustrates.

On a rainy day in Memphis, September 17, 1953, Bessie Faye Tedford stepped out the door of her home onto the porch, slipped on the wet steps, and fell down a short flight of stairs to the sidewalk below. She suffered no broken bones or serious injuries. In fact, it probably wouldn't have been a noteworthy event at all except for the fact that she was seven months pregnant. That fall turned the baby just enough in her womb that the umbilical cord got wrapped around his neck. Later that day, Bessie Faye went into a distressed labor. Within a few hours, Kenny Lee Tedford Jr. was born, two months premature and a "blue baby." He spent his first three months of life in an incubator, his survival each day an uncertainty. He did survive. But being deprived of oxygen for so long resulted in brain damage, deafness in both ears, partial blindness in one eye, and a slight paralysis of the entire left side of his body. Kenny Tedford was destined for a hard life.

Learning to speak when you can't hear is an extraordinarily difficult task. Because his family couldn't afford expensive speech coaches, Kenny was ten years old before he learned to speak fluently. So at the age of six when he entered school, Kenny was relegated to the back of the class. While the other children learned their ABCs, Kenny was assigned a coloring book and a few crayons and told to draw pictures. His teacher was unprepared to handle a student with Kenny's needs. Some days he actually felt special and relished his unique status in class. Those were the days the other kids said they wanted to be "retarded like Kenny" so they could just sit in the back and color instead of study.

But other days he was painfully aware of his situation: the cruel names, taunts, and mocking of the way he walked or talked. And the insults didn't just come from the other children. Kenny recalls a class discussion he was allowed to participate in where the teacher asked students to share what they wanted to be when they grew up. There were the expected voices of aspiring doctors, lawyers, policemen, firemen, and a few astronauts. When it was Kenny's turn, he showed the teacher a picture he'd drawn to answer the question. In it was a tall, thin man standing at a lectern. The teacher asked, "What's this?"

Kenny explained, "Someday I want to teach everyone how to get along and love each other." He didn't have the words for it at the time. But what Kenny wanted to do was to be a professional speaker and storyteller. It was an admittedly bold aspiration for a boy who couldn't hear or speak well. His teacher knelt down beside him and addressed him along with the entire class. She said, "Students, Kenneth, this is a very nice idea." And turning to Kenny she continued, "But you'll never do this. You're retarded, and you have a speech impediment. You'll never be able to do anything except maybe sweep the floors." Such thinking was prevalent in the 1950s and in some circles still is today.

But for our purposes, one of the most instructive moments in Kenny's life came later that year. A psychologist visited the class on a regular basis to assess a few of the children, and especially Kenny. One of the techniques was called art therapy. Kenny was asked to share some of his drawings, which the psychologist used to assess his creativity and cognitive ability. On one visit, Kenny offered him a picture of a butterfly he had just drawn. It was small and almost entirely drawn in black and white. Looking at the picture, the doctor said, "Hmmm, not very colorful or creative." And he wrote a D on the picture and handed it back to Kenny. "Maybe my teacher is right," Kenny thought. "Maybe I'll never be anything but a retarded boy."

Kenny rolled up the picture and put it in his backpack. When school was out, he walked out of class with his head hanging low. Shortly, down the hall, another teacher saw him and stepped out to talk to him. "Kenneth, come here." He walked up to her, and she knelt down to talk to him eye to eye. "What's the sad face for, Kenneth?"

"I can't even draw! I got a D on my drawing, and that's the thing I'm best at."

She asked to see his drawing. When he showed her the butterfly, she said, "He's very pretty. But he looks a little sad. Can I see your box of crayons?"

Kenny pulled out the box and showed it to her. It was a tiny little sample-sized box of four crayons, the kind you get at a restaurant to keep the kids entertained before the meal arrives. She opened it up and inside found these four colors: black, white, gray, and red.

"Are these the only colors you have, Kenneth?"

"Yes, ma'am," Kenny said, a little embarrassed. He knew the other kids were given bigger boxes with more colors. But he was the "retarded boy" in back and apparently didn't deserve any more than that.

"Come into my room, Kenneth," she said. He followed her in and she sat down at her desk. She pulled out an enormous box of crayons, just like the other kids had, and gave it to him. She found several sheets of paper, rolled them up, and placed them in his backpack. Then she said to him, "Kenneth, I want to tell you something. You are very creative. When you talk, even at your age, you tell the most amazing stories. And you seem to love all the kids, even the ones who make fun of you. So I want you to go home and think about that, that you are important and you have a gift.

"Then I want you to draw your butterfly again. Use any colors you want this time. And when you're done you think of a story to make your butterfly come to life." Then she hugged him and sent him on his way.

A few days later the psychologist returned for another visit. "Do you have any more drawings, Kenneth?" he asked.

Kenny handed him a new picture of a butterfly. But this one had a splendid array of colors that would bring a smile to even the most dour critic. "Wow! That's wonderful, Kenneth." Then with a puzzled look on his face, he added, "And is that a woman on the back of the butterfly?"

"Yep," Kenny responded confidently.

"Who is it?"

"That's my momma," Kenny said, smiling brightly.

"What's she doing there?" the doctor asked, genuinely curious what business a woman has on the back of a butterfly.

Then six-year-old Kenny Tedford told the psychologist, "She's there so she can fly around the room here and make sure you give me an A+ this time."

That, apparently, was enough to thaw even the cold heart of this very serious psychologist. With watery eyes, he looked down at Kenny and said, "What a beautiful story." Then he took out his red marker, cupped his hand around it so Kenny couldn't see what he was writing, and scribbled his assessment at the top of the picture. Then he rolled up the paper and gave it to Kenny. "Put this in your backpack and don't look at it till you get home."

With impressive resolve for a first-grader, Kenny dutifully waited till he got home. He ran straight to his bedroom, pulled out the paper, and unrolled it. In big red letters, he saw A+ at the top of the page.

That's when Kenny knew that with the right opportunities, he could do anything he wanted to do. With the right crayons he could be a great artist, and with the right education he wouldn't be relegated to sweeping floors for a living.

Fifty-five years later, Kenny Tedford's life still isn't easy. He's survived numerous life-threatening challenges, including a heart attack, cancer, a broken neck, and a stroke. And of course, he still has the same brain damage, hearing and vision loss, and paralysis he was born with.

But in 2007, at the age of fifty-three, Kenny Tedford earned a Bachelor of Arts degree in theater from the University of Tennessee at Knoxville. In 2011, he completed his master's degree in storytelling from East Tennessee State University. And today, more than half a century after he was ridiculed for believing such an absurd notion, Kenny Tedford is a professional storyteller.[1] He brings a smile, a laugh, and a special kind of wisdom that only his life could teach to audiences all over the country.

Kenny Tedford is living proof of the limitless abilities of "disabled" people when they're given a chance. What he most hopes people take away from his story is that people born with different abilities want to be treated just like everyone else, and given the same opportunities. They want to be talked to like everyone else, not spoken to like an infant. They want to be loved like everyone else, not tormented and teased like an outcast. More important, they want to be challenged like everyone else. They want someone to have high expectations of them, higher than they might even have for themselves. They want to be believed in, to have their dreams and aspirations nurtured, not mocked. Give them the same box of crayons you'd give any other child, and you'll be amazed at the stories they make with them.

• • •

In an age where chivalry is largely extinct, it's sometimes helpful to remind ourselves that some of the oldest traditions are born out of respect for other people.

I learned one of my most memorable lessons on chivalry as a college student. One Saturday, my girlfriend Kelley and I were walking on a downtown sidewalk alongside bustling midday traffic. As we walked past a middle-aged African American man sitting on a bench, he called out to me in a respectful but disappointed tone, "Young man, show some respect. Walk curbside of that pretty lady."

I was instinctively embarrassed, though I wasn't immediately sure why. But I quickly switched places with her anyway. With a few minutes' reflection, it occurred to me he was teaching me a valuable lesson that probably dated from decades earlier. When walking along the side of a road with a companion, the one walking closest to traffic is at higher risk of coming in contact with the cars or horses speeding by. Or less dramatically, that person is more likely to end up wearing the dust, mud, or smell that regularly flies off passing vehicles. The other pedestrian is more protected from those unpleasantries by his or her partner. Chivalry dictates that a man protect his lady by walking curbside, allowing her the safer (and cleaner) position. I wasn't showing Kelley that respect. This stranger taught me how.

But I had more lessons to learn. Just knowing what to do isn't enough. Knowing how is also important.

Proud of my newfound gallantry, the next few times Kelley and I went for a walk I made a show of my chivalrous position curbside. The first time evoked a genuine smile from her. But after two or three such instances, her polite but annoyed smile let me know my pride was overshadowing the good deed. Apparently, part of being a gentleman is doing so without being boastful.

I only came to fully appreciate the value of humility in relationships many years later as a newly married man. I had of course told my wife, Lisa, that I loved her many times in our early marriage. But I asked her one evening when she really knew for certain that I did. She surprised me by saying there was a very specific moment that convinced her so. I had learned that Lisa had a habit of sleeping completely covered with blankets all the way up to and over her head. She left only a small opening in the covers near her mouth, which I affectionately dubbed her "breathe hole."

She answered my question by reminding me of something I had done one evening that I wasn't aware she ever knew about. I had gotten up in the middle of the night to use the bathroom, and when I returned to bed, I noticed I had disturbed the covers just enough to collapse her breathe hole, leaving her entire head covered by the blanket. With her still asleep (or so I thought), I quietly reshaped the blanket to reconstitute a proper opening and rolled over to go back to sleep. Apparently, although she kept her eyes closed, my movement had awakened her just enough to notice what I was doing. And while she did appreciate having her breathe hole fixed, what she appreciated more was that I did so even though I thought she was still asleep and would never know of my deed. That's when she knew that I really loved her.

• • •

There is a difference, of course, between respect and reverence. What's been discussed in the last two stories is showing respect, being considerate and tolerant of other people. In short, treating other people the way you would want to be treated. But reverence is another thing entirely. The *American Heritage Dictionary* defines reverence as "a feeling of profound awe and respect and often love."[2] So while most well-mannered people display respect fairly often, reverence is a much rarer thing. Therefore, deciding for whom, in what situations, and how to show that reverence is a serious matter for many people. If you or your family aren't among them, it's a worthwhile discussion to have.

Seeing what real reverence looks like is perhaps easiest when you're not expecting to see it. That's exactly what happened to an American businessman in Bangkok, Thailand.

Jeff Null and seven members of his team were nearing the end of a three-week stay in Bangkok. After indulging in the local cuisine for the entire trip, they opted for more familiar food at the Hard Rock Café that night. Walking out of the restaurant after dinner, they were hit by a wall of heat, sound, and smells at the center of a city of eight million people. At around thirteen degrees north latitude, Bangkok is deep in the tropics and has an average high temperature of over ninety degrees Fahrenheit year round.[3] And the Hard Rock is on one of the busiest streets in the city. Jeff explains, "The thing you've got to imagine about this street is that it's about as wide as a five-lane road in the U.S., but with about twelve lanes of cars in it. They're all just crammed together end-to-end with motorcycles weaving in and out of what little space is left between them. And the street vendors are fighting for the attention of every passerby. It's hot. And it's incredibly loud."

Down the street, the group saw a pedestrian bridge they could use to get back to their hotel. After navigating the thick foot traffic on the sidewalk, they came to the base of the bridge. But as they started to enter it, a man stepped in front of them and blocked their way. As Jeff recalls, "He was this tiny little man, perhaps no more than eighty-five pounds. And he stood there with his hands stretched out to each side, shaking his head, clearly not wanting us to walk across." But Jeff's group didn't speak Thai, and this man had very little English. The only thing that was clear was that he was adamant that they not enter the bridge. Weary and just wanting to get back to their hotel, the group began to get agitated.

"Eventually," Jeff explained, "the man pulled out a bill from his wallet and started pointing to it."

"I think he wants a bribe to cross the bridge," one of the group offered. But they soon determined that wasn't the case. He was pointing to something *on* the money. Finally, as he began to recall some English, they heard the word "king." Indeed, there was a picture of the king of Thailand on the money. So they parroted back to him the words, "the king, the king." And as they did, they started looking around and began to notice some activity. When they finally put it all together, they realized the king of Thailand was coming.

"We'd not seen the king, so we started getting excited and loud ourselves. But after a few moments of that, this little man turned to us, now with more full grasp of his English. He looked right at us and said in a commanding voice, 'Silence please. My king is coming.'

"We turned around to look and sure enough, the road was now cleared, and everybody as far as we could see was bowed down, head to the ground. And it. Was. Silent." The group watched as a motorcade of official cars moved through the opening in the center of the street. As it passed, activity started to return to normal. "Then this little man turned to us and bowed and let us go through."

Jeff stood there in awe at the situation that had just unfolded in front of him. It was the most potent and sincere display of reverence he had ever witnessed.

To fully appreciate the event, however, it's important to understand three things. First, this man was not a police officer or one of the king's guards. He appeared to Jeff to be a common citizen, and a modestly dressed one at that. Second, Thailand is overwhelmingly Buddhist, with 93 percent of the population claiming to practice it.[4] The position of your head and your feet therefore has deep symbolic meaning. To have pedestrians walking over the bridge with their feet above the head of the king passing underneath would be grossly insulting. And third, reigning since 1946, King Rama IX is the world's longest-serving head of state and the longest-reigning monarch in Thai history.[5] He still serves as of this writing.

When I asked Jeff to explain the significance and meaning this event has to him, he shared that it's something he reflects on often. Once a month or so, the man's words, "Silence please. My king is coming," ring in his ears.

"First," he said, "I am fascinated by the resolve of this ordinary Thai man who stood up to a group of foreigners, pushed through the difficulty of translation, and eventually made his position clear. He was clearly motivated by a huge amount of respect and love for his king, enough to overcome his natural Buddhist tendency to get along with everybody. What would my life be like if I lived like this guy? What would the world be like?

"Second, I am fascinated by the fact that the Thai people believe the king is worthy of such reverence. And in large part, he deserves it. Thailand is a constitutional monarchy, so he isn't the head of the government. But he is widely credited with using his power to help the poor and needy. Like the first point, what would the U.S. be like if we had that kind of unanimity of belief toward anything or anyone?

"Finally, my life is full of distraction and noise. Every Sunday morning I go to church and sing songs and listen to lessons and recommit myself to put God first. And very quickly thereafter I tend to push him to the background as I deal with all of that distraction and noise. A big chunk of reviewing this story with myself is an attempt to be silent and listen for God. To remember what my real priorities should be."

All of Jeff's questions are important ones, very much worthy of consideration. And when you're done, ask yourself, "Whom do I revere?"

TWENTY

Friendship

One thousand friends is too few. One enemy is too many.

—TURKISH PROVERB

Becky Okamoto learned several valuable life lessons from a friendship she almost didn't make.

Becky is an engineer by training and has spent most of her career in and around manufacturing. A few years ago, she was part of the leadership team at a production facility in California. It was one of the most diverse leadership teams she'd ever been a part of. In addition to her as an Asian American, there were two other women on the team and two Hispanic managers as well. In an otherwise Caucasian, male-dominated country and industry, it was nice to be on a team where her culture and values weren't in the minority. She felt comfortable. Until Marvin showed up, that is.

Marvin was the newest member of the leadership team. And as Becky described him, "He was very 'white male,' a man's man, played football in high school and college, loved talking about sports." Her first impression? "I did not like him."

She recalls in one of the first meetings he attended, he was sharing some analogy about Scottie Pippen he thought would help make his point. When one of the Hispanic women asked who Scottie Pippen was, he was astonished. "He plays for the Chicago Bulls!" he blurted out.

To which she replied, quite unimpressed, "What are the Chicago Bulls?" If there was any indication he was out of his element, this was it.

Becky also didn't like that he'd just come from an assignment in marketing (unusual for a team of engineers) and he was very aggressive. She admitted, "I was competitive myself and I probably felt threatened by him." As a result, their interactions were often antagonistic.

Becky soon went to a confidant on the team, Ernie Ahumada, to vent. "Ugh, he's so arrogant! I really don't like him." Since Ernie was a minority manager himself, Becky assumed he'd be sympathetic to her complaints. His response was anything but.

"Becky, it's your fault you don't like Marvin. This has nothing to do with him. This is your problem. If you decided to like Marvin, you'd like Marvin."

How did Becky feel about Ernie's response? "I was so mad! He was supposed to take my side!"

But Ernie wasn't done. He continued, "You need to make an attempt to like Marvin. If you did, you'd find out he's exactly like you."

"Oh no he is not!" Becky shot back.

"Yes, he is," Ernie assured her. "You both have the same values. And I have tremendous respect for both of you. Why wouldn't you respect each other?"

Ernie convinced her that she'd just made a judgment about Marvin because of his cultural differences growing up as a white male versus her as a Japanese female.

"You need to approach Marvin, and you need to like him."

So she decided to follow his advice. She went to Marvin and said, "I want to make our relationship work. I don't want to keep fighting. I apologize because I'm the problem." Recalling that moment, she admitted how hard it was to muster those words. "It darn near killed me. But I'm so glad I did it."

Marvin's response was, "I want to make this better too. It's not working, and it's a shame. We should do something about it." A gracious response, Becky thought, given the circumstances.

She described their progress this way. "As we started working together with more positive intent, we found out Ernie was right. We had the same core values and had the same goals for the organization. We just had different ideas about how to get there. After that, we would still have animated debates about what to do. But we did it respectfully and knew that we both shared the same objective."

Looking back after nearly two decades, Becky sees several lessons in this experience. The first and most obvious is not to judge the proverbial book by its cover. Marvin wasn't the arrogant white male she assumed him to be.

Second, she learned that not liking someone is a choice, which meant that liking that person is also a choice. Liking someone or respecting someone is something you *do*, not something that happens to you without your control.

Third, she learned how powerful a genuine apology could be in taking a relationship in a different direction.

Lastly, she learned from Ernie's example what good friendship looks like. It would have been easy for Ernie to sympathize with her complaints and join her in criticizing Marvin. "But he didn't take the bait," she explained. "He never said a bad word about Marvin."

Today, Becky describes Marvin as "one of my most trusted and respected mentors, coaches, and role models. I admire him greatly." The two enjoy a wonderful relationship. And it all started with a decision to be friends.

• • •

As we just learned, you can make a choice to be friends with someone even if you don't like him. But the opposite is also true. You can choose *not* to be friends with someone, even if you like him. And sometimes that's exactly what you should do. Just ask Vijay Easwaran.

When Vijay was a young boy growing up in Chennai, India, his grandmother shared with him a piece of wisdom that will be familiar to most readers, regardless of where you grew up. She told him that if you put one rotting mango in a basket of good mangoes, soon the entire lot will spoil. In the United States the metaphor chosen is often an apple, and doubtless other fruits are chosen in other geographies.

The message, of course, is the same. Choose your friends wisely, because they will have a significant influence on who you become. For many children, that metaphor is where the discussion and learning ends. Without ever seeing how that might play out in someone's life, it's hard for a child to make the connection. Unfortunately, Vijay had an opportunity to see firsthand how one bad mango could completely ruin the life of another young boy in Chennai.

In the seventh grade, Vijay had a classmate named Bala. Vijay and Bala attended classes together and played kabaddi, a wrestling sport. Vijay describes Bala as a happy-go-lucky sort, one who was always good at getting a laugh from the other students, and even the teachers. He got to school early every morning, would read quietly when he was supposed to, and was a good student, generally obedient, and well liked by most. Bala's father would come to school to have lunch with him once a week, making him the envy of many boys who weren't so lucky.

Then in the tenth grade, trouble moved in. A new boy from Bombay showed up at school, and he was a rule breaker. He quickly developed a close following, and Bala was among them. Soon, all the boys adopted the bad behavior of their new group leader. They started skipping school regularly and were frequently caught smoking and drinking. "They were constantly in the principal's office for one thing or another," Vijay remembers. But for some reason, Bala seemed to take the fall for most of their misdeeds, which he wore as a badge of honor. It almost certainly cemented his place in the group for the valuable service he provided. The slick kid from Bombay always seemed to get away without punishment. Bala was now one of these "cool kids" and had no more use for his dad's lunchtime visits.

In the eleventh grade, this group's behavior continued to escalate. In one particularly memorable event, the boys allegedly hired call girls and took them to Bala's house when his parents were at work. When Bala's father unexpectedly came home midday, the entire group was caught in the act. For once the entire group felt the brunt of the punishment. Unfortunately, it wasn't enough to curb their increasingly dangerous lifestyle.

Later that year, six of the boys decided to party at the seaside resort town of Mahabalipuram, about thirty-five miles south of Chennai. As usual, all were drinking heavily. Then they decided to go for a swim in the ocean. All six went out. Only five came back, and Bala was not one of them. In his drunken state, he couldn't swim well enough. And in their drunken state, his friends were in no position to save him. Bala's barely recognizable body washed ashore a week later.

When word reached the school, Vijay immediately thought of his grandmother's mango story. This kid from Bombay had moved in and spoiled a whole group of good kids. And it cost Bala his life. It left a deep impression on Vijay. Twenty years later, Vijay has two children of his own, and he's taught them both the wisdom of the rotten mangoes. And it seems to be working. At the age of seven, his daughter, Kaveri, came home and asked Mom and Dad if she could have a friend over to play. Without being asked, she made a list of the qualities this little girl possessed that made her want to have her as a friend and presented the list to her parents: "She listens to the teachers, works hard, is kind and polite, and prays to God." And his five-year-old son, Surya, added, "And she's always smiling. I like her too." Vijay was proud of the wise choice his children were making. And of course they invited the young girl to play. Kaveri (and Surya) went to bed that night with the joy of having a new friend. And Vijay went to bed without having to worry about any rotten mangoes in his children's basket of friends.

• • •

Once you've chosen your friends, you'll want to treat them as such. If you don't, you won't keep them long. Marvin Abrinica, whom you met earlier in this book, learned that the hard way in, of all places, Woodstock.

When Marvin was in the fourth grade, his family moved to a new city, which meant Marvin had to make a whole new set of friends. One of the first ones he recalls was Jackson. As Marvin remembers, "Jackson was an awkward and clumsy fellow, and into many of the same things I was, like *Star Wars* and Transformers and rock music. We hit it off instantly." The two spent many a night sleeping over at each other's homes eating pizza and Doritos, playing Nintendo, and watching *Headbangers Ball* on MTV when their parents thought they'd gone to sleep. They were like brothers.

When they entered their teenage years, however, Marvin expanded his circle of friends. As many teenagers do, he started spending more time with what he thought was the "fun crowd," a group more prone to experimenting with alcohol than his best friend Jackson was. That complicated things. In particular, he and Jackson had been planning for some time to attend a concert together in Woodstock, New York, commemorating the twenty-fifth anniversary of the now world-famous event that took place there a generation earlier. They had just graduated from high school and were ready to exercise some of their new freedoms. And some of their favorite bands were on the roster, so it promised to be an event they'd both relish.

But about a week prior to the event, Marvin had a change of heart. Not about going to the concert, but about whom he wanted to go to the concert with. He thought he'd have more fun with his newer and faster friends. He would have asked Jackson to join them. But Jackson wasn't that much of a partier, and Marvin thought he might just be a drag on the whole affair. Besides, Jackson had other friends who were planning to go to the concert.

Now Marvin needed an excuse for backing out. So he simply told him, "I have to work that weekend." He admits it was a lame excuse. But at least it was a safe one. There were more than 300,000 people expected at the concert, and the venue was a sprawling 600-acre dairy farm. As long as nobody squealed, it was a good plan.

On a rain-soaked Saturday that summer, Marvin and posse arrived at Woodstock. The concert began and was everything he hoped it would be. He was in the middle of an "endless sea of teenagers jumping around and going crazy. It was like the world's largest mosh pit." At one point, Marvin's favorite band, Primus, took the stage, which took his excitement to a whole new level. During one of their signature songs, "My Name Is Mud," the crowd burst into a spontaneous and joyous battle flinging mud around like a food fight in a school cafeteria. It was the most euphoric moment of the entire event, and one Marvin knew he would remember for a lifetime. When the song came to a close, Marvin turned around, still with an ecstatic smile on his face, only to find himself standing face to face . . . with Jackson.

"He was just staring at me in disbelief. In that moment, we both knew that I lied to him, that I abandoned him. He'd wanted to go to that concert with me and I agreed to. It was a stupid and immature choice, and one I regret to this day."

The two stood there silently for a few seconds. Then Jackson turned and walked away.

At the end of the summer, Jackson went away to college. Marvin ran into him one winter break and apologized the way he should have done at the time. "He said he forgave me. But our friendship never recovered. And I can't say that I blame him. It was such a nasty thing for me to do. I had known him for ten years, and I just threw it away.

"It's really ironic," Marvin reflects a couple of decades later. "I never really realized the value of being loyal to friends until I betrayed one."

• • •

Of all the reports parents can hear from their child about how things are going at school, few will raise their ire and outrage more than finding out their child is being bullied. And any parent whose child has been in that situation struggles with how to advise his or her young one on how to respond. Do you give the age-old wisdom that "if you stand up to bullies, they'll always back down"? Or is that ill-advised in today's more violent climate? Perhaps you should just instruct your child to go tell a teacher each time and risk the playground ridicule of being branded a tattletale.

Fortunately, after a decade of effort, most schools have significantly reduced the most overt and offensive bullying behavior. In many places, the days are gone of the schoolyard thug extorting milk money, homework papers, or test answers from the smaller kids. What's still prevalent, and probably always will be, are the unkind taunts, teases, name calling, and harassment that are harder to identify and police. How is a child to respond to that kind of mistreatment?

The best response, of course, is dependent on a number of factors. But let's look at how two youngsters responded to a tormentor on two continents and see if we can find some wisdom. We'll start with me.

Despite being a talkative know-it-all with a sarcastic sense of humor, I somehow made it all the way to the fifth grade without having what I would consider a real "enemy." But that's where my luck ran out. I had somehow become the target of ridicule of the class clown, John. For weeks, he made me the butt of his many jokes. If it had stopped there, that might have been tolerable. But his jokes spread to name calling, taunts, and teases. And since the other students admired his sharp wit, many of them soon joined in the chase. My life had become a fifth-grade version of a living hell.

One evening, I went to my father for advice. For some reason I chose the one night a week when his drinking buddies were at our house for a visit. Ironically, that turned out to be a far better choice than the sober hindsight of age would suggest.

The men listened to my dad give me the mature and reasonable advice to have a respectful talk with John, telling him how his comments made me feel, and asking him to please stop. After patiently suffering this apparent affront to masculinity, my father's best friend at the time, Jerry, interjected with this advice: "Bullshit! This is what you need to do. You get to school tomorrow morning extra early. You wait outside the school in the parking lot and wait for this 'John' to get dropped off. Once he's away from his mom and not yet buddied up with his friends, you walk right up to him, get in his face, and you say this: 'John, you and I are either going to be friends, or we're going to be enemies. And you need to decide which it's going to be, right now.'"

"Then what do I do?" I asked.

"Nothing. That's all you have to do."

"But what if he says he wants to be enemies? Or what if he wants to know what I'm going to do about it?" I complained.

"He won't," Jerry assured me. "But if he does, all you have to say is, 'I just need to know where we stand, John. Are we friends? Or are we enemies?' Then no matter what his answer is, say 'Okay' and walk away."

It sounded too easy. But all the men, including my father, seemed to think it was a good solution. So the next morning, that's exactly what I did. I waited to get John alone in the parking lot and executed my lines with the precision and seriousness of a military officer. John's reaction surprised me as much as my parking lot ambush probably surprised him. Despite his being a few inches taller and several pounds heavier, he took a step backwards. His eyes widened. And he stammered out a set of words less meaningful than the tone of voice he used to stammer them. Each of his two or three disjointed sentences contained the word "friends." But his tone was a combination of shock, fear, and shame. Our business concluded, we walked into the school together.

John never spoke an ill word of me again.

In the years since, and having two boys of my own now, I've tried to identify what it was about this response to a bully that made it work. But it wasn't until I came across two other successful examples that I saw it. Read the following stories of young Carson Brooks and see if you can spot the similarities.

Like any nine-year-old boy, when Carson was in the fourth grade he loved recess. One particular week, he found himself playing a game of tag with some other boys. But not just an open-field race to stay away from whoever was "it." This game of tag had as its venue an elaborate set of playhouses and climbing structures. In other words, this was an especially awesome game of tag!

After a few days in a row enjoying tag, one of the boys, we'll call him Jim, intercepted Carson at the beginning of recess and told him he wasn't allowed to play anymore. Apparently, Jim explained, some other player had been sick and absent from school for a few days, and Carson had only been allowed in to fill his place. "But he's back now, so you can't play anymore." And that didn't just mean today. It meant ever.

Of course, the whole decree was silly since there are no player limits in tag. And who appointed Jim as headmaster of the playhouse anyway? But that didn't matter. He had asserted himself as the leader and had the support of the other kids. Carson Brooks was out.

Carson was of course disappointed. It was a really fun game to miss out on. But more important, being excluded hurt his feelings. He wasn't just cut out of the game, but out of the friendship-building time with the other boys. At home that night, Carson's parents could tell something was wrong. When he shared his plight, Mom and Dad had an idea. They knew the boy's parents. So two weeks later, they arranged for Carson and Jim to have something of a play date at the school football stadium when there was little activity scheduled. Carson, as instructed, took Jim around the field and showed him all of his favorite places: the best seats, hiding spots, and play areas. Basically, Carson took an interest in Jim and was nice to him.

Then he asked Jim to sit down on a bench and said to him very maturely, "Hey Jim, about that thing that happened a couple of weeks ago at recess, when you said I couldn't play anymore. That really hurt me. It made me feel really bad." Not exactly the conversation Jim expected.

But Jim's response was equally mature, and probably equally surprising to Carson. He said, "Yeah, I've been thinking about that too. I've been feeling guilty about that ever since. I'm really sorry." And with that, it was over. Carson started playing tag with Jim at recess again. And these boys who had been avoiding each other for days were now at ease.

His parent's well-planned intervention worked. And Carson executed his part flawlessly. Being nice to Jim and then confronting him was the furthest thing from Carson's mind originally. But he had to admit, it did work. They were never best friends. But they did have a better relationship. And Jim never excluded Carson from any game again.

Fast forward two years, and let's see how Carson handled another experience with bullying. This one happened four thousand miles away and involved more than just a game of tag. In his sixth-grade year, Carson's family moved to Geneva, Switzerland. It was unlike any environment he'd experienced before. He was used to the conservative atmosphere of his suburban Christian school back home. At this school, the language and topics of conversation among the boys were, let's just say, worldly. And one of the worldlier of his peers was Brandon.

In addition to bad language, Brandon made a habit of slinging insults at the other boys around the locker room. Each of his targets had the pleasure of a tailor-made set of degrading comments constructed just for him. For Carson, one of his favorite barbs included "fat, stupid

American." He also enjoyed teasing Carson for his foreign accent. But the worst part was when he included Carson's mother in his slurs.

Again, Carson's parents were quick to pick up on his mood and ask what was going on. But unlike the last time, neither Mom nor Dad had any relationship with Brandon or his parents to arrange a meeting. And Carson had even less stomach for befriending this boy through kindness than he had last time. They needed a different plan. So here's what they did.

A few weeks later, on a field trip across the border in France, Carson saw his opportunity. The students were exploring a large cornfield. He waited until Brandon was separated just a bit from the other kids. Then he approached Brandon and asked if they could talk for a minute. He then led him off to the side. Perhaps not out of eyesight, but definitely out of earshot. And that's when he delivered his one and only line he'd been practicing with his dad for two weeks.

He looked Brandon straight in the eye and said calmly, but seriously, "Do we have a problem?"

"What?" was the only response an off-balance Brandon could manage.

"I said, do we have a problem?" And then Carson briefly reminded him of the locker room slurs.

Now in full backpedal, Brandon replied, "Uh . . . oh, that. No, I do that to everyone. Nothing personal, man." Then after nervously stammering out a few more retractions, Brandon finished with, "I don't have anything against you, Carson. Really. I'm sorry."

"Good," Carson responded with a tone of finality. And then he and Brandon walked back to join the other students.

Brandon never bothered Carson again.

Like the last example, this response to bullying seems simple. But also like the last one, it took practice. Carson and his father role-played the entire event several times, sometimes with Dad and sometimes with Carson playing the role of Brandon. When playing the villain, Dad challenged Carson with every potential response. "What? Why do you want to talk to me over there? Do you want to kiss me or something?" After several scenes, Carson was comfortable playing his role.

But let's look at what else these two scenarios have in common, along with the first one involving me. I would argue three key similarities. First, and most obviously, in all three cases the victim confronted the bully face to face, as opposed to leaving the situation to get better on its own or relying on adult intervention.

Second, in each case the victim addressed his tormentor with a statement or a question, not a threat. There wasn't any "if you don't stop being mean to me I'm going to . . ."

Third, and I think most important, in all three cases the victim got the bully away from his friends to have the conversation. Without any witnesses, the bully has nobody to impress and no reason to be defensive. The same confrontation, if played out in front of a cohort of friends, could easily backfire.

Hopefully your young person never has to confront this difficulty. But if he does, now you have a few responses to consider.

• • •

For most people, especially young people, hearing one person demean another is a particularly juicy piece of gossip. It's therefore one of the hardest to keep from sharing, especially from the person the insulting comments are about. They sometimes justify it by telling themselves, "I'm just being a good friend by telling her. After all, I'd want to know if someone said something mean about me, wouldn't I?"

Would you really? Consider what happened to Mandy. Mandy was a high school senior. She was bright and outgoing and had a tight group of friends she had strong relationships with. But her relationship with her mother was another story. The two fought constantly and disrespectfully, much more than the typical teenager and parent. So they'd been attending counseling together to help resolve their differences and improve their relationship.

In one of their counseling sessions, Mandy surprised the counselor, and her mother, by sharing her most recent reason for being upset. Apparently, one of her mother's best friends had spoken of her quite unkindly. "She said I was 'fat and lazy,'" Mandy insisted.

Her mother responded quickly, "I've never heard her say anything like that about you. What makes you think that?"

Mandy was vague and evasive in her response, so the counselor asked her directly, "Mandy, who told you that?"

Mandy answered defensively, "I don't have to tell you that. I don't want to get anyone in trouble. Let's just say that one of my friends overheard her saying it at school in the drop-off line, and she told me."

"Really?" her counselor asked, looking confused. "A friend of yours told you that?"

"Yes, of course. I have loyal friends. They look out for me."

The counselor's response was the last thing Mandy expected to hear. "It sounds to me," the counselor offered, "like you need better friends."

That took Mandy aback. She didn't understand it. But she could also tell there was some wisdom in it that she just didn't grasp yet. So she asked in a humble tone that suggested more genuine interest than the defensive retort one might have expected, "What do you mean, 'better friends?'"

"Mandy, I'm not excusing what that woman said about you. It was unkind and uncalled for. But she didn't hurt your feelings when she said it because she didn't say it to you. Your feelings got hurt when your friend told you about it. A good friend would protect you from hurtful things like that, not bring them to your attention."

Those words hung in the air as Mandy processed them. She'd never thought of it that way. Perhaps her friend had done her a disservice. And she's certain she's done the same thing on many occasions with her friends. She may not have made much progress in her relationship with her mother at that session. But she gained a whole new perspective on what friendship means.

• • •

So being a friend might mean not sharing hurtful comments when you hear them said of someone you care about. But what if you're in the position Mandy was in? What if you're the one on the receiving end of the hurtful comments? What can you do about that? Not long after hearing Mandy's story, I found myself in that exact situation.

A colleague of mine at work confided in me that one of my peers didn't like me. She didn't know why he didn't like me. But it was just apparent to her that he didn't. And as a student of human behavior, she was genuinely curious as to why. A few weeks later she somehow figured it out. And the next time she and I had a conversation, she was eager to share what she'd learned. She started to tell me, but in the middle of her first sentence, I interrupted her and said, "Do I really need to know this?"

She looked confused, so I explained, "Is it some deep character flaw I need to be made aware of, or something I did that I need to apologize to him for? Or is it just something about me this guy doesn't like?"

She thought about that for a moment and said, "Just something he doesn't like."

"Then if you tell me, I'm probably just going to feel bad. In which case, I think I'd rather not know."

We both smiled at what we each considered a good decision. I was happy she'd gotten her curiosity satisfied by knowing the answer. And she was happy that she didn't burden me with it. We continued our conversation about something else.

So the answer is, if you find yourself in Mandy's position, you don't have to let someone share that kind of information with you. You can ask your friend nicely to not share unless it's truly important that you know. If your friend really is a good friend, he or she will be happy to be interrupted.

• • •

We've all heard the advice "don't talk about people behind their backs." But as we just learned above, talking about them behind their backs isn't what hurts them. It's when someone shares it with them that it hurts. Right? So does that mean it's okay to talk about people behind their backs? Consider the following tale of a young military man in France, and you be the judge.

In France, young men between the ages of eighteen and twenty-two serve a mandatory twelve months in military service. So it was for a young Parisian, Henri-Jacques Letellier, when he was of age. He was assigned to Camp de la Horie, in support of the 1st combat helicopter regiment near Phalsbourg, in the northeast of France. Because he had just completed two years of medical school, he was assigned to be a medical assistant in the infirmary, alongside a dozen other young men his age.

At the time, almost all service personnel on the base were male. So it was a notable event for a woman to enter the hospital for any reason. But a few times a year, it did happen. One such occurrence turned out to be so notable that thirty years later, Henri-Jacques still remembers it like it was yesterday.

She was an average-looking woman in her forties, in for what was probably a routine checkup. Now you have to understand what it must be like for a group of young, single men confined to a military base without the company of women. It takes very little to turn the conversation to their baser instincts. And when a woman walks right into their midst . . . well, you can imagine. While she was with the doctor, the boys all traded crude comments about what she might look like undressed or the kind of things they'd like to do with her in bed, all the while having a good laugh.

As soon as she left, they noticed something was wrong. The ambiance had changed. Their boss, the administrative officer of the infirmary, seemed to have changed his mood for the worse. It didn't take long for them to find out why. Around five o'clock, quitting time, he stopped to talk to his staff on the way out. He said, "I'm leaving, boys. And by the way, I have something to tell you. I overheard you talking about one of our patients while she was with the doctor. I wanted you to know that she's my wife." And without saying another word, he turned and walked out.

A room full of guilt-stricken young men stood motionless and in silence. Their eyes exchanged glances as if to ask, "Did that really just happen? Did we really just insult our commander's wife in front of him?" They spent the next few minutes debating what to do. How could they possibly restore their relationship with him? They wondered if he would even talk to them the next day. Would there be any consequences? Would he refuse to authorize their weekend passes?

After some debate, their concern turned from themselves to the party they offended. What kind of evening would he have tonight with his wife? Would he look at her differently now? Would his thoughts linger on the distasteful way they described her? Would he tell her what he heard? Or would he suffer in silence?

The next day they tried to pretend nothing happened. It didn't work. It felt like walking on eggshells every time they passed him in the hallway. Their guilt continued to escalate. After three days, some of them couldn't take the tension any longer. They approached their boss and humbly apologized. To their relief, he accepted their apology. But he took the opportunity to remind them how hurtful their words could be, even if they never got to the person they were talking about.

The following week, the officer called the young men together. He let them know he'd noticed a change in their behavior, and he commended them on the improvement. They'd suffered long enough. So he let them in on his secret. "The truth is, that woman is not my wife."

The young men found this almost as shocking as when he first told them she was. Their first response was not believing they had fallen for the deception. He must have played his part quite well. Their second response was thinking how clever he had been to teach them such an important lesson in such a personal and memorable way. Instead of feeling duped, they were grateful he cared enough about their character to intervene. Lastly, they were relieved. While they had still insulted that woman, at least it wasn't their boss's wife.

What his revelation did not do, however, was undo the valuable lesson they all learned. It didn't matter that she wasn't his wife. She was someone's wife. And she was someone's sister. Someone's mother. And someone's daughter. And she deserved more respect than they had shown her.

After three decades, this remains perhaps the most important, and certainly most memorable, lesson Henri-Jacques learned in his military career.

TWENTY-ONE

Social Intelligence

> Social intelligence is the ability to understand and manage men and women, boys and girls—to act wisely in human relations.[1]
>
> —EDWARD THORNDIKE

Prom night is supposed to be one of the most exciting events of our lives. At least that's what Walethia Aquil thought as a senior at Northwestern High School in Flint, Michigan. Unfortunately for her, it turned out to be one of the worst.

Just a few weeks before the prom, Walethia didn't even think she'd be going. She described herself as "shy, with very little self-confidence, and not very popular." The bottom line was that nobody had asked her yet. As the date got closer and closer, conversation in the hallways turned almost exclusively to the prom: what kind of dress the other girls were going to wear, where they planned to have dinner, and whom they were going with. For Walethia, all that only served as a constant reminder that she didn't even have a date.

But then just a few days before the big night, everything changed. "A guy nobody wanted to go with asked the girl nobody wanted to take. So now, I was going to the prom." Walethia took her preparation seriously. She found a dress on sale she could afford. She styled her own hair and manicured her nails. She already had long white gloves and had a pair of shoes dyed to match her new gown. She was all ready for the prom. Or so she thought.

While she prepared well for how she should look, what she hadn't considered is that she didn't know how to behave. And that, it turns out, was a much bigger deal for Walethia. The reason? This wouldn't just be her first prom. It would be her first date. She had never been out with a boy in what most people would consider an official date over dinner or to a dance. In fact, Walethia had no recollection of ever eating in a restaurant before that night. As one of seven siblings, she explained, "We never had money to feed nine people in a restaurant."

Prom night came and Walethia remembers being excited but nervous as they sat down at the restaurant. When the waiter handed her a menu, she didn't have a clue how to read it. None of the things on it sounded like what she was used to eating at home. Eventually she saw the word "shrimp" in one menu item and at least recognized that as something she might like. So she ordered it. When the waiter delivered it, she was mortified. He laid in front of her a plate of food so enormous she was embarrassed to even be seen sitting near it. And other than the shrimp, she recognized little of what was on it.

She sat there motionless, paralyzed in self-conscious fear. She felt like every eye in the restaurant was on her. And even if she hadn't just lost her appetite or knew what food was on her plate, she didn't know which fork to use or what to do with her napkin. Looking back, she describes herself as just not having any of the social skills to navigate all this strange territory.

Walethia made it through the evening and the rest of high school. But that night left a lasting mark on her, one she would revisit on several occasions. She went on to attend Mott Community College in Flint. After her first eighteen months, she made the dean's list. But she was still shy and insecure, and she struggled with her social skills. It was that lack of social skills that eventually led her to drop out of college entirely. She hoped it had just been the school environment and the social pressures of being a teenager that were so difficult. But she found the working world no different. After taking a job at General Motors, she concluded that "people didn't like me, and I didn't like people. I was missing opportunities right and left."

It was clear the need for these skills wasn't going away. If anything, they were getting more important the older she got. Eventually she decided to attend a finishing school to develop her social skills. And that turned out to be one of her better decisions. It gave her the confidence to handle any situation in business or social settings. After many successes in her career since, she concluded there was nothing she couldn't achieve when she combined hard work with good manners, grace, charm, and poise.

But she never forgot the old Walethia and knew there were others who struggled with the same issues. And that led her to start her own business: Grace & Charm, a training firm for entrepreneurs and young executives to help make sure their personal and professional image doesn't limit their success. For eight years now, she's successfully coached business leaders, politicians, entertainers, and beauty pageant winners.

But she also never forgot that shy little girl who was terrified at her prom dinner. And as frightening as it was for her at the time, she's since learned an even more disturbing scenario that plays out every year at prom time. The social pressure and anxiety surrounding prom night has only increased in the years since Walethia was in school. Now there are kids who fly off to New York to pick out just the right dress or rent limousines and even helicopters to deliver them to their dinner destinations. At times, this has led to all kinds of unfortunate consequences. She learned from a guidance counselor at a local high school of a senior in her school she was concerned about. She was on track academically, with a promising college and working career in front of her. The only thing between her and that future was prom night and the final five months of high school. But she couldn't afford a new prom dress. Her plan to deal with that unfortunate situation? Drop out of school. Seriously. The social stigma of not going to prom, or going but wearing anything but a shiny new dress, was apparently stronger than the stigma and consequences of dropping out. If she weren't a student, there would be no pressure to go to prom. That was her solution. And apparently, this girl wasn't alone in her predicament or her solution.

Situations like that led Walethia to start another venture, but this one is a purely charitable one. As part of her venture, called My Dreams Do Come True, Walethia solicits donations of new or slightly used prom dresses and gives them away to girls in the Genesee County area who need them. But she doesn't just provide the dress. She gives the girls the whole boutique shopping experience. For most, this will be their first experience shopping for a dress. And like Walethia in that restaurant many years earlier, they wouldn't know how to handle themselves shopping for a formal gown. So she teaches them. They come in, get sized, pick out a nice dress, and even have it altered if needed. In the first three years, she's given away more than five hundred dresses to local girls, most of whom otherwise wouldn't be able to afford one. She recalls at least one in a wheelchair and one in the middle of a battle with cancer. But all of them leave with a smile.

And all this came from that one awful night she'd been trying to forget. Looking back at all she's achieved and the difference she's made in countless lives since, Walethia now reflects, "Maybe that wasn't such a terrible night after all."

Today she advises the shy and insecure and tells them they're not alone. "Reach out to a mentor, or join organizations [like hers] that provide coaching and reinforcement." As a successful entrepreneur, author of several books, and one of *Stiletto Woman* magazine's 2013 Amazing Women of the Year, Walethia is perhaps the best example of what you can achieve with a little grace and charm.

• • •

As we've just seen, sometimes social problems come from the difficulty of getting a date or of navigating it once you have one. Other times the trouble is the opposite: how to get out of one. That's the topic of our next story.

When Renée Sicina was a high school freshman in Winslow, Maine, she did what many fifteen-year-old girls do. She developed a crush on a senior. We'll call him Dave, and he was gorgeous. He was also smart, and funny, and mature, and he could drive a car. What was not to like? But he was a senior and not too interested in fifteen-year-olds. But three years later, when Renée was a senior, Dave was still in town and took an interest in her. So after three years of admiring him from afar, Renée was more than a little excited when he asked her out.

The plan for their first big date was a Saturday night movie with just the two of them, followed by a big party many of their friends were going to. But that was a few weeks away. So before then, they had time for a couple of smaller, less formal dates over lunch. These were Renée's first opportunities to meet the real Dave. But unfortunately, she didn't like the man she met.

He seemed far less mature than she expected for a twenty-one-year-old. He kept telling crude jokes and acting childish. And she learned that he'd dropped out of college and seemed satisfied with a job that lacked any challenge for him or interest for her. A few days prior to the big Saturday night date, Renée decided she wasn't interested in going out with him. But she'd never broken a date with anyone before and wasn't really sure if or how she should do it. So she did what most of us do when we're uncertain. She put it off.

Saturday afternoon came and, as planned, Renée went to her high school football game with her girlfriends. Her big date with Dave was still a few hours away. But who should walk over and sit down beside her? Dave, of course. What did Renée do? "I ignored him," she recalls. "And then when he tried to talk to me, I was curt with him. After a while he got frustrated with me and left. He just stood up and said, 'I'll call you later,' and then walked away. I remember my girlfriend saying, 'Renée, you weren't very nice to him,' and she was right. I guess I thought if I wasn't nice to him he would break our date so I wouldn't have to."

Two hours before he was to pick her up, Dave called Renée. After a few pleasantries he said, "I don't think we should go out tonight," and Renée quickly agreed. She even apologized for not breaking the date with him sooner. A moment later the call was over. Renée quickly made another phone call to her girlfriends. She still wanted to go to the party, just not with Dave.

Now you have to understand that at the time most homes only had one telephone. It was usually mounted to the wall in the kitchen, and the handset was tethered to it with a curly cord. That meant conversations were rarely private. So it shouldn't be too surprising that Renée's mother overheard both conversations.

As soon as she hung up, her mother stopped her and said, "You are not going to that party tonight. Call them back and tell them you can't go." This must have seemed as surprising to Renée as it seemed unfair. But her mom explained herself well. "That was not an appropriate way to break a date with a boy. You made a promise to go with him. It's okay to change your mind. But you should have the decency to tell him yourself. And you should have done it sooner so he could make other plans. You don't have to go to the party with him tonight. But you'll not be going with anyone else either."

Mom went on to explain that just because you don't like someone doesn't mean you should treat him unkindly. "Renée, you will always run into people you don't like. Never show it. Treat people, everyone, with the dignity and respect they deserve as human beings."

By this point, Renée's father had walked into the room and picked up on the conversation. Now it was his turn to share some wisdom. "Renée, he will forever think of you in that light. He had a very good image of you in his mind, and you destroyed it. It's a bit like how you now feel about him. You built him up in your mind in a way he didn't live up to. Now he's feeling the same about you. Only he's more justified in his disappointment."

The entire event and her parents' reaction made a lasting impression on Renée that she perhaps only fully realized years later. While walking to a meeting with her boss at work, they ran into a colleague of Renée's she didn't like. Her boss knew she didn't like him and why. But after the brief encounter in the hallway, her boss marveled at how she handled it. "That person will never know you don't like him. You said 'hello.' You asked how he was doing. And you remembered something about him and asked him about it. Most people in your situation would have just said, 'hi' and nothing more, or ignored him entirely."

Renée had indeed learned her lesson well. And through sharing her story, you can make sure others do as well.

• • •

Kids today are growing up in a much smaller world than their parents. Their schools are full of students from all over the world. Their first job will have them sitting next to coworkers from different countries. And even when they're not physically beside someone, they're likely to be virtually working or studying on a team with people from just about anywhere. So it's more important than ever to understand that social norms of behavior can and do vary widely in different places. If you shake your head left to right in most Western cultures, it means "no." Do the same thing in India and it means "yes." Misunderstand that and it can have troubling consequences.

But most differences are more subtle and difficult to pick up on. So your best defense against making the wrong assumption is to not make any assumption at all. Instead, ask. That's the lesson learned by Dorinda Phillips, whom you met already in this book. Early in her career, Dorinda was managing a young lady who constantly interrupted her. As Dorinda recalls, "Every time I tried to explain something important to her, she interrupted me. I couldn't imagine why she thought it was okay to be so rude to her boss. Did she not respect me? Was she just not interested in what I had to say? Well, I finally decided the next time it happened, I was going to say something about it. I would tell her how disrespectful it was and that I didn't appreciate it."

Of course, it didn't take long for Dorinda to have that opportunity. The next morning, the two were having a conversation, and once again Dorinda got interrupted. But instead of confronting this woman like she'd planned, some wise part of her brain told her to just ask, "I've noticed you interrupt me a lot. I'm curious. Why is that?"

The woman's response took Dorinda completely by surprise. She said, "That's because I'm so interested in what you have to say!"

"Really?" was Dorinda's incredulous reaction. "I thought it was exactly the opposite, that you weren't at all interested in what I have to say."

"Oh no, no, no! I'm from the south of Italy and that's how we show we're interested. If I just sat here and said nothing, it would mean I'm bored."

"Oh, how fascinating. I come from the north of England, and we interrupt all the time; it shows we're not interested."

Then the two ladies had a lovely discussion about their cultural differences that they've laughed about for many years since.

It turned out Dorinda's unplanned intervention was exactly the right thing to do. Instead of judging her colleague's behavior as rude and chastising her for it, she just asked, "Why do you do that?" And that's all it took to resolve the problem.

• • •

Growing up in different countries is certainly an indication that cultural differences like this might exist. But you can even find them between two people with the same background. A good example of that is what happened to Hana.

In one of Hana's early working assignments, she had a boss who apparently didn't think too much of her performance. When it came time for her annual performance review, Hana and her boss sat down. The first words out of her boss's mouth were, "You did not meet expectations this year."

"I was shocked," Hana recalls. "I'd never received that kind of feedback before. I didn't really know what to say, so I didn't say anything. I was silent."

That silence clearly offended her boss, because her next words were, "You don't care what I say, do you? You don't seem to value my opinion."

But Hana did care. Her silence was her way of processing what she heard. Accepting criticism isn't much fun, but it's one of the ways we learn. So Hana sat quietly and listened intently to everything her boss had to say. Her boss just assumed that meant Hana didn't respect her. But for Hana, it didn't mean anything of the sort. And in this case, both women grew up in the same country and culture.

Everyone is different. We tend to project on other people the lens we use to see the world. If someone insults you in no uncertain terms, you're probably well within your rights to be offended. But getting offended by the way someone talks, or doesn't talk, or the look on her face, or even the direction she shakes her head, can be surprisingly easy to misinterpret. Next time that happens to you, don't assume. Just ask.

TWENTY-TWO

Forgiveness and Gratitude

Never ruin an apology with an excuse.

—BENJAMIN FRANKLIN

In 1976, Alex Haley published his Pulitzer Prize–winning book *Roots: The Saga of an American Family*. The story chronicles the history of Haley's ancestors, starting in 1767 when an African man, Kunta Kinte, was kidnapped in Gambia, brought to the United States, and sold into slavery. A year after the book was published, it was adapted as a television miniseries that reached a record 130 million viewers. I watched the entire series from the gymnasium floor along with my entire sixth-grade class. It was brutally realistic in its depiction of life as a slave. In one particularly horrific scene, his master repeatedly whipped Kunta Kinte because he refused to accept his slave name of "Toby."

Later that school year, our class went on a field trip. I was lucky enough—or so I thought at the time—to be placed on the one and only school bus that had a radio on board. It was quite a treat to be listening to the local rock and roll station with all my friends at nine o'clock in the morning instead of sitting in class. But after a while, it got harder to hear the music over the din of the conversation. I tried several times to get the bus driver (an African American man in his forties) to turn up the volume. But I couldn't get his attention. I knew if I could shout out his name, he would probably notice my request. But I didn't know his name. So I asked the boy sitting to my right if he knew. He said with an awkward smile, "Sure. His name is Toby."

Being the naive ten-year-old that I was, I believed him. I shouted at the top of my lungs, "Hey Toby! Turn up the radio!" The radio snapped off immediately. The bus lurched to a stop as the driver abruptly pulled off the road. A hush fell over the cabin, and every eye turned to me with a harsh stare. Through the oversized rearview mirror at the front of the bus, I could see the driver glaring at me with a look of anger and disgust I'd never seen in my short life.

I knew immediately I'd done something terribly wrong. But I had no idea what it was. All I could come up with was that perhaps I hadn't asked nicely enough. So with as pleasant a tone as I could muster, I asked again, "Toby . . . would you please turn up the radio?"

The driver's glare intensified. A few muffled gasps filled the otherwise painful silence. I frantically searched the faces of my classmates for help and support, but mostly for an explanation. None of them held any answers, only the same damning and horrified expression. None of them, that is, except for one: the boy sitting immediately to my right. His face had a mischievously satisfied smile that gave me the answer I was looking for.

I knew in an instant I had been duped. The driver's name wasn't really Toby. A sickening feeling hit the pit of my stomach as I realized what a horrible thing I had just done. How humiliating must it have been for that driver to have a ten-year-old boy disrespect him in such a degrading manner in front of a bus full of children? And then for that boy to unapologetically repeat the insult a second time! It was the first time in my life that I truly knew what it felt like to be ashamed.

When we arrived at our destination, I slithered off the bus without saying a word. I was too embarrassed and immature to even make eye contact with the driver, much less apologize to him. I called my mother from a pay phone and begged her to come pick me up at the end of the day so I wouldn't have to ride the same bus back to school.

I suppose I learned three lessons that day. First, from the unforgettable pain I saw in my bus driver's eyes, I learned to appreciate a little of what it must have been like to be an African American man in a small southern town in the 1970s. Second, as a result of what I said, I learned how easy it could be to offend someone if you're not careful. But third, and perhaps most important, as a result of what I did *not* say, I learned the importance of admitting your mistakes early and apologizing for them. How much better it would have been for me (and the driver) if I'd had just the courage to say, "I'm sorry."

• • •

In some cases, like the one above, the person you've offended may be someone you've never met before and will never see again. That doesn't make your offense any less offensive. You just might not be awkwardly reminded of your transgression every day. But what if the person you offend is someone you go to school or work with? That trickier situation is exactly what happened to Steve Blair, the Fleetridge Elementary student from Raytown, Missouri, you met in chapter 7.

When Steve was in the third grade he did something he's regretted for the thirty-five years since. What was his unforgettable and unpardonable sin? He wrote a poem. A very bad poem.

Steve's class had been learning the rhyme and meter of several forms of poetry. One particular week they learned about limericks—a five-line poem in anapestic meter with an unmistakable rhyming pattern. Each student was expected to write his or her own original limerick to demonstrate an understanding of the form and then read it aloud to the class. Steve wasn't much of a class clown. But he was particularly pleased with his poem because, at least in his mind, it was exceedingly funny. And he assumed everyone else would think so as well. When it was his turn, he proudly read the following to the class:

Sally Strobe
Was as fat as a globe
She was so fat
She had a flat
And that was the end of Sally Strobe

Steve finished his limerick and waited with a wide smile for the expected howls of laughter. He got none. Nor did he get the compulsory applause the other students got for even the lamest verse. Even at the age of eight, Steve recognized the unmistakable look of disgust and confusion on the faces of his fellow classmates and his teacher as he panned the room with his eyes. The object of his derision, fellow classmate Sally Strobe (not her real name), struggled with her weight most of her life, both before and since. Steve had just added himself to a long list of tormentors. At the tender age of eight, it never occurred to Steve that his words might offend. It was the first time in his life he remembers being painfully aware that his words had hurt someone.

Steve avoided Sally for the following weeks, surely out of embarrassment. And as many children (and adults) do, he just pretended nothing had ever happened, hoping she'd forget about it. What he didn't count on, however, was that he would be the one who wouldn't be able to forget.

Today, at the age of forty-two, not a month goes by that Steve's thoughts don't drift back to third grade and to Sally Strobe. He relives that awful moment he first uttered his hurtful limerick, his heart still filled with remorse. It's not a debilitating regret that consumes him daily. But in thirty-five years, he's suffered countless times for that one single unresolved transgression. Imagine how much pain and anguish Steve could have saved himself if he'd just apologized to her and put the entire incident behind him. Oh, his teacher made him give the obligatory "I'm sorry" immediately after the poetry reading. But that's different from a genuine, heartfelt apology from someone who really understands what he's done wrong. And the longer he went without giving a true apology, the harder it got to even consider.

Three decades later, in the Internet age of social media, he came across Sally's name on Facebook. He thought about contacting her and asking forgiveness. But doubt set in. "Would this just open up a wound that had long since closed? Would she think it self-serving of me to apologize after all these years, perhaps just to clear my conscience?" So he didn't. And so the thorn remains.

Steve learned two valuable lessons from this experience. The first was this: Despite what you may have heard about "sticks and stones," words can hurt people. To this day, it would be a rare occasion to find Steve saying anything ill of another person. His second lesson was the value of asking forgiveness. Without it, not only does the pain of an offense remain with the victim, but it continues to fester in the perpetrator as well. And the longer one goes without apologizing, the harder it is to do. Resolve to forgive early and often, and you'll never have to suffer decades of remorse, no matter how bad your poem was.

• • •

Skeptical that asking forgiveness can be effective after too many years? Think maybe it's too late for Steve? After all this time, perhaps he's just better off letting it go and not opening up old wounds, right? Perhaps. But that's not the decision Phil made after twenty-five years of guilt. See how it turned out for him, then you be the judge.

Phil spent his elementary school years in New Orleans, Louisiana. At the age of five he met a classmate who would become his best friend for most of those elementary years. We'll call him Doug. Phil and Doug spent much of their time together as best friends will do. Until fifth grade, that is. That year—and for reasons that Phil can't even remember—he decided he didn't want to be friends with Doug anymore. But he had no idea how to break that kind of news to another ten-year-old boy. So he didn't. He just stopped being friends with him, which means he just stopped talking to Doug. He stopped talking to him in class. He stopped talking to him on the playground. He stopped returning his phone calls at home. He just stopped. No conversation. No explanation.

To Phil, it must have seemed the quicker and less painful method for both boys. But to Doug, it surely felt like a cruel and inhumane thing to do. But since he wasn't talking to Doug, Phil didn't really know that, until Doug stopped showing up at school. Phil learned that Doug's parents had taken him out of school and registered him at another nearby elementary school. And while Phil couldn't be sure at the time, his suspicion was correct. That move was a caring act by Doug's parents to protect him from the daily torment of a best friend who wouldn't even face him at school.

As happens with children, both boys grew up and went their own way in the world. Phil ended up in Tennessee and Doug in North Carolina.

"For years," Phil recalls as he fights back tears, "I was haunted by the memory of what I'd done. I ached knowing I was responsible for such a cruel act." Then, as with Steve in our previous story, social media happened. By the year 2008, Phil had already connected with several old elementary and high school friends on Facebook. And occasionally the thought would enter his mind that eventually he and Doug would cross paths. "I was dreading that day. But oddly looking forward to it at the same time," he admits.

And then one day it happened. Doug showed up in a list following the words "You may know these people."

"I saw his name and my heart stopped. I knew this was my moment to make this all right." But before he did that, Phil decided there was one thing he needed to do first. By this time he had two children of his own, not too far from the age he was when he committed his transgression. "I went downstairs for dinner and I told my kids, 'I have a story to tell you.'" And he proceeded to tell them everything: about his friendship, the cruel way he ended it, the two and a half decades of guilt and regret and shame he'd been carrying with him, and finally the opportunity that just dropped in his lap to reconnect with Doug.

"My kids looked completely drained of color. One of them asked me, 'Daddy, why would you do something like that?' And I had to tell them I didn't know. Then they wanted to know if it was all okay with Doug now. And I had to tell them I didn't know that either, because I hadn't contacted him yet. I wanted to tell them about it first. I wanted them to watch me go through with something I should have done twenty-five years ago. I wanted them to see their father struggle a little with his guilt and his shame, and then to see me do the right thing. And I could see they were disappointed in me, which was understandable. I was disappointed in myself."

The next morning, Phil sent a friend request to Doug. In it he said, "I'd like to talk to you about some things I've carried with me for years."

Phil admits to not getting much work done that day, preoccupied with wondering what response he would get. When his kids came home from school the first thing they asked was, "Well, what did he say? Is he your friend again?"

But all Phil could tell them was, "I don't know yet. He hasn't responded."

That of course set off a chain of speculation on their part about why. "Maybe he hates you and doesn't want to talk to you." Perhaps. They would all have to wait to find out. It was a cliffhanger for everyone. On the following day, the suspense was broken. Doug responded, accepting Phil's friend request along with a message that said he was excited to connect after all these years. The two men traded several messages that day that surely included the requisite small talk about family life and careers. But Phil quickly got to the point: his apology. And it wasn't the kind of wishy-washy nonapology a bigger ego might have offered, like "I don't know if you remember, blah, blah, blah . . . but if anything I did offended you way back then, I guess I'm sorry." It was a full-on, no-holds-barred apology: "Doug, I was so very wrong for the way I treated you in the fifth grade. And I am truly sorry. Would you please forgive me?"

Much to Phil's relief, Doug accepted his apology. And he went on to try to shoulder some of the blame. "Phil, we were just kids," he said. "And you know, I was kind of a nerd anyway. I guess I maybe brought some of that on myself."

But Phil knew better and wouldn't let that pass unchallenged. "No, Doug. You didn't deserve any of that. It was my fault. I'm to blame."

And with Doug's blessing, Phil felt a twenty-five-year burden lifted from his shoulders. "It was the most cleansing and freeing thing I've ever felt." He didn't know whether he should cry or shout for joy. But he did know what he had to do next. When his kids got home from school he told them everything that happened. "I'll never forget the look on my kids' faces when I told them. Their disappointment was gone. And I could tell they respected me even more."

It's ironic really, that something as vulnerable and humbling as asking for forgiveness can give you so much energy and strength, even after twenty-five years.

• • •

When psychologists study human character strengths, they tend to study gratitude and forgiveness in isolation from all the other strengths.[1] They appear to be more highly related than the others, and actually build on each other. It turns out grateful people are less likely to respond with anger after being hurt by others, and less angry people are more likely to extend forgiveness. With that, let's turn our attention for the final story in this chapter to gratitude.

"It's better to give than to receive" is an oft-quoted platitude. But the relationship between giving and receiving is a little like that between a leader and a follower. Before you can be an effective leader, you have to learn to be a good follower. So it is with giving. You'll be a more caring, generous, and humble giver once you learn to be a gracious receiver. That's the hard lesson Don Carter learned one Thanksgiving week several years ago.

Don had been the pastor at the First Baptist Church in Eureka Springs, Arkansas, for four years. During that time he worked with a number of local charities and mission groups to bring food and clothes to the needy, some of whom were parishioners in his church. Shortly after he left that position, and just a few days prior to Thanksgiving, Don got a call from Jim, the head of the Passion Play organization, with a request similar to many he'd received before. "Don, can you come down here sometime today? We've got something for you."

Don arrived later that day, and one of the staffers asked him to help load some supplies into Don's car, a dozen or more bags of food and clothing. New clothes, mind you, not used—some for men, some for women, and some for children. And the food included an entire turkey and several bags of canned food. In all, it barely fit into Don's roomy Dodge Caravan.

When the last one was in, Don went into Jim's office and told him, "Okay, it's all loaded. Where do you want me to deliver all this?"

"Huh? No, you don't understand, Don. All that's for you."

In a tone somewhere between confusion and disbelief, Don could only stammer out, "What?"

"Yeah," Jim replied. "We heard things were hard at home right now. So we got it for you."

"But Jim, I didn't know I was needy."

"Don, just take it as a gift and a blessing," Jim told him. And with that, Jim went back to work.

Don piled in his now cramped car for the four-mile drive home, still reeling with confusion. But that quickly faded as he processed what was going on. "They think I'm poor and can't take care of myself," Don thought. Somebody was treating Don Carter, a man who'd spent his life giving to the less fortunate and leading mission trips and community outreach, like he needed a handout. "It made me almost mad," he explained.

When he got home and walked in the door with the first bag, his wife, Lesa, noticed the look on his face. "What's wrong with you?" she asked.

"I need your help unloading the car. I can't even talk about it right now."

As they unloaded bag after bag, Don took stock of the generosity of the gift. "What are we supposed to do with all this stuff?" he wondered. He told his wife where it came from, that someone heard they needed it and just gave it to him. Then, perhaps for different reasons, Don and his wife hung their heads at the kitchen table and wept.

He would later realize that those gifts carried his family not just through Thanksgiving, but through the entire winter. Lesa tried to get him to write a thank-you note to Jim right away. But he couldn't bring himself to do it. He hadn't asked for any of this stuff. But whether he could admit it or not, the truth was that they did need it. Don had quit his job as pastor of the church four or five months earlier and hadn't found a full-time position yet. In the meantime, he was doing a little part-time electrical work with a friend to make ends meet. And Lesa had some part-time hours at a day care facility. But even combined, that wasn't bringing in enough to support his family of four. At one point Don even took a job washing dishes at a local restaurant.

About two weeks after Thanksgiving, Don was finally able to overcome his pride and send a thank-you card. "Gratitude was a hard lesson for me to learn," he explained. "That experience taught me that gratitude is a heart condition, not a need-based thing." Whether he needed it or not was not really the issue. Being able to accept the gift with grace, dignity, and gratefulness was a matter of choice, not a matter of meeting some financial criteria.

Don moved on to other full-time pastor and ministry jobs soon after. But how did that experience affect his ability to be generous? "It changed my attitude for how to help other people because I know what it's like to be on the receiving end of giving.

"Plus now it's even more joyful for me to give to other people. Because I know firsthand what a difference it can make in their lives."

TWENTY-THREE

Appreciation of Beauty

> Everything has beauty, but not everyone sees it.
>
> —CONFUCIUS

Peter learned a lifelong lesson about appreciating beauty in arguably one of the most beautiful places on earth—Rocky Mountain National Park, outside Boulder, Colorado. Perhaps not too surprising a place to learn a lesson about beauty. But the way he learned the lesson was far less expected: he forgot his camera.

Peter visited the park the summer before his senior year of high school as part of a two-week church trip. On one of those days, their agenda was a full-day hike to Bear Lake, one of the most popular locations in the park. They left their campsite first thing in the morning and wouldn't return until 4 p.m. About one hour into the hike, Peter realized he'd left his camera in the tent. "I was crushed," he said. Of all the days to forget his camera, he had to pick the day of the hike to Bear Lake?

When they arrived at the lake, all the other kids began madly taking pictures of the amazing vistas. All Peter could do was watch. This was before the days of digital cameras, so it wasn't like his friends could easily send him copies of their pictures. He simply wasn't going to have pictures today. So he decided to try something else, something amazing as it turned out. He sat down, faced out across the lake to the stunning mountain peaks on the opposite side, and just stared. One minute, two minutes, three minutes. Just stared. Then he closed his eyes and tried to remember what he was just looking at. He couldn't remember enough detail. So he opened his eyes again. Four minutes, five minutes. Then he closed his eyes again. He did this until he could see in his mind's eye every jagged cliff, every snow-capped peak, the timberline where the trees stop growing and the barren rock begins, even the shadows of the clouds as they drifted across the side of the mountain.

Thirty years later, Peter still has wonderful memories of that entire two-week trip. And he has hundreds of pictures he can show you if you have time for him to dig them out of a closet somewhere. But there's only one scene—one amazingly beautiful scene—he can describe to you in breathtaking detail. And it's Bear Lake. The only place in Rocky Mountain National Park he doesn't have a single picture of.

To truly appreciate something of beauty requires the one thing we seem to have less and less of these days: focused attention. In a typical vacation, we're so rushed to snap photos of every possible thing of interest that we fail to actually take interest in the things we've rushed to see. What Peter learned through that experience is the value of truly being in the moment. Stop. Truly see what you came to see. If you do it right, you won't need pictures anyway.

• • •

On January 12, 2007, at 7:51 a.m., Joshua Bell walked into the Washington, D.C., subway at L'Enfant Plaza Station and set up his music stand. Like dozens of other street and subway performers in D.C., he opened his instrument case and seeded it with a few dollar bills and change, hoping to encourage passersby to throw money in. Then he picked up his violin and he began to play. His first piece was the Chaconne from Johann Sebastian Bach's Partita No. 2 in D Minor. In the course of forty-three minutes, he played a total of six classical violin pieces he knew well.

More than a thousand people walked by during those forty-three minutes. Only seven of them stopped for any measurable time to listen.

Twenty-seven dropped money in his case (that's less than 3 percent). And not one person applauded. He left with just over $32 in small bills and change.[1]

This scene is hardly unique. It's played out at street corners and subway stations around the world countless times a day. And it wouldn't be noteworthy here except for these facts. Joshua Bell isn't an out-of-work musician. He's an internationally renowned concert violinist. His instrument is a $3.5 million, eighteenth-century Stradivarius. And just three days prior to his subway performance, he played to a sold-out crowd at Boston's Symphony Hall, most of whom shelled out an average of $100 or more for the privilege of hearing him play.

There are probably many lessons to learn from this event. Some have criticized the D.C. subway patrons for their astonishing lack of appreciation for fine music. But I think that's unfair. Most were busy commuters on their way to work, without the time to stop and listen no matter who the performer was. I believe the more important lesson is this: Appreciation is better understood not as a noun, but as a verb—to appreciate. It's an active choice we make to do something. It's possible that at least one of those busy commuters who walked hastily by Joshua Bell that morning in the subway also sat in Symphony Hall three days earlier enjoying every note of his performance.

Appreciation of beauty isn't some rare thing that some people "possess" and other people do not. It's something some people *do* and other people *do not.* I find that encouraging. That means we can all have an appreciation for Joshua Bell's music, or anything else for that matter. We're each in control of what we choose to appreciate and when. One thing I take away from the story above, however, is that we could probably all make a choice to do that a little more often than we do.

• • •

In the Joshua Bell experiment above, we learned to let ourselves appreciate beauty when we find ourselves in its presence. In the story below, we learn the role we can play in letting other people appreciate beauty they encounter, as well as how fleeting that beauty can be.

Bob Woolley (the aspiring astronaut you met in chapter 1) had been running his Astronomical Adventures program in Arizona for several years. He gave tours of the Grand Canyon and other sites during the day, and at night his guests enjoyed tours of the night sky with his massive homemade telescopes.

On one particular tour, Bob and his guests had just arrived at their first stop at the Grand Canyon. Unlike other tours that simply show their guests the canyon or offer them mule rides to the bottom, Bob takes his guests on an awe-inspiring scientific journey spanning four billion years. With the deftness of a professional storyteller, Bob explains the original formation of Earth and its many layers over the eons. He then tells how over several million years, the Colorado River cut a mile-deep and ten-mile-wide canyon through the Arizona plains. Looking out at the canyon, his guests saw each layer as Bob described what Earth was like when that particular layer was at the surface and active with life. He described what the plants and animals looked like at the time and if they would have been standing on solid ground or buried beneath miles of ocean water.

Then, in the middle of this fascinating story, one of Bob's guests blurted out, "Look! A hawk!" as she pointed excitedly to the sky over Bob's shoulder. Like a Broadway actor's speech stopped in mid-sentence by an unsilenced cell phone, his performance screeched to a halt. His whole audience turned their attention to the hawk gracefully soaring over the canyon.

Frustrated at such a rude interruption to his well-rehearsed routine, Bob barked at her, "Hey, are you more interested in a hawk or in the Grand Canyon?" Her smile and elation vanished as quickly as they had appeared. Embarrassed and humiliated, this grown woman started to cry. Bob continued his scientific discussion, but with a gloomy pall hanging overhead. Afterwards, it became clear that some of the other guests were upset with Bob for mistreating her. Once he took a few minutes to digest that, he realized the mistake he'd made. Bob had seen lots of red-tailed hawks. But she hadn't. His even more interesting insight was this: Bob was thinking that she could see a hawk in lots of places, but you can only see the Grand Canyon at the Grand Canyon. What he realized was that the beauty of the hawk was fleeting. It would only be there for an instant. Thirty seconds later, those rocks would still be there.

The whole ordeal made him rethink his priorities for appreciating beauty. Sometimes the thing that you should pay attention to is the thing that won't be there a moment later. It's worth the distraction. Like that moment just after sunset when the entire western sky turns a deep reddish-orange, just moments before the gray dusk consumes it. Or the butterfly that lands on your shoulder to say hello and then flits away. Or the look of joy and wonder in your child's eyes right after saying, "Daddy, look what I did!" But if you look five seconds later, all you'll hear is, "Aw, you missed it."

Bob ended up apologizing to the woman. Looking back, what he might rather have done is thank her for the countless fleeting things of beauty he hasn't missed ever since.

TWENTY-FOUR

Getting Started

> The goal isn't to leave a better world for your kids, it's to leave better kids for the world.
>
> —SALMAN KHAN

You've reached the end of this book, but hopefully only the beginning of an exciting and fruitful journey with your young person. As mentioned in the Introduction, if all you do is read this book, much of its value will be lost. To put it to good use, you have to share these stories with the people you care about and talk to them about each one. Hopefully you've already downloaded the free discussion guide (www.leadwithastory.com/resources) and started to put it to use.

To help you get off to a productive start, this final chapter will address the three biggest barriers most people have to putting stories to better use.

BARRIER #1: I DON'T HAVE ANY GOOD STORIES TO TELL

This is by far the biggest barrier most of us have to using stories more often. Fortunately, if you're reading this, you already have it largely solved. You have 101 stories in your hands right now ready to share. The appendix includes a story matrix that lists all 101 stories in this book by topic to help you find exactly the right story when you need it. And there are books listed in the Additional Reading section where you can find others. But you'll want more. So let's look at two other productive places to find them.

Stories from Your Past

Yes, there are great stories lurking in your own past; you just may not know it. When I asked people to be interviewed for this book, the most common response I got was, "Sure, I'd be happy to. But I don't really have any good stories. My life isn't that exciting." And if that were true as often as I heard it, I would have never been able to complete this book. But fortunately, it turns out, that was never true. Never. Read this closely: Every single person I interviewed had at least one compelling story inside. And most people had several. I'm only disappointed I couldn't fit all of them in the book. But many of them didn't know they had such great stories because they'd never been asked (or asked themselves) the right questions to uncover them.

What I learned through interviewing hundreds of people over the past several years is that you don't find people's best stories by asking them to tell you their best stories. That's because we don't think of the most inspiring, insightful, and meaningful moments in our lives as "stories." We think of them as events. This became clear to me after one of my early interviews. I'd sent a draft of a story I'd written to the person interviewed, and the response was, "Oh, I didn't know that's the kind of thing you were looking for. That's not really a story. That's just something that happened to me." Exactly. And once you write it down or tell it to someone, it becomes a story.

So it turns out that the best way to unearth those events is to ask questions about specific moments in life. Below are the questions I found most productive during the research for this book. Ask yourself these questions and you're certain to come up with powerful stories of your own to share.

1. Tell me about a time in your life when you learned an important but completely unexpected lesson, or learned it in an unexpected way.
2. What's the biggest mistake you've ever made? Why?
3. What have been your biggest regrets thus far in life? Think of one thing you did and wish you hadn't, and one thing you didn't do and wish you had.
4. What are three of the smartest decisions you've ever made?
5. Describe a vivid memory you have as a child where you felt terrible about how you made someone else feel.
6. Describe a time when you faced someone or something you were truly afraid of. How did it turn out?
7. Can you remember a time as a child when you did something you had been told not to do and you did it anyway? How did it turn out? Do you wish you had obeyed and hadn't done it? Or are you glad you did it anyway?
8. Tell me about a time in your life when you learned a hard lesson about the value of __________. Then fill in the blank with a topic of interest. For example, see the list of chapter titles for this book.

The only two questions I found useful that used the word "story" were the two below. The reason I think they worked is because they weren't vaguely asking for someone's "best stories," which can be wide open for interpretation. (Would that be my favorite stories? The ones other people like to hear the most? The most effective ones? The funniest ones?) They ask for specific stories most of us can identify as soon as the question is asked.

9. What stories do you find yourself telling over and over again as an adult to teach someone a lesson?
10. What stories do you remember hearing as a child that taught you so valuable a lesson you still remember them to this day?

Stories Other People Tell

The richest source of stories you'll ever have are the stories you hear other people tell. There's only one of you, but there are about seven billion other people on the planet. You can have an endless supply of great stories just by paying attention to the stories you hear from others. When you hear a great story with an insightful lesson, instead of just enjoying it and letting it pass from your consciousness, make note of it. Maybe even write it down. Then think of when you might use it. Who in your life could benefit from hearing it, and when might they need to hear it?

But you don't have to wait to hear great stories from other people. You can go in search of them. Identify a few people in your life and interview them using the same questions you asked yourself above. Your parents, grandparents, aunts, and uncles are wonderful sources of wisdom and life lessons. They've had more time to earn successes and make mistakes.

BARRIER #2: I'M NOT SURE WHEN TO TELL THESE STORIES

When our parents and grandparents were children, families sat around the dinner table and told stories. It was just part of their daily routine. Not many of us do that today. Our kids have overscheduled lives outside the home and a team of electronics fighting for their attention for the little time they spend inside the home. We've lost the most traditional venue for storytelling. So it's natural to wonder when exactly we are supposed to be sharing all these tales of wisdom.

You have several options. First, you can always do yourself and your young ones a favor and reinstate the dinner storytelling routine. Author Rachel Naomi Remen observes in her book *Kitchen Table Wisdom*, "The less time we spend together at the kitchen table, the more how-to [self-help] books appear in stores and on bookshelves."[1] Once my nine-year-old Ben found out I had a stash of stories, he started asking me to tell one every night at dinner. Try it. You'll be amazed how quickly they come to appreciate it and yearn for more.

For younger kids, bedtime is still a great time for stories. Bedtime stories don't have to be the kind you read from a children's book with illustrated pictures.

But I believe the best time to share stories like these isn't at a scheduled time and place. It's more opportunistically, the moment they're needed. In her book *Bringing the Story Home*, Lisa Lipkin recalls, "When my father told me his most affecting stories, they weren't during 'story hour.' They were while he was opening a can of peas or changing a light bulb."[2] It's that moment when the need for it arises naturally in the course of your parenting. In fact, I'm of the mind that if you have to say, "Sit down and be quiet and listen. I'm going to tell you a story now," you're probably doing it wrong.

BARRIER #3:
I DON'T KNOW HOW TO TELL STORIES VERY WELL

First of all, relax. You're not filming a Hollywood movie. Your kids don't care if you flub your lines. You're just telling a story to people who love you. You're also not expected to "perform" these stories like a professional storyteller jumping around on stage and taking on voices for each character. The best advice I can give you is to just tell these stories to your children like you were talking to your best friend. If you do it right, someday they will be.

The most common question I get about how to tell stories is about how to memorize them. And my answer is simple. Don't. It's too hard to do, and nobody wants to hear a story that sounds like it's been memorized, especially your kids. And for the same reason, reading the story directly from the book isn't the best idea either.

In her book *The Parent's Guide to Storytelling,*[3] Margaret Read MacDonald suggests that when you find a story you want to tell, read through it two or three times to yourself until you understand generally what happens. Then imagine that it actually happened just down the street and you were an eyewitness to the whole thing. Now go tell someone what happened. If you do it that way, it won't sound like a story you read in a book. You'll have made the story your own.

Also, when you do it that way, you'll instinctively tell the story in language that's appropriate for the age and background of your listener. If you're telling your five-year-old daughter, you should be using smaller words and simpler sentence structures than if you're telling your eighteen-year-old nephew. You naturally do that when talking to those two very different people. Your storytelling should work the same.

For more advice on how to craft your own stories, see my first book, *Lead with a Story: A Guide to Crafting Business Narratives that Captivate, Convince and Inspire.*[4] It has detailed chapters on proper use of story structure, emotion, metaphors, surprise, realism, style of prose, and even creating events for your audience to participate in.

To illustrate what this all might look like in practice, consider the following example of a parent overcoming all three of these barriers by (1) having exactly the right story, (2) sharing it at exactly the right time, and (3) doing so in an enormously effective way. That parent just happens to be my father. And the child he was sharing it with was me when I was still a month shy of my forty-sixth birthday.

I'd recently found myself struggling with the toughest career decision of my life. I was trying to choose between two very different options. One was to stay in my current job, which provided lots of reliable income and benefits, but it wasn't work I was unusually excited about doing. The other option was to become a full-time writer and speaker, something I was truly passionate about, but that provided no long-term financial security and no steady paycheck.

I figure you're never too old to benefit from someone older and wiser. So I wrote my eighty-year-old father a letter and asked him what I should do. But instead of just giving me advice, he shared a story about himself as a young boy that I'd never heard before. His letter said:

> Son, when I was 5 or 6 years old I knew exactly what I wanted to do when I grew up. I wanted to be a singer—yeah, a singer—like Bing Crosby, Frank Sinatra, or Tony Bennett. My mother always had the radio on listening to all the popular music of the day, and I listened. And I just knew that's what I wanted to do.

By the time I started 1st grade I knew all the popular songs—words and music by heart. About the 2nd or 3rd week of school the teacher asked if anyone in the class had some talent like dancing or singing or doing magic tricks—things like that. Well, I put up my hand and said I could sing. So she asked if I would sing a song for the class. Despite the fact that I'd never sung in front of anyone except my mother, I said yes. I picked my favorite song, and I did it. I sang the whole song—all the right words and melody. I still remember the song. It was "I Don't Want to Set the World on Fire" by the Ink Spots.

When I was done, the teacher and students applauded. And that's when I was certain that's what I was destined to do with my life.

Well, that turned out to not only be the first time, but also the last time I ever sang in front of an audience. Life got in the way. But it really remained my dream for the rest of my life. I just never had the courage to pursue it. One day, son, you'll wake up and be 80 years old like me, and it will be too late.

And as if that story by itself wasn't enough to motivate me, my father closed the letter with two sentences that literally took my breath away and changed my life. He said:

I'd love to see you pursue your dream. But that doesn't mean in *your* lifetime, son—that means in mine.

Love, Dad

Those words hit me like an unexpected kick in the head. Everything stopped except for my heart, which was now beating out of my chest and loud enough to hear. I read his words again. "Did he say what I think he just said?" Yes, he did. My father had laid down the gauntlet in front of me and challenged me to pick up. Not sometime in the future, many years down the road. But right now.

It was like that scene in the movie *Rocky II*, where Adrian tells Rocky to "Win!" The theme music starts with a loud orchestra hit. And Rocky starts the most inspirational workout in cinematic history. Except in my scene, I'm Rocky, and this isn't a movie. It's real life.

More important, my dream was no longer just my dream. It was now my father's dream too. At this point, he'll probably never achieve his dream of being a professional singer. But through me, if I have the courage to go through with it, he can enjoy the closure he never had with his own dream. I can think of no more inspiring and worthy challenge. And I find it poetically ironic that the man who in 1967 gave me life would forty-six years later give me the courage to truly live it.

I hope you get something out of my father's letter too. Many of us harbor a secret dream we're too afraid to pursue. And as long as we are the only one we're disappointing, I suppose that might be okay. But we all probably have someone in our lives we care about who also wants to see us pursue our dreams. That might be a parent, sibling, spouse, friend, coworker, or child.

Whoever that is for you, if you won't pursue your dream for your own sake, do it for him or her. You'll make two people happy in the process.

Oh, by the way, the week after reading those words from my father, I walked into my boss's office and resigned from my twenty-year career to pursue my dream.

Thanks Dad—for giving me that courage, and for showing me you're never too old to benefit from parenting with a story.

An Invitation

Congratulations! You've taken your first step to sharing wisdom through story and helping your young person develop life's most important character traits. But there's much more to explore. Visit me at www.leadwithastory.com and continue the journey. There you can sign up for my newsletter and podcasts to get a regular dose of wisdom stories.

But I'd love to hear your stories as well. If you have a story you'd like to share, or just want to tell me what you think of the book, email me at paul@leadwithastory.com. Who knows? Your story or comments might make it into a podcast or my next book!

Most important, if you like what you read in this book and think the world would be a better place if more people read it, here's what you can do to help spread the word, and the stories, to others:

- *Write a review on Amazon or another online bookseller.* People want to read a book other people like.
- *Tell your friends.* Post something about it on your Facebook, blog, Twitter, etc. Or just tell your friends about it at work. It's still okay to just talk to people.

I also invite you to follow me on social media for the latest news, events, and stories.

Facebook: www.facebook.com/LeadWithAStory
Twitter: @LeadWithAStory
LinkedIn: http://www.linkedin.com/in/smithpa9

Lastly, if you liked these stories for your personal life, you might like my book of leadership lessons for your work life, called *Lead with a Story: A Guide to Crafting Business Narratives that Captivate, Convince, and Inspire*. When you've got great stories for home and work, there's no limit to the difference you can make in the world.

APPENDIX

Story Matrix

FIND JUST THE RIGHT STORY WHEN YOU NEED IT

Chapter	Story #	Instead of saying something like this:	Share this story:	Page
Introduction	1	Stand up to peer pressure	Eating the quiche	1
		Part 1: Who You Are		
1) Ambition	2	Set lofty goals	On becoming an astronaut	11
	3	Never settle for "good enough"	National Merit scholar picks local college	14
	4	Be a big fish in a small pond	Better to be the head of a dog than the tail of a lion	15
	5	Define success your way	Best Crash in the Pinewood Derby	16
	6	Let go of unworthy goals	Letting go of the status and the suit	18
2) Open-Mindedness	7	Maybe you're wrong	Women's voices in the men's room	20
	8	See things from a different angle	Solving the matrix... horizontally	22
	9	There's a good reason for most things	The Japanese maple tree	24

Chapter	Story #	Instead of saying something like this:	Share this story:	Page
	10	First, assume there's a good reason. Then find it.	Wrestling coach out of her seat?	26
3) Creativity	11	See what isn't there, but could be	"Michael, what do you see?"	28
	12	Don't spend your time in noncreative ways	No toys with batteries	30
	13	Creativity needs room to play	James and the tea kettle	31
4) Curiosity and Learning	14	The joy of discovery leads to curiosity	Boy Scouts finding the dry wood	33
	15	We go toward our focus, for good or bad	"Don't hit the flagpole!"	35
	16	What does success in school look like?	Scouting vs. theater, and valedictorian vs. choir	37
	17	College opens up opportunities	Leaving Negros for college: Fifty years later	38
	18	Don't stress too much over choosing a major	"I started as a geneticist. Now I'm an artist."	41
5) Courage	19	Join the team. What do you have to lose?	Not joining the softball team	43
	20	Don't let opportunities pass you by	Passing on the basket of oranges	45
	21	It's okay to go alone	Going to *Les Mis* all by myself!	46
	22	Stand up for what you believe in	Staying in Austria	47
	23	Go for it, and don't look back	Beating Matt Cooper	49
	24	If you can't be brave, at least be smart	Standing up without getting your nose broken	52

Chapter	Story #	Instead of saying something like this:	Share this story:	Page
6) Integrity	25	Don't bear false witness against your neighbor	"She put the peanut in my nose!"	55
	26	No stealing	Taking the Teenage Mutant Ninja Turtle	56
	27	Keep your word	The long division contract	59
	28	Stand by your con-victions	How Larry Bird picked his agent	61
7) Self-Reliance	29	Don't just stand there. Do something about it. (Part 1)	The Steve Blair sidewalk	64
	30	Don't just stand there. Do something about it. (Part 2)	Free Wheelchair Mission	66
	31	Have you tried everything you can think of?	Paying for Ritvik's leukemia treatment	69
	32	You miss every shot you don't take	The only applicant getting the intern-ship	71
8) Grit	33	Never give up, even after repeated failure	Persistence to be president	74
	34	Practice, practice, practice	Learning the kip	76
	35	Focus on the current task	Losing the wrestling tournament	78
	36	Perfectionism makes you give up too soon	Quitting the team before tryouts end	80
9) Hard Work and Struggles in Life	37	Take pride in your work	Ahmad the caddie	83
	38	If you're going to work, look like you're working	"Why are you sitting on your ass?"	86
	39	That which we obtain too easily, we esteem too lightly	Paying for the psy-chiatrist	87

Chapter	Story #	Instead of saying something like this:	Share this story:	Page
	40	Even a jilted love has benefits	Staying in Germany after a lost love	88
	41	Don't like your job? Make it better.	Junior Achievement Teacher of the Year	90
10) Self-Confidence	42	Never do something just to get someone else to like you	Killing the rabbit	93
	43	"What do you care what other people think?"	Physicist grills a steak	95
	44	Early wins build confidence	The international soccer match	97
11) Self-Discipline: Money and Delayed Gratification	45	A penny saved is a penny earned	The magic of compound interest	98
	46	Learn to be happy with less stuff	Summers in Bombay	103
	47	Do you really need that fancy red sports car?	Wrecking the Mazda Miata	105
	48	Delayed gratification is a virtue	Looking for presents before Christmas	107
	49	Watch your language!	"I want some f'ing candy!"	108
12) Health	50	Take care of your body and it will take care of you	Know the symptoms	110
	51	Watch your weight	Battling obesity and anorexia	114
13) Positive Mental Attitude	52	A challenge is just an opportunity in disguise	Hurricane at the hardware store	118
	53	Happiness is a choice (Part 1)	"Because the sky is blue"	119
	54	Happiness is a choice (Part 2)	The happiest place in the hospital	121

Chapter	Story #	Instead of saying something like this:	Share this story:	Page
	55	Look for the good in things, not the bad	"One thing I didn't know" at the stat course	122
	56	Don't worry. Be happy.	"Happy birthday, John Ray!"	124
	57	Let your great attitude infect others	Climbing Kilimanjaro	127
14) Dealing with Loss	58	Relationships are more important than things	The great Berkeley fire	131
	59	Families grow stronger after losing a member (Part 1)	"One Dark Branch"	134
	60	Families grow stronger after losing a member (Part 2)	The passing of my Japanese father	136
Part 2: How You Treat Other People				
15) Kindness	61	Be kind to strangers	Free hugs	143
	62	Be kind to the people you see every day	Walk of shame to the nerd table	145
	63	Take a stand against cruelty	Basketball team has lunch with Jenny	147
	64	Be kind to all creatures, great or small	Ants on their way home from work	151
	65	Give to those less fortunate than you	A street corner in Caracas	152
	66	No money? Give of your time.	Gleaning rice fields for hungry kids	155
16) Patience	67	Be patient with others	Canoeing the rapids	157
	68	Listening is patience in action	Quitting Notre Dame	159
	69	Asking good questions is not talking, it's listening	A probing question at the pub	163

Chapter	Story #	Instead of saying something like this:	Share this story:	Page
17) Fairness and Justice	70	Illegal and wrong aren't the same thing	No fireworks on July 4th	165
	71	Compromise	The Christmas Tri-angle	168
	72	Treat others the way you want to be treated	The shared blanket	170
18) Humility	73	Show respect to your elders	Carving the Thanks-giving turkey	172
	74	Pride comes just before the fall	Nailing the solo and blowing the one-liner	174
	75	Bragging about yourself won't win you any friends	Sixty seconds at the dinner party	175
	76	A little humility will get you a long way	Learning to "play the game"	177
19) Respect for Others	77	Confront bigotry with civil disobedi-ence	"It's five o'clock! Time to play basket-ball!"	179
	78	Subconscious bias makes you treat peo-ple differently	Suicide bomber in class	180
	79	Disabled people want to be treated like everyone else	More crayons, please	183
	80	Chivalry is not dead. Show some respect.	Walk curbside of that pretty lady!	187
	81	Reverence is different from respect. Whom do you revere?	"Silence please. My king is coming."	188
20) Friend-ship	82	You could be friends if you just tried	Deciding to be friends with Marvin	192
	83	Choose your friends wisely	One bad mango	194
	84	Be loyal to your friends	Betraying a friend at Woodstock	196

Chapter	Story #	Instead of saying something like this:	Share this story:	Page
	85	Stand up to bullies and they always back down (Part 1)	Friends or enemies? You decide.	198
	86	Stand up to bullies and they always back down (Part 2)	Carson and his bullies	200
	87	Friends protect you, not hurt you	"I think you need better friends."	203
	88	Don't listen to gossip that might hurt you	"Do I really need to hear this?"	204
	89	Don't talk about people behind their back	"That woman is my wife."	205
21) Social Intelligence	90	Mind your manners	Avoiding the prom?	208
	91	You don't have to like everyone, but treat them as if you do	Breaking my date with Dave	211
	92	Beware of cultural differences (Part 1)	Dorinda's interruptions	214
	93	Beware of cultural differences (Part 2)	Hana's silence	215
22) Forgiveness and Gratitude	94	If you hurt someone, say you're sorry (Part 1)	"Toby, turn up the radio!"	216
	95	If you hurt someone, say you're sorry (Part 2)	"Sally Strobe was as fat as a globe"	218
	96	It's never too late to say you're sorry	The twenty-five-year-late apology	220
	97	Be grateful for all gifts	"But I didn't know I was needy."	222
23) Appreciation of Beauty	98	Be in the moment	Forgetting my camera at Bear Lake	226
	99	Stop and smell the roses	Violinist in the subway	227

Chapter	Story #	Instead of saying something like this:	Share this story:	Page
	100	Stop to appreciate fleeting beauty	"Look, a hawk!!!"	228
24) Getting Started	101	Pursue your dreams	Dad's seventy-five-year-old dream	236

Additional Reading

STORIES FOR TEACHING WISDOM AND CHARACTER:

All I Really Need to Know I Learned in Kindergarten, by Robert Fulghum. New York: Ballantine Books, 1988.

Kitchen Table Wisdom: Stories that Heal, by Rachel Naomi Remen. New York: Riverhead Books, 1996.

The Book of Virtues: A Treasury of Great Moral Stories, by William Bennett. New York: Simon & Schuster, 1993.

My Grandfather's Blessings: Stories of Strength, Refuge, and Belonging, by Rachel Naomi Remen. New York: Riverhead Books, 2000.

30 Lessons for Living: Tried and True Advice from the Wisest Americans, by Karl Pillemer. New York: Hudson Street Press, 2011.

This I Believe: Life Lessons, edited by Dan Gediman. Hoboken, NJ: John Wiley & Sons, 2011.

John Chancellor's *Lessons in Life* newsletter. Subscribe at www.teachthesoul.com.

One Hundred Wisdom Stories from Around the World, by Margaret Silf. Oxford, UK: Lion Books, 2003.

Stories to Live By: Wisdom to Help You Make the Most of Every Day, edited by James O'Reilly, Sean O'Reilly, and Larry Habegger. Palo Alto, CA: Solas House, 2005.

The Prophet, by Kahlil Gibran. New York: Alfred A. Knopf, 1923.

Seven Lonely Places, Seven Warm Places: The Vices and Virtues for Children. Cincinnati, OH: St. Anthony Messenger Press, 2003.

Daddy Teller: How to be a Hero to Your Kids and Teach Them What's Really Important by Telling Them One Simple Story at a Time, by K. Sean Buvala. Tolleson, AZ: Creation Company Consultants, 2009.

HOW-TO GUIDES ON CREATING AND TELLING PERSONAL STORIES:

Lead with a Story: A Guide to Crafting Business Narratives that Captivate, Convince, and Inspire, by Paul Smith. New York: AMACOM Books, 2012.

The Power of Personal Storytelling: Spinning Tales to Connect with Others, by Jack Maguire. New York: Tarcher/Putnam, 1998.

The Storytelling Coach: How to Listen, Praise, and Bring Out People's Best, by Doug Lipman. Little Rock, AR: August House, 1995.

The Parent's Guide to Storytelling: How to Make Up New Stories and Retell Old Favorites, by Margaret Read MacDonald. Little Rock, AR: August House, 1995.

Bringing the Story Home: The Complete Guide to Storytelling for Parents, by Lisa Lipkin. New York: Norton, 2000.

To Our Children's Children: Preserving Family Histories for Generations to Come, by Bob Greene. New York: Doubleday, 1993.

Telling Your Own Stories: For Family and Classroom Storytelling, Public Speaking, and Personal Journaling, by Donald Davis. Little Rock, AR: August House, 1993.

Creative Storytelling: Choosing, Inventing, and Sharing Tales for Children, by Jack Maguire. New York: McGraw-Hill, 1985.

Awaken the Hidden Storyteller: How to Build a Storytelling Tradition in Your Family, by Robin Moore. Boston: Shambhala, 1991.

ON VIRTUES AND CHARACTER:

How Children Succeed: Grit, Curiosity, and the Hidden Power of Character, by Paul Tough. Boston: Houghton Mifflin Harcourt, 2012.

Character Strengths and Virtues: A Handbook and Classification, by Christopher Peterson and Martin E. P. Seligman. New York: Oxford University Press, 2004.

The Seven Deadly Sins and The Seven Cardinal Virtues, by Reverend James Stalker. Carol Stream, IL: NavPress, 1998. Originally published as two separate tracts in 1901 and 1902, respectively, by the American Tract Society.

The Art of Living: A Classical Manual on Virtue, Happiness, and Effectiveness, by Epicteus, with A New Interpretation by Sharon Lebell. New York: HarperCollins, 1995.

Humility: The Forgotten Virtue, by Wayne Mack. Phillipsburg, NJ: P&R Publishing, 2005.

Notes

INTRODUCTION

1. Hannah Arendt, *Men in Dark Times* (New York: Harvest Books, 1968–70), p. 105.
2. Paul Tough, *How Children Succeed: Grit, Curiosity, and the Hidden Power of Character* (New York: Houghton Mifflin Harcourt Publishing, 2012).

CHAPTER 1: AMBITION

1. http://en.wikipedia.org/wiki/NASA_Astronaut_Corps.
2. http://www.spacecamp.com.

CHAPTER 3: CREATIVITY

1. Andrew Carnegie, *James Watt* (New York: Doubleday, Page & Co., 1905).
2. William Bennett, *The Book of Virtues* (New York: Simon & Schuster, 1993), p. 347.

CHAPTER 4: CURIOSITY AND LEARNING

1. Steven Vannoy and Craig Ross, *Stomp the Elephant in the Office: Put an End to the Toxic Workplace, Get More Done, and Be Excited About Work Again* (Lakewood, CO: Wister & Willows Publishers, 2008), p. 140.
2. American Community Survey and Puerto Rico Community Survey, 2006. United States Census Bureau, http://en.wikipedia.org/wiki/Higher_education_in_the_United_States.
3. www.pronoiart.com.
4. http://online.wsj.com/news/articles/SB1000142405274870420680457546816280587799 0.

CHAPTER 5: COURAGE

1. Rachel Naomi Remen, *Kitchen Table Wisdom: Stories that Heal* (New York: Riverhead Books, 1996), p. 50.
2. Often attributed to Edmund Burke.

CHAPTER 6: INTEGRITY

1. Peter May, *The Big Three* (New York: Simon & Schuster, 2007 [1994]), p. 57.

CHAPTER 8: GRIT

1. A. L. Duckworth, C. Peterson, M. D. Matthews, and D. R. Kelly, "Grit: Perseverance and Passion for Long-Term Goals," *Personality Processes and Individual Differences* 92, no. 6 (2007): p. 1087.

CHAPTER 9: HARD WORK AND STRUGGLES IN LIFE

1. *The Log Cabin Democrat*, July 2, 2001, http://thecabin.net/stories/070201/edu_0702010005.shtml.

CHAPTER 10: SELF-CONFIDENCE

1. Richard Feynman, *What Do You Care What Other People Think?* (New York: W. W. Norton & Company, 1988), p. 46.

CHAPTER 11: SELF-DISCIPLINE: MONEY AND DELAYED GRATIFICATION

1. The exact number is 2,147,483,647 pennies. I suspect many readers will try this calculation themselves (good for you!) and come up with only 1,073,741,824 pennies like I first did and race to send me or my publisher a note to correct the error. To save you the embarrassment, that number is how much you would receive on the thirty-first day of the month. But you have to add to it the money you got on the thirtieth day, and the twenty-ninth day, and every other day of the month before that. The total will equal the 2.1 billion shown.
2. http://www.nytimes.com/2013/08/22/us/politics/us-median-income-rises-but-is-still-6-below-its-2007-peak.html?_r=0.
3. http://www.bankrate.com/finance/credit-cards/rate-roundup.aspx.
4. http://www.creditcards.com/credit-card-news/average-credit_card_debt-1276.php.

CHAPTER 13: POSITIVE MENTAL ATTITUDE

1. http://www.altitude.org/air_pressure.php.
2. If you'd like to read a full account of Dan's adventures on Mt. Kilimanjaro, check out his engaging book, *Kissing Kilimanjaro: Leaving It All on Top of Africa* (Seattle, WA: The Mountaineers Books, 2011).

CHAPTER 14: DEALING WITH LOSS

1. Captain Donald R. Parker, Oakland Fire Department, http://www.sfmuseum.org/oakfire/overview.html.

CHAPTER 15: KINDNESS

1. You can learn more about Kristin at www.storytellerkp.com.
2. In an ironic twist of fate, nine years later Chad learned firsthand much of what Jenny's daily struggles in life were like. When he was twenty-seven, a two-thousand-pound bale of hay shattered his neck, leaving him a quadriplegic. Today Chad speaks to audiences all over the world sharing this and other stories to inspire them to overcome their barriers.
3. "The World Factbook: Venezuela," cia.gov.
4. "96 homicidios por cada 100.000 habitantes," *El Pais*.

CHAPTER 17: FAIRNESS AND JUSTICE

1. James Stalker, *The Seven Cardinal Virtues* in *The Seven Deadly Sins and The Seven Cardinal Virtues*, by Reverend James Stalker. Carol Stream, IL: NavPress, 1998. Originally published as two separate tracts in 1901 and 1902, respectively, by the American Tract Society.

CHAPTER 18: HUMILITY

1. James Stalker, *The Seven Deadly Sins* in *The Seven Deadly Sins and The Seven Cardinal Virtues*, by Reverend James Stalker. Carol Stream, IL: NavPress, 1998. Originally published as two separate tracts in 1901 and 1902, respectively, by the American Tract Society.

CHAPTER 19: RESPECT FOR OTHERS

1. Kenny Tedford Jr., http://www.kennytedfordjr.com.
2. *The American Heritage Dictionary of the English Language*, Third Edition (Boston: Houghton Mifflin Company, 1992).
3. http://www.worldweatheronline.com/Bangkok-weather-averages/Krung-Thep/TH.aspx.
4. Pew Research Center's Religion & Public Life Project: Thailand (Pew Research Center, 2010).
5. http://en.wikipedia.org/wiki/Bhumibol_Adulyadej.

CHAPTER 21: SOCIAL INTELLIGENCE

1. E. L. Thorndike, "Intelligence and Its Use." *Harper's Magazine* 140 (1920): pp. 227–35.

CHAPTER 22: FORGIVENESS AND GRATITUDE

1. William E. Breen, Todd B. Kashdan, Monica L. Lenser, and Frank D. Fincham, "Gratitude and Forgiveness: Convergence and Divergence on Self-Report and Informant Ratings," National Institute of Health, http://www.ncbi.nlm.nih.gov/pmc/articles/PMC2943233/.

CHAPTER 23: APPRECIATION OF BEAUTY

1. *Washington Post*, April 8, 2007, http://www.washingtonpost.com/wp-dyn/content/article/2007/04/04/AR2007040401721.html; http://www.youtube.com/watch?v=hnOPu0_YWhw.

CHAPTER 24: GETTING STARTED

1. Rachel Naomi Remen, *Kitchen Table Wisdom: Stories that Heal* (New York: Riverhead Books, 1996), p. xxxviii.
2. Lisa Lipkin, *Bringing the Story Home: The Complete Guide to Storytelling for Parents* (New York: W. W. Norton & Company, 2000), p. 22.
3. Margaret Read MacDonald, *The Parent's Guide to Storytelling: How to Make Up New Stories and Retell Old Favorites* (Little Rock, AR: August House, 1995), p. 9.
4. Paul Smith, *Lead with a Story: A Guide to Crafting Business Narratives that Captivate, Convince, and Inspire* (New York: AMACOM Books, 2012).

Index